Lady of Burlesque

Lady of Burlesque

The Career of Gypsy Rose Lee

ROBERT STROM

Foreword by John Fricke
Afterword by Noralee Frankel

McFarland & Company, Inc., Publishers
Jefferson, North Carolina, and London

"Unconventionally Speaking" by Henry Morton Robinson, reprinted with permission from *Reader's Digest*. Copyright © April 1946 by The Reader's Digest Association, Inc.

LIFE articles reprinted with permission from LIFE.

"How to Undress Gracefully in Front of Millions," article courtesy of *TV Guide Magazine* , LLC © September 1964 TV Guide Magazine, LLC.

The May 1942 *Argosy* magazine cover copyright © 1942 by Popular Publications, Inc. Reprinted by permission of Argosy Communications.

Gypsy's letters to the editors at *Inner Sanctum Mysteries* regarding her work on *The G-String Murders* are in the Gypsy Rose Lee Collection, Manuscripts Division, Department of Rare and Special Collections, Princeton University Library. Reprinted with permission from the Princeton University Library.

Articles from the *Chicago Tribune*, "The Girl with the Big Golden Harp," and "Meet the 'New' Gypsy Rose Lee — She's a TV Yakker Now," reprinted with permission of the *Chicago Tribune*; copyright Chicago Tribune; all rights reserved.

The three featured Springmaid ads, *Tea with Mrs. Julio de Diego, The Bed of Nails* ad, and *The Napolena Bonaparta* ad, are reproduced courtesy the Springs Close Family Archives, The White Homestead, Fort Mill, S.C.

"Naked Genius: Gypsy Rose Lee's Greatest Fantasy Was Herself," originally published in the November 1988 issue of *Washington–The Evergreen State Magazine,* reprinted with permission from C.R. Roberts.

"To Catch a Musky" was originally published in the July 1957 issue of *Sports Afield. www.sports afield.com*

LIBRARY OF CONGRESS CATALOGUING-IN-PUBLICATION DATA

Strom, Robert, 1961–
Lady of Burlesque : the career of Gypsy Rose Lee / Robert Strom ;
foreword by John Fricke ; afterword by Noralee Frankel.
p.   cm.
Includes bibliographical references and index.

ISBN 978-0-7864-3826-6
softcover : 50# alkaline paper ∞

1. Lee, Gypsy Rose, 1914–1970.   2. Stripteasers — United States — Biography.
3. Authors, American — 20th century — Biography.   I. Title.
PN2287.L29S77 2011   792.702'8092 — dc22   2010052391

BRITISH LIBRARY CATALOGUING DATA ARE AVAILABLE

On the cover: Gypsy Rose Lee, circa 1930s (Photofest)

Manufactured in the United States of America

*McFarland & Company, Inc., Publishers
Box 611, Jefferson, North Carolina 28640
www.mcfarlandpub.com*

This book is dedicated to
six extraordinary gentlemen:

Gene Arceri
Mark Gebhardt
Arnie Goodpasture
Kinmont Hoitsma
Erik Preminger
Erik Strom

and to six extraordinary women:

Dr. Claire Borkert
Jacqui Diaz
Linda Goppert
Marti "Lady" Hicks
Ellie Hoffman & Barb Raboy
And my beloved mother — Lana Strom

Table of Contents

Acknowledgments

There are, of course, numerous people to acknowledge and thank. For their assistance in making this book possible, I would like to acknowledge:

Phyllis Diller, an American Original if there ever was one, a gifted painter and pianist, an earthy and sophisticated lady who is still going strong in her nineties.

Donna Anstey, Kaye Ballard, Richard Blum, Regina Feiler, Charles E. Green and AnnaLee Pauls, Noralee Frankel, John Fricke, Ronald Hussey, Matthew Kennedy, Matthew Keough, Karen Nickerson, Leonard Maltin, Eileen O'Malley Spangler, Denise Mort, Diana Rupp, Don C. Skemer, Robert Weinberg, Randall F. Weissman, and Sue Woody. Thank you all for your generosity.

There are numerous family members and friends who support all of my creative endeavors. Some of them are: Joan Arthur, Joe and Diane Cohen, Larry Dunlap and Bobbe Norris, Celia Esposito-Noy, Michael Feinstein, Bob and Vietta Fuller, Duke and Marsha Hill, Jen Hill, Rick Hocker, Ray Holt, Lynn Hicks, Rae Ann Innanello, Christopher Kendrick-Stafford, Juanita Kirby, Sally Knox, Dennis Kohles, Rachel LePell, Carlos Lopez, Beth Lorber, Ramona McMaster, Penny Peck, Allan and Michaele O'Leary-Reiff, Nanette Rubio, James O. Rugland, Toni and Luanne Prima, Sal Russo, Roger Schram, Mertis Shekeloff, Keely and Piggy Smith, Kay Starr, Debbie Strom, Sally Strom, Mark Vierra, Sara Wiener and Joanne Richter, Bella Wiener, Gaynel Wray, and Marika Young. Thank you all for your support.

Love and thanks to members of my family: the Garriety Family, the Goppert Family, the Kellner Family and my "cousins by the dozens" (you know who you are)!

More love and thanks to the people who keep me alive and loving life: the *entire* staff of EBAC, and The Angel Nurses: Carol, Janet, Carrie and Lisa.

Last, but absolutely not least...
Ladies and Gentleman, thanks to the one, the only, the incomparable Queen of Burlesque—Gypsy Rose Lee!

I have been in awe of you and inspired by you for more than forty years. You have never ceased to amaze and entertain me. You, and the soundtrack of *Gypsy*, have made me smile on both dark and sunny days. Thanks for living an unbelievable life, a life worth writing about. A life that shows others that anything is possible. The spotlight will never dim for you. Take another bow, Gypsy. Encore! Encore!

Foreword

by John Fricke

Gypsy Rose Lee fulfilled virtually every glowing adjective that defined "celebrity" back in the day.

But what separates Rose Louise Hovick from most of today's media darlings and demons is the simple fact that Gypsy was also able to "take stage"—and fulfill and sustain the concept of "let me *entertain* you."

She wasn't famous for being famous. She grew to legendary status because she had the goods and (ultimately) the history and experience to amuse, captivate, titillate, and delight any audience anywhere.

She delivered—as an entertainer.

She also knew how to intelligently meld and disport her own unique qualities of humor, common sense, and self-awareness. Across four decades, she came to be recognized as an amalgam of punch-it-across performer and sophisticated sage—as successful as the best of her breed (and better than all the rest).

Handsome rather than beautiful, she was a determined human being and business woman who simultaneously managed to define "glamour." And in Gypsy's case, the glamour was enhanced by her singular, tongue-in-cheek punctuations of sass, superstition, and self-preservation.

Seek out her autobiography, with its now-renowned and acknowledged blend of fact, fiction, and fancy. Revel in the fine biographical portrait written by her son, Erik.

But first peruse Robert Strom's gloriously assembled "reader's guide" to a self-created, self-perpetuated, self-sustained star. It was a career and persona founded on a one-of-a-kind woman—who could, depending on what would best work at any given moment, slip from guise to guise as a regular broad, a great dame, a joyous entertainer, and a first class lady.

John Fricke is the Emmy Award–winning co-producer or co-writer of Judy Garland: By Myself *(PBS-TV "American Masters") and* Judy: Beyond the Rainbow *(A&E Cable Network "Biography"). He is the author of* The Wizard of Oz: An Illustrated Companion to the Timeless Movie Classic *(with Jonathan Shirshekan) and* Judy Garland: A Portrait in Art and Anecdote.

Preface

Gypsy Rose Lee is on that list of rare individuals who are American Originals. A list that includes performing arts icons such as Louis Armstrong, Fred Astaire, Rosemary Clooney, Doris Day, Jimmy Durante, Judy Garland, Billie Holiday, Eartha Kitt, Peggy Lee, Bette Midler, Marilyn Monroe, Frank Sinatra and Keely Smith. Like most of these stars Gypsy, especially during the last decade of her life, was also called "a living legend." She knew she would not be forgotten.

It has been said that when Gypsy attended the premier of the Broadway musical *Gypsy* she entered the theatre as a star and left it as a legend. Over the years this has proven to be true: the evidence is in the fact that *Gypsy* has had more revivals than most Broadway musicals. As of this writing, there have been four major revivals, each starring one of the theatre world's most acclaimed stars — and American Originals — in the role of Mama Rose: Angela Lansbury in 1974, Tyne Daly in 1989, Bernadette Peters in 2003, and Patti LuPone in 2008.

There is also the film version of *Gypsy* starring Rosalind Russell as Mama Rose, and a perfectly cast Natalie Wood as Gypsy. In 1993 Bette Midler took on the challenging role of Mama Rose in the only television adaptation of the musical, to date.

Further proof that our fascination with Gypsy is unending are the two books published in 2009: Noralee Frankel's *Stripping Gypsy: The Life of Gypsy Rose Lee* and Rachel Shteir's *Gypsy: The Art of the Tease (Icons of America)*.

While their books, and this one, are about the same person, the approaches are different. Ms. Frankel's and Ms. Shteir's books are biographies. This is a reference book, a chronological record of Gypsy's career, and an historical account of Gypsy's accomplishments from many perspectives.

This book follows Gypsy's career from Vaudeville to Burlesque, Broadway to Hollywood, and the overlapping intersections beyond. It gives the reader a chronological account of what Gypsy accomplished in her multifaceted career as a striptease artist, star of stage, screen, radio and television, a playwright and screenwriter, murder mystery author, memoirist, activist, raconteur par excellence and master of public relations. Her ability to put on all of these hats with ease and skill, along with her talent for re-creating herself in order to remain famous for five decades, is the foundation of her status as an icon and has ensured her place among American Originals.

This book has hundreds of interviews and articles, presenting the stories of Gypsy's early life, achievements, marriages, travels, and legendary career. And that's exactly what they are: stories. Similar stories with differing details have been included because Gypsy was too changeable to be pinned down by the facts of her life.

Gypsy was a master storyteller, prone to embellishment. On the dust jacket of her autobiography *Gypsy*, another teller of tales, John Steinbeck, proclaimed, "I found it irresistible. It's quite a performance. I bet some of it is even true, and if it wasn't, it is now."

Therefore, I feel that it is necessary to offer as many of her fascinating tales as possible in the hope that you might be able to find the truth, or at least the version you like best. That's what Gypsy did.

The majority of research is based on the books, films, magazines, programs and newspapers I have purchased over many years. Another important source comprises the articles, short stories and books written by Gypsy herself.

I hope this book entertains you. That's what the incomparable Gypsy would have wanted. Her entire life was devoted to entertaining. With the numerous revivals of *Gypsy* on Broadway and the three new books inspired by her life and legend, she continues to fascinate and thrill us. She is now and forever will be the First Lady of Burlesque: Miss Gypsy Rose Lee!

CHAPTER ONE

Born in a Trunk

Born January 9, 1911, Gypsy Rose Lee began her life as Rose Louise Hovick, the first daughter of Rose and John Hovick. Rose was 15 when she married John Hovick. According to Gypsy's 1911 birth certificate, her father sold ads to local newspapers.

Sources occasionally give Gypsy's date of birth as 1913 or 1914. *Halliwell's Who's Who in the Movies* claims she was born in 1913. The discrepancies exist for two reasons. Gypsy's mother didn't want anyone to know the age of her daughters (Rose Louise and younger sister June), wanting them to be a "kiddie" act for as long as possible, and as years went by Gypsy's "faulty" memory clouded the issue further.

June, also known as "Baby June" and "Dainty June," was born Ellen Evangeline Hovick on November 8, 1913. Rose Louise (Gypsy) grew up on the road, touring with her mother and her sister in a vaudeville act known as "Dainty June and Newsboy Songsters." It was a popular act on several vaudeville circuits, including the Pantages circuit. Later, the act joined what was recognized as vaudeville's ultimate destination: the Orpheum circuit. Dainty June and company were making an estimated fifteen hundred dollars per week. This was a tremendous amount of money in the late 1920s.

Rose Louise Hovick at age six. The fact that the photography studio was DeHavers of Chicago suggests that the young Rose Louise was already on the road with her sister's vaudeville act. Circa 1917 (Culver Pictures).

June and Rose Louise on the steps of what was most likely a theatrical hotel or boardinghouse. June is approximately six, Rose Louise is eight. Circa 1919 (Culver Pictures).

Much to Mama Rose's dismay the act ended when June eloped with dancer Bobby Reed, in 1929, when June was sixteen. Mama Rose had Reed arrested. When she went to the jail to retrieve June she drew a gun and attempted to shoot Reed. Luckily, the safety catch was on and Reed escaped unharmed. However, the damage had been done. Eventually, June left the act for good.

June later changed the spelling of her last name to Havoc. As June Havoc she appeared in several films and enjoyed success on Broadway. She wrote two biographies, *Early Havoc* and *More Havoc*, and as a playwright she penned *Marathon '33*. The play was based on June's experience as a marathon dancer during the Great Depression.

Without her sister, Rose Louise found herself unhappily thrust into the spotlight along with a handful of other, more eager, girls recruited for the show. The act first became "Mme. Rose Debutantes," then "Madam Rose's Dancing Daughters." When Rose Louise bleached the other girls blonde they were known as "Rose Louise and Her Hollywood Blondes." Louise, the only brunette on stage, stood out. The new act could not overcome the fact that vaudeville was dead. It was killed by Hollywood and the movies.

In 1927 the sixteen-year-old Rose Louise Hovick knew she was the breadwinner. Mama Rose and the girls in the failed act depended on her to provide their living. Summoning up her courage she decided to become a stripper. While watching her name go up on the burlesque theatre's marquee, she suddenly realized that Rose Louise Hovick did not look right. She made up a name on the spot (or so she said), and instructed the theatre's manager to put Gypsy Rose Lee up in lights.

Most articles written about Gypsy Rose Lee tell the story of her humble beginnings, her trouping in vaudeville and her stardom in burlesque. Each time the story changes, sometimes slightly, sometimes boldly.

Chapter Two

You Gotta Have a Gimmick

> Before the woman who became known as Gypsy Rose Lee arrived in New York in the 1930s, striptease took place more frequently on tables in saloon backrooms or in whorehouses than on Broadway or in Hollywood.
> — Rachel Shteir, *Gypsy: The Art of the Tease*

After Gypsy's New York debut things started to change quickly. Her meteoric rise to fame emboldened and inspired composers, lyricists, and choreographers to incorporate striptease into Broadway musicals. Most of the time these were spoofs of the "art" of stripping. Musical comedy stars such as Gypsy's friend Fanny Brice, Imogene Coca, Beatrice Lillie and Mary Martin impersonated Gypsy. They copied her costumes, hairstyle, movements, voice and attitude. Even male burlesque and Broadway comics dressed in drag to get in on the fun. And why not?

The signature aspect of Gypsy's striptease was the fact that she talked as she stripped. She spoke knowledgeably of art, literature and classical music. In many cases she wrote her own monologues and quickly became known as "The Intellectual Stripper."

Rachel Shteir encapsulates Gypsy's comedic talent, which was based on incredible timing: "She was not the Circe of undressing — she was ... its Dorothy Parker."

• 1930 •

The act "Gypsy Rose Lee and Her Hollywood Blondes" appeared at the Gayety Theatre in Kansas City, Missouri, in January of 1930. More often than not, Gypsy claimed she started her career as a striptease artist in Kansas City. In some interviews she said it all started in Toledo, Ohio. Either way, there is a general consensus that she began stripping, at age 18, in the autumn of 1929 (or at the very beginning of 1930).

• 1931 •

Gypsy performed at the following theatres in 1931: Gayety Theatre, Kansas City; Garrick Theatre, St. Louis; Minsky's Burlesque, New York, and the Empire Theatre in Newark, New Jersey. At the Gayety Theatre in Washington, D.C., in June of 1931 Gypsy's act was called "Gypsy Rose Lee and Her Rhumba Girls."

In *Gypsy—The Art of the Tease* author Shteir offers the following regarding Gypsy at this point in her career:

The young Rose Louise has become Gypsy Rose Lee in this early photograph taken at the beginning of her career in burlesque. According to her memoirs Gypsy made her burlesque debut at age sixteen, when her vaudeville act was booked into the Gaiety Theatre in Toledo. She is slightly older in this photograph, seventeen or eighteen perhaps. The photograph was taken at the John Gilmore Studio in Cincinnati, Ohio. Circa 1929.

... a few things about Gypsy's early numbers (she rotated them) are known. She sometimes stripped to Cab Calloway's "Minnie the Moocher." ... Gypsy did not strip to the altogether, at least not at Minsky's in 1931. When she was arrested ... the morning after her premiere, telegrams offered to protect her.... One tabloid quoted Gypsy as explaining that she made the detective wait outside while she dressed.

The *New York Evening Graphic* documented the gifts Gypsy raked in after her arrest. Among them were many bouquets of American Beauty roses, a case of ginger ale, more than

The original caption of this photograph simply reads: "Gypsy Rose Lee, featured in Allan Gilbert's Irving Place Theatre production." Mr. Gilbert's production was presented at Minsky's Burlesque. Gypsy was twenty. Circa 1931.

forty "mash notes," numerous boxes of candy, a pet rabbit and at least six marriage proposals. Best of all, her arrest brought with it free publicity. Gypsy learned early on the value of publicity, and free publicity was all the better.

Gypsy also performed at the Empress Theatre in Chicago at this time. Ads for her show ran in the *Southtown Economist* on September 18, 1931, and *The Dunkirk Observer* on October 10, 1931. The advertisement read:

EMPRESS

HALSTED AT 63rd
UNDER NEW MANAGEMENT
Twice Daily 2:30 — 8:30
Phone Normal Arts
Week Commencing Saturday Matinee, Sept. 19th
Columbia Burlesque
ED RYAN PRESENTS
GYPSY ROSE LEE
AND HER
GIRLS FROM THE FOLLIES
One of the Most Colorful Productions on Tour
LADIES MATINEE   ALL SEATS RESERVED
DAILY   25 RESERVED
MIDNIGHT REVELS
EVERY SATURDAY NIGHT AT 12 O'CLOCK

• 1932 •

Gypsy Gets Hot. The young Gypsy appeared in the original musical comedy *Hot Cha!* The show ran from March 8 to June 18 of 1932, for a total of 119 performances, at the National Theatre and the roof-top Ziegfeld Theatre, which was located at 6th Avenue and W 54th Street. Gypsy, billed as Rose Louise, had the role of "Girl in Compartment."

• 1933 •

Gypsy and Sigmund. Between February 14 and April 22 of 1933, Sigmund Romberg's *Melody* played at the Shubert Theatre in Newark, New Jersey, and the Boston Opera House. *Melody* had a total of one-hundred twenty-two performances. A rare 1933 playbill provides the following about the pre–Broadway engagement *Melody* at the Boston Opera House in Boston:

> The musical starred Evelyn Herbert, Walter Woolf, Hal Skelly, Ina Ray, Louise Kirtland, Everett Marshall, Jeanne Aubert, George Houston, Vivian Fay and Victor Morley and featured Rose Louise (later known as Gypsy Rose Lee, in one of her earliest stage roles [Claire Lolive, Pierre's mistress]). Credits: Book by Edward Childs Carpenter; Music by Sigmund Romberg; Lyrics by Irving Caesar; Choreographed by Bobby Connolly; Sets designed by Joseph Urban; Costumes designed by Charles LeMaire; Orchestra conducted by Al Goodman; Produced and Directed by George White.

Gypsy's in the Pink. In 1933 Gypsy appeared in a Broadway musical entitled *Strike Me Pink*,* which starred Jimmy Durante. Little is known about this show other than it had a

*Since the performance dates of *Melody* and *Strike Me Pink* overlap, it is likely that Gypsy left the cast of *Melody* before the March 4, 1933, opening of *Strike Me Pink*.

short run from March 4, 1933, to June 10, 1933. *Strike Me Pink* was seen at the Majestic Theatre at 247 W 44th Street. Gypsy quickly moved on to other productions.

Gypsy Goes to Harvard. The December 7, 1933, edition of *The Harvard Crimson* newspaper ran the headline: "Burlesque Queen Likes Harvard Men; Football Stars Too Handsome — Make Her Very Nervous. Calls Repeal Marvelous, and Says 'Stinger' Best Drink for Going Out on Binges."

> "How would I make the Harvard football team? Well, that would be pretty hard to say; they're all so handsome that I'd be awfully nervous," said Miss Gypsy Rose Lee, enticing star of Boston's new home of burlesque, when interviewed last night by the *Crimson* Backstager. Sitting easily back, puffing a cigarette, her shapely legs resting on the dressing table, Miss Lee gave her opinions of Harvard men and many other things. "I've never known many Harvard men, but from what I've seen of them they sure are handsome real men."

• 1935 •

Gypsy's New Face. In the September 16, and November 24, 1935, issues of *The New York Times* it was mentioned that producer Leonard Sillman had signed Gypsy to star in his latest production of *New Faces*. Sillman produced this yearly revue to introduce talent, and new faces, to Broadway audiences. Over the years Sillman launched the careers of several future stars including Imogene Coca, Henry Fonda, Madeline Kahn, Eartha Kitt, Carol Lawrence, Paul Lynde, Maggie Smith and Inga Swenson. Unfortunately for Gypsy, Sillman's *New Faces* was never produced.

Gypsy Mingles. "Burlesque Queen Reaps Rich Rewards" was the headline of an article seen in the *Hartford Courant* on November 17, 1935. The article states that Gypsy was making $900 weekly, and enjoyed the perk of mingling with "Smart New York Society...."

Gypsy's Dream. At some point in 1935 Gypsy rented an apartment in Gramercy Park. It was close to Irving Place (where she was working at the time), and farther away from her mother. She saw her sister more often. The sisters were becoming confidants.

• 1936 •

Gypsy and Mrs. Flanagan. The headline "Mrs. Flanagan Speaks to the Actors — Other Matters Along Broadway" ran in the January 1, 1936, issue of *The New York Times*. Mrs. Hallie Flanagan was the director of the Federal Theatre, which was one of the new projects launched as a part of Franklin Roosevelt's New Deal. The article reported that Gypsy would be among those attending Mrs. Flanagan's speech, referring to Gypsy as "... an artist from Burlesque — or, maybe it's The Artist...."

The Federal Theatre closed in 1939. Mrs. Flanagan said that the end had come "because the ... forces marshaled in its behalf came too late to combat other forces...." She went on to say that those against the theatre could be found in "two congressional committees" where the negative forces "found a habitation and a name." The two committees to which Flanagan referred were the House Committee on Appropriations and the House Committee on Un-American Activities. The latter, also known as the Dies Committee, was headed by Martin Dies. Gypsy would be hearing from the Dies Committee in the near future.

Gypsy's Second New Face? On April 30, 1936, *The New York Times* once again mentioned Gypsy as a player in *New Faces*. The paper reported that she was making an appearance in a skit written by John Held, Jr.

Gypsy in *The New York Times*. On May 9, 1936, Gypsy was mentioned in the "News of Stage" column in *The New York Times*. She performed at the Vanderbilt that evening. The headline read: "'Spring Tonic' Revue Given At Vanderbilt":

Gypsy's Intellectual Pursuits

Somewhere in the past, I once mentioned the intellectual pursuits of Gypsy Rose Lee, queen of the strip tease dancers on Forty-second Street burlesque runways. That was when Gypsy began to dabble in painting, writing and dramatic acting, while she was not artfully removing her costume for the customers.

Since then, the strip tease dancer has achieved a career as a dainty diseuse, my pretties. Don't be alarmed. It is not contagious. Lately, Gypsy Rose has been enlisted in various programs, given by the cognoscenti, to recite sophisticated lyrics. (Sophisticated is Broadway's other word for risqué.) Her monologues are popular in the most polite mixed company. And it has been a pleasant surprise to Gypsy Rose to find that she can entertain a crowd and still keep her clothes on.

She was in the paper again on May 11, 1936, this time in George Ross' syndicated column "In New York." The column ran in various newspapers, including the *Frederick News*, on May 19, 1936.

Gypsy's Easy Money. The rare pulp magazine *Easy Money* featured an article in its June 1936 issue. While the article ("Strip Girls" by George Shute) is about the burlesque world in general, Gypsy is definitely the star.

Eve's tempting of Adam was amateurish compared to the persuasions of a burlesque strip gal. These ladies of the G-String, known as "strippers" to the trade, can make strong men weak and weak men helpless.

Sally Rand feathered her nest with a pair of ostrich fans, reaching the four figure brackets when she juggled a bubble along a stage, while a dim, blue spotlight bathed her unclad body. Overnight, the former screen player changed Chicago's World's Fair from a super-carnival to a national necessity.

Just as Sally became an institution in the nightclubs and presentation theatres, so Gypsy Rose Lee's name has become synonymous in burlesque for zippy stripping.

Now whether or not you are a patron of the burlesque industry, it's three, two, and even, you've heard of Gypsy. Breathes there a man who doesn't know of this darling of the strippers? Recall her as tall, dark, gravely beautiful; her face crowned with wild, dark hair? Her fame is undying. She brought a new technique to the well-undressed stripper.

Stripping is an art. It is not the mere disrobing of garments. A strip girl must be a modern Circe and a Mae West rolled in one. A strip teaser, to reach the top of her profession, must be able to give a Cleopatra cards and spades.

Topflight strippers are rare. You can count them on the fingers of your left hand. Use the right too, if you want. Let's see now. There's Gypsy, Carrie Fennell, Margie Hart, Ann Coreo* [sic], Evelyn Myers, "Peaches" Strange, June St. Clair, May Joyce, and Nadja. And one finger left over.

Gypsy is the undisputed queen of these gals who make their easy money by tossing the torso. In many cities, strip girls have built up personal followings that lure thousands of extra dollars into the box-office.

*The correct spelling is Corio. In the 1960s Miss Corio created and headlined the popular Broadway show *This Was Burlesque*.

Strippers are the triple-threat girls of burlesque; tantalizing, tormenting and thrilling. They banished the $5.50 musical show with its elaborate tableaux of lovely forms and brought into being the $1.50-and-see-what-you're-getting policy.

In the best stock houses, where burlesque might run week after week for as many as ten months, the first dozen rows are sold out in advance for the entire season. In houses featuring a runway (usually out-of-town since Manhattan's self appointed censor frowns upon the practice) the best seats are next to the lane. Otherwise bald head boulevard is occupied.

Although the shows vary but slightly each week, a patron's voice is never raised in dissent. Discontented murmurs are sometimes audible though, when a disgruntled young blade of fifty is forced to sit in the fourteenth row until some of the fresh kids of seventy-five die off and vacate the choice spots.

The vigorous supporters regard the girls as personal friends. Frequently, they take pen in hand and indite well-meaning, sometimes rambling and improper missives, suggesting new "bits" that might be tried, such as bumping to the left, and doing a hop, skip, and jump through a scarlet-in. Presents from "unknown admirers" are not uncommon; in one town, a certain old boy, who has never even met the girl, sends his limousine to take her to and from the theatre.

And now arises the question that has puzzled many minds. Where do strippers come from? Ohio and Pennsylvania contribute a considerable number of the sturdy stock. There is a predominance of Poles; a few Italians are also garment-wreckers. Some strangers are recruited from the chorus, but a majority starts out as a tease artist.

Margie Hart perhaps is the outstanding example of the girl who rose from the chorus ranks to strip to stardom. Conservatively estimated, Margie rates about $500 a week.

This season's sensational girl is named Annette, a discovery of Nat Morton's. Morton, a burlesque agent, found the girl ushering for Minsky in a Miami burlesque house, taught her a routine and today, at eighteen she is outstripping the field.

Newcomers find it difficult to muscle into the business. With the average life of a stripper ranging from two to three years, the stars zealously protect their art, from interlopers. The most effective way of stifling a newcomer is to teach her outrageous techniques and faulty timing, under the guise of lending a helping hand.

Strip girls may receive anything from $75 a week up. Salaries depend on popularity. Gypsy Rose Lee receives around $1,000 a week, while Ann Coreo plays for straight percentage netting as high as $1,500.

In stripping individual technique is everything. The current rage is a rather hefty blonde at the Apollo Theatre in New York City. Her name is Carrie Fennell and she lays 'em out in the aisles with her stuff, which will not be described herein.

Evelyn Myers, gorgeous platinum blonde from California, is another great favorite with audiences. A good teaser, Evelyn introduces plenty of class into her work, stripping to soft, intimate music. The audiences sit enraptured while she glides along the stage, shedding this garment and that until the denouement is reached.

"A girl doesn't have to tear off all her clothes to make a hit with an audience," Nat Morton says. "If she takes off just enough, like her brassiere and maybe running around in a G-String—but cultured—that's plenty."

Challenging this optimistic declaration is Margie Hart, who can tease with the best of them. Margie, it is said, can even make a hardened stagehand blush. She has a technique even the censors can't reach.

It remained for Gypsy Rose, though, to cause the burlesque producers to raise horrified hands and cry in anguished Oxonian accents: "Vot's de metter; you gone nuts?"

Sophisticated songs did it, Gypsy wanted to go highbrow, bring burlesque into the top hat class. She never accomplished the latter objective but she did introduce sophistication. And they ate it up.

Singing numbers of the Dwight Fiske type, Gypsy takes her time about stripping. The audience waits willingly. When she concludes her song, she breaks into a languid strip.

The audience might not appreciate the double meanings of the song, but they do laud the strip.

Gypsy doesn't give them too much. "Now, darlings," she'll protest, "I'm so tired." A smile, a thrown kiss, and she's off. That is, unless she indulges in her favorite indoor sport, flirting with bald headed men.

The real show begins when the rays of a colored spotlight pierce the darkness of the stage, revealing a beautiful young woman, clad in evening gown. The girl moves slowly down the stage, gliding with a curious, fascinating undulation. The spotlight continues to follow her. She walks to the right of the stage, still at that mincing pace, which is dissolving into an insinuating rhythm. Her hands go to her shoulder, hesitantly; and a strap falls. Her progress now is to the left of the stage. Again, her hand is raised, and joining the fallen strap the gown slips from her body, as the girl suddenly disappears into the protecting embrace of the wings, a salvo of applause following her. A moment later, she reappears, this time clad only in a pair of tights and a revealing veil, which is powerless to conceal her peering bosom.

"Take it off, baby, take it off." The cry resounds from the balcony. Faces are framed in smiles, knowing smiles, as the young lady allows the flimsy covering to slip from her shoulder, exposing an undraped torso. But she's not finished yet; the audience is tense. Her hand steals toward a pair white tights as a string is fingered. The girl is edging towards the left wing of the stage. She completes a small circle, much like a waltz-like motion, the tights disappear. A flash of flesh and the young women is gone. Again the audience applauds and whistles. The girl emerges smilingly, but now a dress drapes her form, drapes it not carefully, but carelessly. The young lady smiles, waves her hand and, if she is of a particularly good-humored nature, might even wiggle the lower part of her anatomy, before proceeding off.

Immediately, the tiny orchestra swings into another popular tune and the next number, usually a sketch, is on. The skin game is over. At least for ten minutes. The show must go on. And clothes must come off.

Gypsy's New York. Newspaperman James Aswell wrote a column entitled "My New York" in the 1930s. On August 4, 1936, the column was devoted to Gypsy, about whom Aswell wrote:

> Having just completed a research, for another spot, into the art, mystery and personality of Miss Gypsy Rose Lee, "the greatest stripper in the world," I am as it were, full of my subject. I believe there is more to be said about this saucy gal and her fantastic vocation and if you will shoo children off to bed and turn down the radio, I propose to say it.
>
> Now the mere words, "strip dancer" are apt to summon horrified gasps from the family circle. The curious fact is that Gypsy is not more immodest than any of the chorus girls who prance across the stages of the swank revues and night clubs out-of-towners see without a blush; she is actually, in a technical sense, no more revelatory of her charms than many impeccable ladies in evening dress who swoosh around the city constantly — and across country club ballroom floors throughout the land, for that matter.
>
> The more curious fact is that Gypsy has reached the apex of her profession by being more restrained and mindful of draughts than any of her sister practitioners. She has become the greatest strip dancer — or rather, the highest paid — in town because she has consistently removed less of her covering. Shortly she goes into the "Ziegfeld Follies" and becomes an American institution, along with Dr. Townsend and the tossing of pop bottles at ball games.
>
> Therefore, for any serious students of the fauna and flora of 1936 Manhattan, Gypsy Rose Lee is rapidly becoming a "must." I am myself immune to her art; I find it, if truth must out, excruciatingly dull — along with that of all other strip dancers. But she is herself an engaging young woman, utterly without self-consciousness, and it is certainly true that the Park Avenue set is giving her and some others of her calling a big rush.
>
> Where did she come from and how did she arrive in her present eminence (she makes $1,000 and more weekly)?

She was born in Seattle, Washington, and her mother took her to Hollywood and got her a job in the early cinema as the child actress in "Daddy Long Legs," with Mary Pickford — so you see early environment could not have had anything to do with her trend. Her career as a strip dancer began in Chicago by accident; she had some trouble with a reluctant evening gown's shoulder straps and the audience applauded.

It is, perhaps, a tip-off on the state of mind of this age when Gypsy says she changed her name (from Hovick) because she did not want her grandfather to find out what she was doing. Not her parents (her mother is her constant cheering section) but her grandfather! It shows you how far back into the past the conservatives are retreating.

Mr. Jean Cocteau, the professional esthete from Paree, recently visited here and declared that strip dancing was a marvelous, vital art form. This seems to me to be the sheerest nonsense. But certainly it is catching on. The afternoon I interviewed Miss Lee another reporter had been there earlier and several pundits were doing learned essays on her for the uppity magazines.

What the hell does it mean? Is the moral tone of the land and specifically New York (assuming the town ever had any) falling? I doubt it. I suspect, rather, that the bored gentry of the penthouse brigade have pounced upon another source of material for a fad.

It will rage and roar for awhile, and Gypsy is in the top flight because she is a smart gal, with a flair for satire and a handsome one. But she had better continue her elocution studies and keep her eye toward dramatic acting (she has a mellow and well-modulated voice) so that when the smarties take up bagatelle or bagpipes she will be prepared.

Ziegfeld Girl. On September 14, 1936, the latest version of the *Ziegfeld Follies* opened at the Winter Garden Theatre in New York, which was located at 1634 Broadway. The show ran for 112 performances. The Shuberts produced this latest version of the *Ziegfeld Follies* as a tribute to Billie Burke's late husband, Florenz Ziegfeld.

A great beauty, Burke went on to worldwide fame when she portrayed Glinda the Good Witch in the 1939 classic film *The Wizard of Oz*.

In addition to Gypsy the cast included Bobby Clark, Jane Pickens, Cass Daley and Ziegfeld legend Fanny Brice. Gypsy and Fanny became close friends during this production.

The show also boasted sets and costumes by the up-and-coming Vincente Minnelli, music by Vernon Duke and lyrics by Ira Gershwin. After closing in New York the show went on the road and played various towns including Chicago and Milwaukee.

Gypsy's Grand March. The *Chicago Times* ran an Associated Press item about Gypsy on October 29, 1936. Seems Gypsy was going to college — well, at least for one night. The short piece began, "Gypsy Rose Lee, former burlesque star and now a headliner in musicals, will head the grand march of the senior formal dance of Columbia University...."

Time **Magazine.** Coverage of the Columbia event also appeared in photographic form. In the November 9, 1936, issue of *Time* there is a photo of Gypsy with two gentlemen. *Time* described the evening:

> With Columbia Student Ben Brown as escort, Burlesque Stripper Gypsy Rose Lee attended the Senior Formal Dance as Queen. She went through part of her Follies strip act without stripping, recited some of Dwight Fiske's smutty monologs, and was applauded for encores.

Gypsy's Gems. In late November of 1936 Gypsy was robbed while entering her apartment. The robbery was reported in the *Los Angeles Times* on November 29, 1936. The newspaper claimed Gypsy's jewelry was worth $20,000, but the November 29, 1936, coverage by the *Chicago Tribune* matched the $25,000 originally reported. The story was also in the

This photograph and caption were published in the November 9, 1936, issue of *Time*. "*Columbia Prom Queen and Subjects:* The Two Columbia campus leaders, Kenneth Steffan (left) and Jim Casey, basketball captain and chairman of the Student Board, pictured with Gypsy Rose Lee in the latter's apartment here Oct. 29. Miss Lee, a 'Ziegfeld Follies' star, has been chosen Queen of the Senior Formal Dance the night of Oct. 31, marking the Senior's Social Farewell to the Columbia campus."

This International News Photo was taken on November 28, 1936. "Gipsy [sic], Stripped of Her Gems, Tells Press": "While reporters listen sympathetically, Gypsy Rose Lee, famous strip-tease, ex-burlesque queen and now a Follies star, recounts the sad story of how six thugs held her up in the vestibule of her mid-town apartment and stripped her of $25,000 in gems. 'Too bad, Gyps,' said the leader of the thugs, keeping his pistol steady, 'We're broke or we wouldn't be doing this.'"

November 29, 1936, issue of the *San Antonio Express-News* with the headline, "Gypsy Rose Lee's Fastest Costliest Strip in Apartment Lobby."

Another Texas newspaper, the *El Paso Herald-Post*, had a December 5, 1936, article by Heywood Broun. The journalist announced that because of the theft of Gypsy's jewelry he would not be buying any "... silver rings or brooches or bracelets ... at Christmas, not even for his wife, Connie."

Gypsy's Turn for Society. The robbery didn't slow Gypsy down at all. On November 29, 1936, *The New York Times* announced: "Burlesque Queen to Dance at Gotham's Beaux Arts Ball," and the article began "Gypsy Rose Lee to do a 'turn' for society." Gypsy's appearance at the famous ball was also covered in the December 4, 1936, issue of *The Evening Independent*.

Gypsy Goes to the Ball. On December 5, 1936, *The New York Times* ran the headline "Beaux Arts Ball Is Cosmic Pageant; 'Fete de Rayon Fantastique' at Hotel Astor Attracts a Throng of 2000." The article included mention of Gypsy's act as "The Full Eclipse of the Sun."

Another International News Photo, dated December 8, 1936: "A Treat For Gem Suspects": "New York ... People pay a lot of money to see Gypsy Rose Lee, who soared from striptease in a burlesque to spotlighted stardom in Follies. But a group of suspects rounded up by police were treated to a close-up of Gypsy today, Dec. 8, gratis. When the star attended Tombs Court, seeking to identify the thugs who robbed her of $25,000 in gems in a hold-up recently. Here you see Miss Lee awaiting the call to do her duty as a citizen."

***Collier's* Magazine.** The December 19, 1936, issue of *Collier's* featured an article by Kyle Crichton, excerpted below, entitled "Strip to Fame — The brilliant career of that shapely artist, Miss Gypsy Rose Lee, who has risen to fortune and social prominence through unadorned merit."

> Anybody who doesn't think America is the Land of Opportunity will get no free meals at the home of Miss Gypsy Rose Lee. Gypsy Rose is the young lady who leaped from the stage of Irving Place Burlesque theatre to the Ziegfeld Follies in one generation. She accomplished it by taking off her clothes in public, bit by bit, and feels that any other American may do likewise, granted the same symmetry and ambition.

Miss Lee is known in the trade as a "strip-tease" artist, and brooks no wise-cracks from the *cognoscenti*. In the days of the dear late Queen she would undoubtedly have ended up in gaol but different times, other morals. As it is she has a very good dressing room at the Winter Garden, receives featured billing and has captured the interest of the more sedate dramatic reviewers.

What started Gypsy Rose on the way to fame was the attention of a certain New York couple who may as well answer to the name of Squimpfenhupple, members of the old Knickerbocker aristocracy. The blood in the veins of a Squimpfenhupple is three stains bluer than a Duke Ellington rhythm and to be tapped socially by a Squimpfenhupple is the equivalent to the Order of the Garter. Well, Gypsy Rose was thusly tapped. She was appearing twice daily at the Irving Place, taking off her clothes with distinction at each performance and minding her affairs, when the lady taxi driver who patrolled the beat around Fourteenth Street came in to her dressing room with a note. It was the Squimpfenhupples asking her to make her acquaintance and inviting her to a party.

"They think I'm some kind of freak," said Gypsy Rose, and ignored the royal summons. But the Squimpfenhupples are not of a breed to be tossed around. With the tenacity which made the fortune of the original Squimpfenhupple, they persisted. There were later notes and finally an embossed stationery. Would Miss Lee honor the Squimpfenhupples, etc.

"I decided that if they had seen nobody like me, I had seen nobody like them," says Miss Lee. "So I went."

It was very pleasant. The Squimpfenhupples talked to her about books and she talked back at them about books and they restrained their amazement at finding a burlesque queen who could read, and it ended in a lovely friendship.

Within a short time the friends of the Squimpfenhupples were hurrying down to Irving Place to see this astonishing creature and her name was appearing in the gossip columns and eventually in the casts of some awfully nice private benefits and the national reputation of Gypsy Rose Lee was established. Since she was an intelligent person who had figured out that the divesting oneself of one's garments was better artistry than depending upon free lunches at the Actor's Club, it was natural that offers should soon come to her from uptown.

Ziegfeld Follies had been halted last spring by the illness of Fanny Brice and the Messr. Shubert was now re-launching the exhibit.

"How about Gypsy Rose Lee for that part played by Eve Arden?" asked the agent of Miss Lee with some insistence.

"She strips," said the Shubert representative. "She doesn't talk."

"She talks," said the agent downrightly, and told the Shubert gentleman about Miss Lee's books.

After that it was only a question of haggling and Gypsy Rose and her man out haggled.

"Nine hundred a week and extra for the midnight show," Miss Lee said referring to her appearances at the Irving Place. She hinted that the Follies were paying her about a third of that....

* * *

During the tenure of Gypsy Rose (a name given to her by Minsky [the Minsky brothers of Minsky's Burlesque]; the first time she knew about it was when she saw it in lights) the Irving Place played a full 52-week schedule and she passed the $1,000 mark in salary (midnight show Saturday included).

"Where can you find any better work?" she asks. "Immoral? Why, I'm not embarrassed in the Follies. I never took off as much as that down at Irving Place. And these nightclubs...! They don't have anything on and they're so close to the ringside tables the customers can reach out and touch them. Nobody ever yells about that but you'd think burlesque was awful."

Gypsy has a house in the country (fully paid for, this time), where her mother and grandmother live, an apartment in town, a secretary, a personal maid, a cook and a collection of diamonds which look like an assemblage of shooting stars.

She is tall and shapely, extremely dislikes nightclubs, dislikes to dance, likes brandy, is about twenty-seven in age, and has become something of a personage in New York, where she entertains and is entertained by the Squimpfenhuppels and their set. Interviewers have been known to soften their approach by a preliminary token of orchids and Miss Lee, on her part, has torn the autographed words of E.E. Cummings out of a book because of something he had written about after her departure.

But she has her enemies and they include members of the burlesque-going group. "She makes a joke of the thing," they complain. "You can't be funny about anything as serious as that."

In complaint, and possibly because the Follies top is $3.85, they've been staying away from the uptown performance. The better class audience, however, adores her. They think its Life.

Gypsy in _The New York Times._ "POLICE ACT TO END 4 AM GEM THEFTS" was the headline seen in the December 12, 1936, issue _The New York Times_ after thieves made off with $25,000 of Gypsy's jewelry and her $16,000 mink coat at 3:00 A.M. in front of Gypsy's home.

CHAPTER THREE

You Oughtta Be in Pictures

• 1937 •

***Real Screen Fun* Magazine — January 1937.** A Murray Korman photo of Gypsy appears in this proto-type of the 1950s "men's magazines" filled with scantly clad beauties and would-be stars. Gypsy's photo is part of a section called Follies d'Amour. The caption reads:

> *It's the Gypsy in us. Seems like you good people can never tire of seeing glamorous Gypsy Rose Lee's picture. Now a "Follies" attraction, this former strip girl possesses one of the most beautiful bodies in the world. Count 'em!*

Gypsy the Opera Diva. The *Ziegfeld Follies* performed in Chicago's Grand Opera House opening on January 4, 1937. "Ziegfeld Follies Come to Town and Chicago Fans Enjoy Them," announced the January 5, 1937, edition of the *Chicago Times.* The article described Gypsy as one of "The new generation of entertainers…"

Gypsy's Second Time. In the January 11, 1937, issue of *Time* Gypsy "appeared" in a composite photograph with Mrs. Harrison Williams, as a parody of the first issue of *Look*:

Gypsy Rose Lee had a genius for publicity. Here, in one ad, she manages to advertise herself, the Ziegfeld Follies and the Flameless LektroLite.

A "composograph" (frankly doctored picture) of Gypsy Rose Lee in conversation with Mrs. Harrison Williams, "world's best-dressed woman." Sample imaginary dialogue:
Mrs. Williams: "I never wear the same thing twice. And you?"
Gypsy Rose Lee: "I never put off today what I can put off tomorrow."

Gypsy in *The New York Times*. On January 20, 1937, *The New York Times* ran another article about the jewelry robberies plaguing New York. Gypsy was again a victim of one of these robberies, as was Mrs. Jean E. Herbs. The thieves also attempted to rob Mr. and Mrs. Emile Mathis at the Plaza Hotel.

Gypsy was in *The New York Times* again on January 31, 1937: "Gypsy Rose Lee — Queen of Stage's Artful Undress." The article began, "A TALL, handsome girl with an eccentric coiffure who bears the pseudonym Gypsy Rose Lee has put the entire country into a flutter...."

A Gypsy in Silk Stockings. A Murray Korman photograph of a very sexy Gypsy appeared as the centerfold in the February 1937 issue of *Silk Stockings Stories*. The photo was accompanied by this short poem:

> Her every curve is tantalizing
> Her eyes are bold and enterprising
> Her lips are mine I'm very sure
> Would send me sky-high my temperature
> She sends my racing pulse reeling
> A really most delightful feeling —
> I'd give one eye to embrace her glories...
> But she's only the center of *Silk Stocking Stories*

Gypsy Beats Smithsonian. On February 5, 1937, the *Sheboygan Press* reported in the "Vital Statistics Dept.": "More people saw Gypsy Rose Lee during the past six months than visited the Smithsonian Institute during the same time period."

Gypsy's Valentine. On Valentine's Day (February 14, 1937) an article appeared in the *Ogden Standard-Examiner* about Gypsy's role in the *Ziegfeld Follies*. The article began: "Gypsy Rose Lee considered by many the star of those who undress under a spotlight on a stage for a living is being featured in the revised Ziegfeld Follies. She is the first girl who ever has appeared in any Ziegfeld show minus clothes through bows."

Gypsy in the *Washington Post*. This headline was seen in the February 25, 1937, issue of the *Washington Post*: "Gypsy Lee's Strip Act All in Fun." The article summed up Gypsy's attitude toward her act: "'It's all just pure — well, anyway, pretty pure — fun,' that strip-tease act of hers, says Gypsy Rose Lee! She doesn't take it seriously, heavens no...."

Gypsy American Artist. "MINSKYS SEE PERIL TO AMERICAN 'ART': Burlesque Producers at House Hearing Ask for Ban on Alien Strippers." On February 25, 1937, *The New York Times* reported that the Minskys, Herbert and Morton, spoke before the House Immigration Committee. The brothers feared that aliens, legal and otherwise, were ruining the chances for American girls to make a career in burlesque. The Minskys spoke of American girls as the greatest strip teaser artists and claimed that "stripping" was a typical American art.

Burlesque, the art of stripping, was established in the 1840s, and it thrived in New

The cover of the April 1937 issue of *Romantic Stories* was based on this portrait.

York until 1937, when it was outlawed by Mayor LaGuardia due to its "indecency." Gypsy made the transition to the *Ziegfeld Follies* at just the right time.

Gypsy in Milwaukee. The *Ziegfeld Follies* opened at the Davidson Theatre on March 14, 1937.

Romantic Stories. A beautiful portrait of Gypsy, as she appeared in the *Ziegfeld Follies*, graced the cover of the April 1937 issue of *Romantic Stories* magazine.

Bachelor Magazine. The April 1937 issue of *Bachelor Magazine* included a stunning portrait of Gypsy by veteran photographer Murray Korman. The short caption read: *From the purlieu of Irving Palace to a high spot in "Ziegfeld Follies"; has now been signed by Hollywood for (aside from her obvious charms) her ability as an actress.*

Gypsy in Hollywood. On April 3, 1937, the *Los Angeles Times* noted that Gypsy, "... is definitely scheduled to appear in *Ali Baba Goes to Town*...."

Gypsy's Pure American Art. "Gypsy Rose Lee advanced the cause of this purely American art." So said an article in the April 9, 1937, edition of the *Jefferson City* [Mo.] *Post-Tribune*. The art in question? The striptease, of course. An art that was in trouble again. One John S. Sumner, the secretary of the New York Society for the Suppression of Vice, was on the case. Sumner is quoted as saying, "We have a check on the striptease situation. And from now on burlesque, on the rise in popularity for several years past, will have to be tamer." The article called Sumner "... [long] a foe of indecency in the theatre...."

Gypsy's Up to Date in Kansas City. On April 17, 1937, the *Chillicothe Constitution-Tribune* covered the arrival of the *Ziegfeld Follies*. The article began, "Gypsy Rose Lee, Jane Pickens and other stage celebrities in the Follies at the Kansas City Music Hall this season were seen by many Chillicothe people...."

In the April 19, 1937, edition of the *Chicago Tribune*, Gypsy describes the type of roles she hoped to play. Always good for a memorable quote, Gypsy said, "Mother wanted me to play Camille, but Garbo beat me to it." The *Chicago Tribune* also featured articles about Gypsy's early days in Hollywood. In the April 20, 1937, edition a headline read: "Gypsy Rose Lee Dons Lots of Clothes for Her Role in Movie."

Just five days later, on April 25, Gypsy was mentioned in *The New York Times*. The paper ran an article with the title "Vote for Gypsy Rose Lee." The story began: "Gypsy Rose Lee, burlesque actress, was voted the 'most prominent woman today' by senior students of the Peddie School...."

Other contenders for the title included first lady Eleanor Roosevelt and aviatrix Amelia Earhart.

On April 30, 1937, the *Chicago Tribune* ran an article with this headline: "Gypsy Rose Lee Bashful on Film Set."

Sunday with Gypsy. On Sunday May 2, 1937, a glorious full color photo of Gypsy graced the cover of *Sunday News: New York's Picture Magazine*. Gypsy is wearing a runaway sparkling red dress, a fringed shawl covers her breasts, while the bottom half of the dress slides off her body, showing a great deal of hip.

On that same day the *Chicago Tribune* ran a story boasting "Hollywood Tames Gypsy Rose Lee."

Gypsy and the Nudespaperman. On May 8, 1937, the *Montana Great Falls Tribune* published the following "interview" by Paul Harrison, a journalist reporting from Hollywood. Often Gypsy wrote articles and interviewed herself. This piece has her writing style, and fingerprints, all over it. Whether Gypsy wrote this, or Harrison actually interviewed her, Gypsy was always good at suggestive quotes.

She also makes the familiar false claim, "I had invented the strip-tease!" And as usual, she mentions money — this time it is the tidy sum of one million dollars.

By PAUL HARRISON

HOLLYWOOD, May 8 — A nudespaperman interviews a burlesque queen.

Q — Your name is Gypsy Rose Lee?

A — Well, yes. Originally it was Rose Louise Hovick, but my public began to confuse it with "Havoc," so I changed it to Lee.

Q — You were a strip-tease artiste or "stripeuse" in burlesque, were you not?

A — I was, but I'm not. I have discarded the habiliments of my earlier profession down to the last spangle and fragment of black lace. I now am a motion picture actress, and if you don't believe it you can ask the Hays Office.

Q — I have asked the Hays Office, Miss Lee, and it says that you will not do any stripping for the screen.

A — Say, listen! — these people are so cautious that I'm not even allowed to remove my coat for fear it will be misunderstood. The studio wouldn't let me fly out here from New York for fear the papers would say, "Gypsy Rose Lee takes off for Hollywood!"

Q — How do you like the California climate?

A — It's pretty warm for these long-sleeved, high-necked dresses that I have to wear. Of course, as the old adage had it, "There's never a slip twixt frock and hip." And all my clothes have zippers on them. Do you mind if I...

Q — No, no, please, Miss Lee! I know that you were No. 1 on the list of 10 Best-Undressed Women of the American Stage.

A — You don't know the calf of it.

Keeps in Shape

Q — How tall are you, Miss Lee?

A — Five feet, 10 inches. And I weigh 126 pounds in my stepouts and my slippers. I always wear slippers.

Q — Do you like sports?

A — Yes, good sports. Now that I am no longer dancing, I shall have to take exercises to keep in shape. There was a lot of waist motion in burlesque dancing, anyway. It exercised everything except discretion. As for diet, I eat apples. Look at the way they reduced Eve.

Q — Would you be willing to reveal the secrets of your success, Miss Lee?

A — Of course. I have nothing to conceal. A strip-tease artiste, or stripeuse, soon learns a few simple rules, which govern sexcess. These are: "Never put off tomorrow what you can put off today," "It's a great life if you weaken just a little" and "Brevity is the soul of It."

Q — That's fine, Miss Lee. I'm sure that many ambitious actresses will find those axioms helpful. Tell me, where do you live?

A — I live in an apartment, but I am going to get a house on that new part of Sunset Boulevard known as the Sunset Strip.

Q — Heh-heh, very appropriate, indeed. Are you married or engaged, Miss Lee?

A — Certainly not. No man ever has hid behind my skirts! There is a ridiculous story that I have been married and divorced, but I am neither green nor a grass widow.

Lucky Accident

Q — Will you tell your fans how you happened to take up the art of strip-teasing?

A — Well, I was playing in a little drama called "The Gay Nineties" and a terrible thing happened: a shoulder strap broke. These days I wouldn't care a wrap, but then I blushed. I blushed so hard that the other shoulder strap broke, and suddenly I realized that the audience was actually enjoying it. One less thing led to another, and soon I was just standing there blushing all over. I had invented the strip-tease! Next day we changed the name of the show to "The Gay Nineties," and in a few months I had made my first million.

Q — A million dollars, Miss Lee?

A — Well, maybe not million. Maybe you could say "barely a million." Anyway I did all right. The customers thronged to see me take off my clothes, and the money they paid was the price of emission. I never made an ostentatious show of my wealth, though. Nobody could accuse me of putting every little thing I had on my back.

Talented

Q — Who is your favorite movie actress, Miss Lee?

A — Well, Jean Harlow shows certain qualities that I admire. But she doesn't work for Twentieth Century–Fox, does she? Maybe you'd better say Shirley Temple.

Q — What do you think of Mae West?

A — Mae West reminds me of the weakest link in a Vassar daisy chain.

Q — What do you expect to accomplish in your cinema career, Miss Lee?

A — Well, I will do anything that Darryl Zanuck wants me to do, but I modestly believe that I have varied talents.

Q — For example...

A — I could do straight drama because I believe in stark realism. I could do comedy because I have learned to grin and bare it. After all, a girl can't be born long-faced and broad-minded. Also, I could be a fairly good imitator because I know how to do take-offs.

Gypsy La Belle Grand Star. Hollywood gossip maven Louella Parsons reported this item on May 19, 1937:

> Chatter in Hollywood: Looks as if Gypsy Rose Lee hasn't made up her mind whether to be a "regular" or La Belle grand star in Hollywood. After consenting to be Bruz Fletcher's guest at the Ball where they were planning to snap pictures of Alice Faye, Alice Brady and others who had attended Bruz's "high" party in their amusing costumes for a national magazine Gypsy nearly blew up when she discovered the two Alices were not present. At first she refused to pose with the rest of the gang if the two other stars were not present. When she heard that both were planning to pose at home, Gypsy regally protested: "But suppose they change their minds — then you'll have my picture and no other stars."

Five photographs from the June 1937 issue of *Foto* magazine show Gypsy practicing the fine art of the strip-tease. *Above:* (1) "... The Gypsy Rose is well-nigh dressed for an outing as she demurely counts on her crimson fingertips the number of things she will take off." (2) "Whoops! The rip-cord is pulled, and a luxurious expanse of chiffon hosiery and rounded thighs greets the goggle-eyed cash customers." (3) "The Minskys swear it is American art, but in this pose Gypsy exhibits a smile and stance that makes art go primitive and berserk." *Opposite, upper:* (4) "It's fast work, with a concealed zipper that makes the gown disappear like magic, leaving the lady protected by two muffs and a G-string." *Lower:* (5) "... Music is faster now, and bald-headed business men in the $6.60 seats forget their fatigue and strain their eyes at this final phase. Lovely limbs, Gypsy — but watch that double chin!"

Gypsy's Simple Life. On May 26, 1937, the *Hartford Courant* revealed that Gypsy wanted a simple life. The Associated Press article began as follows: "The mainstream of Manhattan ogled Gypsy Rose Lee for years, but it remained for the movies to see a dramatic actress under all her strip-teasing."

***Foto* Magazine.** *Foto* magazine debuted in June of 1937 and contained three-hundred candid shots. The front cover entices readers with "Intimate pictures of the Duke of Kent, Gypsy Rose Lee, Roosevelt Romances, Backstage Scenes, Murder Mysteries, Artists and Models, Plus Complete Hollywood Section!" Photos of Gypsy stripping in the Ziegfeld Follies are accompanied by the following text.

Burlesque's strip tease is an American art, aver the famous Minsky brothers, who purvey it at a price. Argues a prominent psychologist: "It's a method of giving an audience sexual gratification." Art or sex, Foto considers it a noteworthy phenomenon, and herewith presents the world's most famous strippers, Gypsy Rose Lee, divesting herself of all save the law's negligible minimum. Only the sensuous music which accompanies the act need be imagined.

Gypsy Protested. The *Los Angeles Times* ran this headline in the June 4, 1937, issue: "Flood of Protest Greets Gypsy Rose Lee in Films." The article focused on the "Organized letter-writing opposition to the screen debut of Gypsy Rose Lee...."

Gypsy's film career would be short and troubled. She and producer Darryl Zanuck were in for a rough time compliments of the Hays Office. Zanuck and Gypsy would have to deal with one Joseph Breen, who had made it his personal goal to tame the movie industry's most provocative actresses. Breen and the Hays Office tried to clean up Mae West's sex-laden persona, and now they had their sights set on Gypsy.

Unfortunately, Mr. Breen had the Catholic group the National Legion of Decency on his side. Having stripping in movies was, in their minds, indecent. Zanuck received thousands of letters protesting Gypsy's appearance in movies. The number of letters ranged from 4,000 to 20,000 depending on who was telling the story (Gypsy used the higher figure in interviews).

Gypsy Rose by Any Other Name. A short piece on Gypsy appeared in the June 5, 1937, issue of *The Literary Digest*:

Owing to the decline of the strip-tease as a major national pastime and protests from various organizations, the name of Gypsy Rose Lee was changed by cautious executives of Twentieth Century–Fox Film Company. Henceforth, as a dramatic screen actress, she is known as Louise Hovick, her real name. In the picture on this page, Jack Haley, comedian, Walter Winchell, columnist, and new film star, and Whitney Bolton, Screen and Stage Critic of *The Literary Digest*, now summering in Hollywood, are shown discussing the change with the most famous of the latter-day burlesque queens.

Gypsy Vanishes. On June 13, 1937, the *Harford Courant* ran an article titled, "Gypsy Lee Vanishes in Hollywood; She's Demure Louise Hovick Now."

Gypsy Best Undressed. On June 24, 1937, the *El Paso Herald-Post* reminisced about fourteen-year-old Gypsy's adventures in Mexico.

Gypsy Rose Lee No. 1 on the list of the Ten Best Undressed Women of the American Stage. Back in 1925 she was one of ... six girls of a song and dance act. Calderon recalled they came here under the management of Miss Lee's mother, Mrs. Hovick of Seattle.... Calderon said they were traveling in a big automobile. They played at Lobby No. 2 in Juarez ... then started on a tour of Mexico that ended in Parral when a revolution forced them to leave the country.

Cinematic Gypsy. The July 1937 issue of *Cinema Arts* magazine included a feature piece on Gypsy's debut film *You Can't Have Everything*. The article, entitled "Rose by Another Name," included five photos of Gypsy with the cast which included Don Ameche, Alice Faye and Charles Winninger.

Rose by Another Name

The world's best-undressed woman lost a famous and spectacular name when she went to Hollywood to become a film star. We mean, of course, Miss Gypsy Rose Lee, the celebrated strip artiste, who uses her real name (Louise Hovick) in the 20th Century–Fox production *You Can't Have Everything*.

Miss Hovick's advent into the cinema followed a stage career which ran from Ziegfeld (*Hot-Cha*) to burlesque and back to Ziegfeld. As undisputed queen of an art which, whatever its spiritual shortcomings, earned her $600 a week, she was the petted darling not only of Irving Place but of Park Avenue....

In *You Can't Have Everything* Miss Hovick, properly clothed, plays Lulu Riley, the expensive playmate of a theatrical impresario (Charles Winninger). Alice Faye plays Judy, an inexperienced and highly impecunious young playwright. In a restaurant Miss Faye meets Don Ameche, a successful pot-boiling playwright. Somewhat warmed by wine, Mr. Ameche amuses her by leading the orchestra (conducted by Rubinoff) using a long breadstick as a baton.

High spots of comedy are provided by the three mad Ritz brothers, who, acting in the roles of self-appointed Cupids, seek to bring Miss Faye and Ameche back together again, after a misunderstanding. They do it by persuading Ameche to rewrite Alice's classical musical drama, *North Winds*, turning it into a light, popular show.

The remainder of the film is concerned largely with the efforts of the impure Lulu to entice Mr. Ameche away from the pure Miss Faye. It's all pretty complicated, but it works out in the end.

Gypsy is also seen in a photo from her burlesque days in another article entitled "Calculus."

... Hollywood is not unlike Calculus, inasmuch as it is an exact science with a mathematical formula which may be expressed as: *PA* (Press Agent) + *SA* (Sex Appeal) = *EA* (Eye Appeal). This formula may also be expressed as: G (*Girl*) + L (*Legs*) + O (as little as possible) = *Art*, or what passes for Art.

Gypsy vs. Sally. On July 4, 1937, in the "Looking at Hollywood" column, it was noted that "Gypsy Rose Lee [Louise Hovick] was eyeing Sally Rand at the Troc and Sally Rand was eyeing Gypsy Rose Lee...." The "Troc" is the Trocadero, one of Hollywood's famous nightclubs.

Firecracker Gypsy. Star spangled Gypsy was in *Time* again on July 4, 1937.

This photograph of Gypsy from *You Can't Have Everything* proves the observation made by a journalist who noted that Hollywood gave Gypsy the two things she needed least: a new name and clothes. In typical Hollywood fashion Gypsy made three films in one year.

In *Ali Baba Goes to Town* Gypsy was paired with one of the 1930s' most popular entertainers, Eddie Cantor. Here she is seen as Sultana to Cantor's Ail Baba. Other cast members included Roland Young, John Carradine and singer Tony Martin (Culver Pictures).

Gypsy in the *Chicago Tribune*. In the July 6, 1937, issue of the *Chicago Tribune* George Shaffer wrote about Gypsy's role in *Ali Baba Goes to Town*. The headline read: "Gypsy Rose Lee Put on Display in Cantor Film."

This was followed up with an article in the July 12, 1937, edition of the *Los Angeles Times* that explained the costumes Gypsy wore in *Ali Baba Goes to Town*. "The Around and About in Hollywood" column claimed that Gypsy would wear more jewels "... than adorned the coronation gowns of Queen Elisabeth...."

A *"PIC"* of Gypsy. The cover of the August 1937 *"PIC"* magazine featured a stunning picture of Gypsy at the height of her beauty. The popular magazine was divided into sections that included: "Hollywood," "Sport" and "Broadway." It cost ten cents at the time. Alongside Gypsy's photo are the words "The History of Burlesk."

The article itself is titled "The Rise and Fall of Burlesk" and presented numerous photos of former showgirls and burlesque queens and comics, including Lillian Russell, Joe Weber and Lew Fields, Bozo Snyder, Little Egypt, Mlle. Fatima, Josie Gregory, Libby Lawson and Gypsy's contemporary, Ann Corio.

There is one photo of Gypsy, in which she appears perched on a round cushion with pieces of white fur strategically arranged. The caption reads: *Gypsy Rose Lee, the strip-teaser, graduated from burlesk to "Ziegfeld Follies," and will soon appear in movies as Louise Hovick.*

Gypsy Marries. On August 15, 1937, the *Washington Post* announced: "Gypsy Rose Lee Defies 13th Jinx, Marries at Sea." This was the first mention of Gypsy's marriage to Robert Mizzy. "Louise Hovick, who rose to fame and won a movie contract as Gypsy Rose Lee, America's No. 1 strip tease dancer, defied superstition and accepted proposal...."

Gypsy in *Time*. When Gypsy's debut film *You Can't Have Everything* was reviewed in the August 16, 1937, issue of *Time*, the magazine concluded the film was "bound to disappoint the admirers of Gypsy Rose Lee, whose sultry gifts are confined to such lines as 'I'll cut out your heart and stuff it like an olive.'" Sadly, Gypsy's gifts were similarly confined in all of her early films.

In the "Milestones" section of the August 23, 1937, issue of *Time* the following notice appeared:

> Married. Louise Hovick, 23, famed Burlesque Stripper Gypsy Rose Lee until she turned to the cinema; to Robert Mizzy, 25, wealthy dental supply dealer. Unwilling to wait the 3 days required in California between posting of intention to marry and wedding, they hired a water taxi, went 20 miles out to sea and in the presence of two witnesses were married by the captain.

Gypsy's Wedding at Sea. The August 30, 1937, issue of *Life* reported in the "Private Lives" section: "Gypsy got married at sea." The one photo of Gypsy and husband Robert Mizzy was captioned:

> *Robert Mizzy and Gypsy Rose Lee were married 20 miles at sea Aug. 13. Because this failed to comply with California's three-day-notice requirements they planned to get married again on dry land in Santa Ana. Miss Lee, who graduated last year from Manhattan's Irving Place burlesque to the Follies, has since graduated to the movies and is currently working for Twentieth Century–Fox in a picture named Ali Baba Goes to Town. To minimize Miss Lee's reputation as a strip-teaser, Hollywood censors are making her act under her real name, Louise Hovick. At her wedding she remained completely clad. Her husband is a New York manufacturer.*

Gypsy, now named Louise Hovick for her film appearances, is seen here with the cast of her 1937 film debut, *You Can't Have Everything*. From left to right: Charles Winninger, Louise Hovick, Don Ameche and Alice Faye. Gypsy played the part of Lulu Riley.

Gypsy's Folly. Gypsy appeared in the August 1937 issue of *Sheer Folly* magazine.

Gypsy on the *Silver Screen*. The September issue of the popular *Silver Screen* magazine ran a full page ad for Gypsy's new movie *You Can't Have Everything*. Gypsy was billed as Louise Hovick, and beneath her name were the words: *Bringing a new personality to the screen.*

True Romances Magazine. A beautiful color portrait of Gypsy graced the September 1937 cover of *True Romances Magazine*. The photo was a publicity shot for her film debut in *You Can't Have Everything*.

Gypsy in *Time*. Gypsy and husband Robert Mizzy were mentioned in the September 6, 1937, "Milestones" section of *Time* magazine. "Married. Louise Hovick (Stripper Gypsy Rose Lee); to Robert Mizzy; in Santa Ana, Calif. They had already been married at sea (*Time* Aug. 23). The second ceremony was to satisfy California law."

First husband Robert Mizzy samples his famous wife's cooking. The newlyweds are seen here in Gypsy's custom made trailer. Gypsy has signed this photograph with her stage name and her movie star name.

Gypsy — Sleek, Slithery and Sauvé. The September 7, 1937, issue of the *Chillicothe Constitution-Tribune* expressed how Gypsy's legion of male admirers felt about her connubial bliss:

> Gypsy Rose Lee was about the most glamorous thing that ever heightened the humidity of a Broadway stage. She went from 14th Street to the Follies and college boys named her their ideal woman. She was sleek and slithery and sauvé.... Then what happened? She went to Hollywood and got married ... there goes the glamour ... there goes the illusion....

You Can't Have Everything. Film critic Leonard Maltin gave *You Can't Have Everything* three stars and summed it up as follows: "Good show-biz musical ... Faye writes drama ... only succeeds as musical. Ritz Brothers have good material, Louis Prima adds music."

A Warner Bros. synopsis of the plot of *You Can't Have Everything* reads as follows:

> Penniless and hungry in New York, where she has come from her provincial home town to seek success as a serious playwright, Judy Wells (Alice Faye) attracts George Macrae (Don Ameche), successful musical comedy writer, in a restaurant. Judy's plays are of the uplift variety and she can find no market for them. George comes to her rescue. Sorry for her, he secretly persuades the distinguished producer, Sam Gordon (Charles Winninger), to buy the performing rights of one of her plays, "North Winds," promising that he will reimburse Gordon. Judy is delighted and turns her attention to "reforming" George, whose identity she does not know, thinking he is a mere waster. Unfortunately there is another girl in the case. She is Lulu Riley (Louise Hovick), a very determined young woman who intends to land George for herself. When the leading lady walks out at a rehearsal of George's new musical comedy, Gordon is persuaded by

Gypsy poses with her trailer, which enabled the frugal star to tour the country without ever having to dine in restaurants or stay in hotels. Hollywood, 1937 (Covered Wagon Co.).

George and the Ritz Brothers to substitute Judy for they find she can sing. Lulu sees her chance of stirring up trouble. She tells Judy who George really is, and furious at being deceived, Judy walks out of the show herself and returns to her home town.

Other cast members included Arthur Treacher, Tony Martin and Tip, Tap and Toe. Directed by Norman Taurog. The title song was recorded by MGM's young star, Judy Garland.

Gypsy was fast becoming the favorite cover-girl of American magazines. She appears on the cover of *True Romances*, September 1937.

Ali Baba Goes to Town. In her second Hollywood outing, Gypsy played opposite the popular 1930s comedy star Eddie Cantor. Like Gypsy, Cantor (known as "Banjo Eyes") came up from ranks of vaudeville and burlesque. *Ali Baba Goes to Town* was made in 1937 and featured a cast that included Tony Martin, Roland Young, June Lang, John Carradine and Virginia Field. Gypsy was billed as Louise Hovick and played the role of Sultana.

The finale took place at a 1937 premiere with footage of stars like Tyrone Power and Shirley Temple. The film was directed by veteran director David Butler. Butler's credits include four Shirley Temple films: *Bright Eyes* (1934), *The Little Colonel* (1935), *The Littlest Rebel* (1935) and *Captain January* (1936). Butler also directed one of the popular Bing Crosby and Bob Hope "Road" pictures, *The Road to Morocco*, in 1942.

Leonard Maltin gave the movie three stars.

> This funny, sophisticated satire takes on Hollywood, American society, and the politics of Roosevelt's Depression-Era New Deal. Cantor is in top form as Al Babson, an autograph-seeking, movie star–loving hobo, who wanders onto a set and is knocked out in an accident that disrupts filming. He overdoses on a medication and dreams he is in old Baghdad where he is hailed as the magician, Ali Baba, and proceeds to reform an ancient empire along the lines of the New Deal.

Gypsy Is Popular. Gypsy can be seen on page 21 of the November 1937 issue of *Popular Photographer*. Her photo is one of six Murray Korman photos that accompany an article titled "Broadway's Murray Korman." The article by M. Robert Rogers begins with this subtitle in bold print—"The glamour of theatrical Broadway lured Korman from his job as a newspaper cartoonist and led him to fame as a photographer. Here is the story of his brilliant career."

Gypsy sits on a short pedestal in an elegant black dress, her gorgeous legs are crossed. The caption simply reads, *Gypsy Rose Lee, famous strip tease dancer now in the movies*. She is mentioned briefly in the article with these words: "There is the one-time burlesque stripper now married and in the movies, Gypsy Rose Lee. She wouldn't pose nude for Murray because, as she said, 'The Shuberts are paying me nearly a grand for that privilege.'"

Suicide at Witchwood Manor? On November 27, 1937, *The New York Times* announced: "Trace Teacher's Suicide—Grand Jurors Visit Gypsy Rose Lee's Summer Home in Newburgh."

> NEWBURGH, N.Y., Nov. 26 (AP).
> A grand jury investigation of the death of Genevieve Augustin, 29-year-old New York City school teacher, shifted today to "Witchwood Manor," Summer home of Gypsy Rose Lee, former strip-tease artist and now Louise Hovick of the screen.
> The jurors were guided in their inspection by Mrs. Louise Hovick, mother of Gypsy Rose.
> Miss Augustin, a native of Kenosha, Wis., was found dead in a bedroom, a rifle by her side, during a week-end party of a group of showgirl friends of the actress. Although her death was listed as a suicide, the jurors are investigating "certain conditions" at the request of Miss Augustin's mother.

Gypsy and Ali Baba. Gypsy appeared in the November 1937 issue of *Movie Life* magazine to promote *Ali Baba Goes to Town*.

Gypsy Gets Serious. "Louise Hovick Takes Her New Job Seriously," proclaimed the December 21, 1937, issue of the *Washington Post*. The journalist recalled the "... sunny afternoon we spent in the living room of Miss Gypsy Rose Lee...." The article began: "Former Gypsy Rose Lee Aspires to Be Fully Clothed 'Vamp.'"

• 1938 •

In 1938 Gypsy made three more films: *Sally, Irene and Mary*; *Battle of Broadway*; and *My Lucky Star*.

Louise Hovick, the 20th Century–Fox movie star, as rich divorcée Joyce Taylor, in the 1938 film *Sally, Irene and Mary*.

In *Battle of Broadway* Gypsy was wooed by Brian Donlevy (left) and Victor McLaglen (right). The film was released in 1938.

Sally, Irene and Mary. This film starred the extremely popular musical stars Alice Faye and Tony Martin. Gypsy was cast as Joyce Taylor. Others in the cast included comics Fred Allen, Joan Davis, and Jimmy Durante. The film featured Faye and Martin singing "This Is Where I Came In" and "I Could Use a Dream."

Battle of Broadway. *Battle of Broadway* found Linda Lee (Gypsy) caught between two American Legionnaires, Victor McLaglen and Brian Donlevy.

Gypsy's Movie Life. Gypsy was in the April 1938 issue of *Movie Life* magazine. Child star Deanna Durbin was on the cover as part of the "Babies in Hollywood" feature. Gypsy's photo accompanies an article "Night Clubbing" in New York and is captioned: *"Her stage name is Gypsy Rose Lee. On the screen she's Louise Hovick. Has she a Stork Club name too?"*

Gypsy Clothed. The April 26, 1938, issue of the *Chicago Tribune* featured a review for *Battle of Broadway* titled, "Gypsy Rose Lee Film Sensation (in Her Clothes)."

My Lucky Star. On May 5, 1938, *The New York Times* reported in a "News of the Screen" article that "Billy Gilbert and Louise Hovick (Gypsy Rose Lee) have been added to Sonja Henie's "My Lucky Star" at Twentieth Century–Fox...."

By her fourth Hollywood film, *Battle of Broadway*, producers and directors at 20th Century–Fox still saw her as a clotheshorse, overlooking her gift for comedy.

The star of *My Lucky Star* was Olympic gold medalist ice skater Sonja Henie. Gypsy played a character named Marcelle. Cesar Romero, Buddy Ebsen, Joan Davis, Billy Gilbert and Arthur Treacher were also in the cast.

Gypsy's Charm. On August 8, 1938, Hedda Hopper, the queen of showbiz gossip, wrote in *Hollywood* about meeting Gypsy in a "Charm School." Hopper also reported that film star Roland Young, who appeared in *Ali Baba Goes to Town* with Gypsy, told her that Gypsy was "one of the swell-est eggs he'd ever come across...."

Gypsy finished her career at 20th Century–Fox with the film *My Lucky Star*, in the role of jealous girlfriend, Marcelle (Culver Pictures).

Gypsy Nixes Hollywood. On November 4, 1938, the *Morning Avalanche* of Lubbock, Texas, announced that Gypsy had "... deliberately given up her movie career to return to the stage ... striptease made her famous. She has started ... transcontinental tour ... will feature her system of taking off her frilly garments. But she will not do it in theatres ... going to appear in the biggest movie palaces...."

In Hopper's September 22, 1938, column she wrote, "I love Gypsy Rose Lee's line about herself after seeing *My Lucky Star*: "If that's me, something's got to be done about it."

Gypsy Advertises. Gypsy was mentioned in the "Front Views and Profiles" column of the November 12, 1938, edition of the *Chicago Tribune*: "Miss Gypsy Rose Lee, in a black and red gown with a female torso clipped to her belt ('Advertising,' says Miss Lee)...."

Gypsy Sees Red. During November and December of 1938 numerous articles appeared in newspapers across the nation regarding Gypsy and the Dies Committee (House Un-American Activities Committee).

November 26, 1938—*Hartford Courant.* "Gypsy Rose Lee to Testify on Un-Americanism." The article begins: "Representative Harold Mosier, Democrat, Ohio, a member of the congressional committee investigating un–American activities, called upon Gypsy Rose Lee today...." On November 28, 1938, the *Hartford Courant* ran the headline: "Gypsy Rose Lee Won't Be Called to Testify."

November 26, 1938—*Washington Post.* "Gypsy Rose Lee Will Bare All—but Not About Reds." The article began, "Gypsy Rose Lee, strip-tease artist, said tonight she could not go to Cleveland to appear before members of the Dies Committee on un–Americanism...."

On that same day *The New York Times* had a piece titled: "Dies Invoked Law on Reds and Bund...." This article got to the heart of the reason behind Gypsy being asked to testify. The article began, "He [Dies] said he had no intention of interviewing Gypsy Rose Lee, actress, concerning Hollywood efforts to raise funds for Spanish Loyalists...."

November 26, 1938—Missouri's *Daily Capital News.* "Gypsy Rose Lee to Testify on Hollywood Drive to Aid Loyalists." In part, this article read: "Two members of the Dies Congressional Committee alleged Communist activities in Ohio schools today summoned Rose Lee for testimony about a Hollywood campaign to raise money for the Spanish Loyalist government. Committeeman Harold Mosier who with Representative Noah Mason is conducting the inquiry here telephoned Miss Lee at Columbus where she is doing a striptease act...."

December 3, 1938—*The New York Times.* Gypsy's now infamous fundraising efforts were mentioned in the "News of the Stage" column: "Gypsy Rose Lee will head the cast of the second annual "Stars for Spain" to be held on Dec. 11 at Mecca Temple."

• 1939 •

Gypsy the Teaser. In January of 1939 *Stage—The Magazine of After Dark Entertainment* included "Teasers," which chronicled the "ancient and honored history" of the striptease:

Adah Isaacs Menken is shown in tights during the 1861 production of a show called *Mazeppa*.

England's Lydia Thompson "created quite a stir" with her 1869 troupe of ample women known as Burlesque Blondes.

Rose Sydell and her London Belles were the rage of the "gay nineties."

1930 brought us the nationally famous Ann Corio.

The great British comedienne, Bea Lillie, is pictured in a show called *The Show Must Go On* in which she wore a coiffure and gown similar to those worn by Gypsy.

The equally hilarious Imogene Coca is shown doing a spoof of the striptease in a show titled *New Faces*.

Finally there is a photo of Broadway star Mary Martin who did a strip to the Cole Porter song "My Heart Belongs to Daddy" in the Broadway show *Leave It to Me*. Martin's strip catapulted her to fame.

The January 1939 issue of *Stage — The Magazine of After Dark Entertainment* featured these eight photographs of Gypsy's predecessors, peers and contemporaries.

The photo of Gypsy, which appears between those of Ann Corio and Beatrice Lillie, includes the caption:

Gypsy Rose Lee, another notable of Corio's generation, brought the strip-tease into the public eye in The Follies of 1936 when she sang a song filled with scraps of Nietzsche and Freud, showing even strippers have serious thoughts.

Gypsy in *Time*. The January 3, 1939, issue of *Time* covered Gypsy's continuing troubles with the Dies Committee: "Last November Representative Martin Dies's Congressional Committee of Un-Americanism threatened to summon Louise Hovick (strip-name: Gypsy Rose Lee)...."

Reverse Roles in *"PIC."* A beautiful full-page black and white photo of Gypsy graced the inner cover of the Hollywood section in the January 10, 1939, issue of *"PIC."* The caption read: *Queen of the Strip-teasers, Gypsy reigned in almost nude splendor on N.Y.'s Forty-second St. until a role on a Shubert show sent her to movies.*

The next photo of Gypsy was from *You Can't Have Everything*. The caption heading labels Gypsy a FLOP: *Gypsy Rose Lee of burlesque became Louise Hovick (her real name) of the films. She lost the opulent flamboyance that made her a success, played some unimportant roles and vanished from Hollywood.*

Gypsy in *De Film*. Gypsy appeared in the January 22, 1939, issue of Holland's *De Film* magazine, with co-stars from *My Lucky Star*: Sonja Henie and Richard Greene.

In *"PIC"* Again. "They call them 'Queens,'" reads the title of a two-page photo spread in the February 7, 1939, issue of *"PIC"* magazine.

> The stage has its stars, the opera its divas and the ballet its prima-ballerinas — but burlesque has its queens. They are the stars of the show and the backbone of the burlesque industry. Touring the country, they get all the ballyhoo and draw in most of the customers at the burlesque houses in the big cities.

The photo spread featured pics of the following "Queens": June St. Claire, Margie Hart, Georgia Sothern (Gypsy's great friend), Margie Kelly, Ann Corio, and Gypsy, whose caption read:

> *Gypsy's long reign was interrupted when she went to Hollywood. Though technically considered a "graduate," she is now touring in vaudeville with an act similar to that which first brought her fame.*

Gypsy Keeps Her Clothes On. In spite of earlier performances in *Hot Cha*, *Strike Me Pink* and *Melody*, the production of *I Must Love Someone* is considered to be Gypsy's first attempt at "legitimate" theatre. It also marked her return to Broadway and New York. *I Must Love Someone* ran for 191 performances between February 7, 1939, and July 22, 1939, at the Longacre Theatre, which was built in 1913 and is still operating.

Gypsy in *Time*. The May 15, 1939, issue of *Time* ran the following in their "People" section:

> In Leftist and Liberal weeklies appeared this ad: "Clothes? Any New Clothes, Old Clothes? … for Spanish Refugees … Gypsy Rose Lee is chairman of the clothing division of the Spanish Refugee Relief Campaign…."

Her efforts were again referred to in "People" section in the June 26, 1939, issue of *Time*.

> To raise Spanish relief fund, aphrodisiantic Louise (Gypsy Rose Lee) Hovick auctioned off autographed best-sellers: Eleanor Roosevelt's *This Is My Story*, Thomas Mann's *Joseph in Egypt*. To make them real collector's items she added her own signature.

Burlesque on Broadway. In August of 1939 Gypsy appeared in the Broadway play *Burlesque*. Her co-stars were Paul Stewart, Vivian Vance, Frank Rowan and Lionel Rand. The show was also seen at the Spa Theatre in Saratoga Springs.

In *The Other Side of Ethel Mertz*, authors Frank Castellucio and Alvin Walker observe:

> Gypsy Rose Lee starred in the next play of the Saratoga Players, a vehicle appropriately named *Burlesque*. In the 1930s, Lee's burlesque act made her the most famous stripper in the country. In fact, Arthur Laurent's musical *Gypsy* is based on Lee's memoirs of the same name.
>
> *Burlesque* deals with the backstage gossip and private lives of burlesque actors. Vivian played Mazie, the best friend of Gypsy Rose Lee's character. Lee's notoriety pulled in huge audiences but her charisma and hard work could not sustain her performance.
>
> As this review points out: "It is unfair to compare (Miss Lee's) acting ability with that of the veterans who supported her — Vivian Vance provided in generous quantity and superb quality

any acting ability which may have been needed to balance the show. We like Miss Vance better every time we see her, and we thought she was excellent the first time."

"PIC" Magazine — September 19, 1939. This issue of *"PIC"* has a unique cover. At first glance it looks as if there are three magazines overlapping each other with only the "C" from *"PIC" Magazine* visible on the titles "underneath." Under the top title "PIC" is the Broadway section with a picture of Gypsy. Under the "C" of the second title is a picture of the popular comic book hero, boxer Joe Palooka, representing the Sport section. Underneath the "C" of the third title is a picture of movie star Paulette Goddard, representing the Hollywood section.

Gypsy has a two-page photo spread, with four photos. The first shows Gypsy at age eighteen or nineteen, at the beginning of her career in burlesque. The next three photos are almost as long as the magazine itself.

The first of the three is captioned as follows:

Burlesque — Gypsy made her Broadway debut at Minsky's Republic Theatre in 1931. She played the house for twelve weeks — a record for a strip teaser. By 1935 her salary was a straight $900 a week, and she was undisputed queen of strip teaser.

The second shows Gypsy in costume for the Eddie Cantor movie *Ali Baba Goes to Town.* Its caption reads:

Movies — Gypsy's first picture was "You Can't Have Everything!" followed by "Ali Baba Goes to Town" (above). Hollywood kept her under wraps and gave her no opportunity to display her talent for comedy.

The Third and final photo is captioned:

Stage — In "I Must Love Someone," Gypsy won critical applause on her first venture into the "legitimate." Having seen her in everything else, Broadway won't be surprised if she turns up in opera next year.

The short article accompanying these pics in *"PIC"* has no by-line. In part it reads:

Gypsy Rose Lee is typical of the Great White Way as the bright lights that gave it its name. Like most big-name entertainers, she was born in the provinces — Seattle, Washington, was her home town. Working her way up from the bottom, she hit the top and stayed there by using her head, selling her personality, and taking advantage of the beautiful body she brought with her from Seattle. There have been many beautiful bodies and charming personalities on Broadway, but it was Gypsy's wit and intelligence which have made her one of the most exciting characters in the theatrical world — both on stage and off.

"PIC" Loves Gypsy. Even though Gypsy's film career was over, the publicity department at Twentieth Century–Fox was working overtime. For the fourth time in a year Gypsy appeared in the pages of the popular *"PIC"* magazine. In this issue, dated October 17, 1939, she is seen in one photograph accompanying an article about ruthless showbiz agents. The article is entitled "Don't Be a Sucker!" Her photo bears the caption:

Gypsy Rose Lee was sued by the William Morris agency because she was not giving them her cut of her Hollywood pay, although she had a contract with them. Gypsy answered the Equity had advised her to shift agents and she no longer was signed with Morris. A compromise split the ten percent.

Author Rachel Shteir includes a fitting ending to Gypsy's life in Hollywood in *Gypsy: The Art of the Tease.* Gypsy's own words are poignant:

The studio rewarded Gypsy for her cinematic failures. The *Los Angeles Times* listed her as one of the biggest money-makers in Hollywood that year. But in a column for Walter Winchell she complained, "I let them change my name … they gave me tragic eyes."

Shortly after her return to New York Gypsy was back on Broadway. She took over the role of May Daly for a vacationing Ethel Merman in Cole Porter's new musical *DuBarry Was a Lady*. Here she is seen between legendary comic Bert Lahr (left), as Louis Blore, and co-star Benny Baker who appeared as Charley.

DuBarry Was a Lady. Cole Porter's Broadway reign continued with *DuBarry Was a Lady*. The show was an enormous hit. It was a showcase for the talents of the great burlesque comedian, Bert Lahr. To add to the show's box office draw Lahr was cast alongside the queen of Broadway musicals, Ethel Merman.

When Merman needed a vacation the producers came calling for Gypsy to play the role of May Daly. Gypsy and Lahr enjoyed a year-long run at the Royale Theatre. They opened on December 6, 1939, and closed on December 12, 1940.

CHAPTER FOUR

Star & Garter

• 1940 •

New York World's Fair—1940. Gypsy appeared at the 1940 New York World's Fair in a show called *Streets of Paris*, which was her first professional collaboration with master showman Mike Todd. Eventually, the two became lovers.

In 1940 Gypsy met theatre impresario Michael Todd. He created a show for her called *Streets of Paris*. The spectacular show was staged during the second season of the 1940 New York World's Fair.

Gypsy: the ultra glamorous star of Mike Todd's *Streets of Paris*. Gypsy's sister, June Havoc, once remarked that the meeting of Todd and Gypsy was "Money at first sight." As a matter of fact, Gypsy helped bankroll the many productions in which she and Todd were collaborators.

Gypsy at the February House. In her highly acclaimed book *February House* Sherill Tippins takes her readers on a fascinating tour of the unique house at 7 Middagh Street in Brooklyn. During 1940 and 1941 the house was a salon of sorts for a wide variety of artists: writers, painters, musicians, literary figures and intellectuals of all stripes, one of whom was Gypsy Rose Lee. Gypsy's roommates included W.H. Auden, Carson McCullers, Jane and Paul Bowles and Benjamin Britten. It was during this time that Gypsy began writing *The G-String Murders*.

She did so under the tutelage of George Davis, who was one of the most respected editors of the 20th century. The following extract details the factors that influenced Gypsy's decision when she had to choose between staying at the house and finishing her book or following Mike Todd to Chicago where he was launching his latest extravagant production.

> Much as she enjoyed spending time a 7 Middagh Street and working with George, the writing business had turned out to have a serious downside — the necessity for a beginning novelist to finish her book before getting paid. Gypsy loved the process of churning out the chapters with George, but writing had turned out to be hard work — and not having a contract with a publisher was "like being all made up, ready to go on ... and not knowing what theatre you were playing." Despite George's assurances, it was hard to tell whether her writing was any good. When the tea was just right during her morning work sessions and her business interests were going well, she found that she could write just fine. But "if I have night lunch with a smarty pants like Saroyan," she wrote, "I want to spit on the whole damned manuscript."

In short, Gypsy was fed up with the full-time literary life. The continued chaos — increased considerably now that the house was open to visitors — and the squalor of a home shared by so many got on her nerves. Nor did she approve of all the drinking that went on at 7 Middagh. Now, with the refugees arriving by the shipload and Britten playing the piano all day, the house seemed to be turning into a Noah's Ark, with two of every species, making it impossible to concentrate. Gypsy began to think she'd be better off writing backstage. The sight of her sister having the time of her life in *Pal Joey* helped make up her mind. She missed the spotlight and she needed more money. And she didn't want to write any more — or much more — unless she got paid.

A little before Christmas, Gypsy broke the news to George that she had decided to join Todd in Chicago. George, stunned that Gypsy would leave before the book was done, tried to talk her into staying, at least until they had completed a few more chapters. But Gypsy had already packed her bags. In the previous month, she had completed two chapters to George's satisfaction. She agreed to write a third in Chicago and send it back for editing if he would find a publisher and try to get her an advance.

Despite her abrupt departure and George's sharp disappointment, there was no denying that each had profited considerably from their brief partnership. Gypsy's presence had lent a unique twist to the household and attracted the most sought-after names in cultural New York — names that George was certain would continue to travel out to Brooklyn. And Gypsy herself was leaving not only with the completed chapters and the material for others, but also with an address book full of impressive new names. During the weeks she spent among the Brooklyn literati, Gypsy had formed warm and lasting friendships with Janet Flanner, Carson McCullers, Louis Untermeyer, Pavel Tchelitchew, Cheryl Crawford, the poet Muriel Rukeyser, and the noted biographer Carl Van Doren. Marcel Vertes was now peppering her with charming cartoon letters that transcended his English. Gypsy, recognizing an opportunity when she saw one, sweetly requested the rights to a sketch he had made of her: she was sitting at a dressing table in a pink negligee and high heels, typing madly on her Underwood with a cigarette between her lips. Vertes gallantly agreed to the gift, and Gypsy used the image as her personal logo for the rest of her life. "Dammit, I love furriners!" she wrote jokingly to a friend. "Aside from the hand kissing they really make like gents."

> Gypsy's departure in December left not only an empty suite on the third floor of 7 Middagh but an equally empty hole in George's life. Over the winter, George had grown as dependent

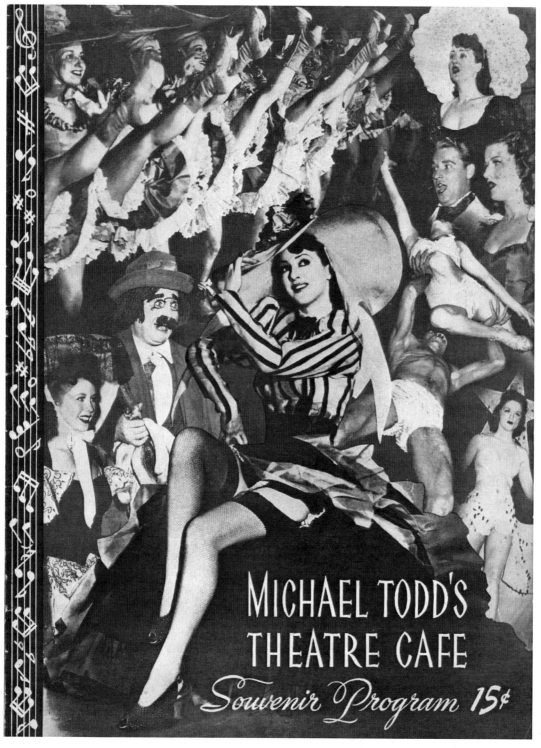

The cover of the 15-cent Souvenir Program for Michael Todd's "Gay New Orleans." The program describes the amenities for sale at the Theatre Café: "For half a dollar the customer gets a seat at a table or at the bar commanding a view of the stage. He gets his choice of table d'hote dinners from seventy-five cents up, and if he likes champagne cocktails they're his for a quarter. ALL THIS AND GYPSY ROSE LEE TOO!" (1940).

as Carson on Gypsy's sympathetic ear and bracing, no-nonsense attitude. He dutifully wrote to her a number of times as he carried on with his duties as nominal landlord—providing all the juicy details on the holiday party: their cook, Eva, "got plastered, but not objectionably," and both Chester Kallman and Susie the maid became very friendly with a group of British sailors. But George felt let down by Gypsy's refusal to stick it out at 7 Middagh until she fully understood the writer's craft. By deciding that she had learned what she needed to know and moving on, he felt, she was giving up her best chance to escape the destiny her mother had handed her. "You've learned that there are other things in life worth acquiring—and for the time being it seems to you that they can be bought with the same coin, pushed across the counter," he wrote. "It isn't so but you won't discover that until that makeup is forever off, and you will no longer be an illusion."

Parisian Gypsy. Gypsy appeared at a fashion event where Parisian gowns brought top dollars to benefit France. The show was covered by *The New York Times* in its May 10, 1940, issue. The headline read: "GOWN BRINGS $700 AT FRENCH BENEFIT; PARIS IMPORTS AT FASHION FETE...."

Dear Gypsy. In 1940 Gypsy wrote a Dear Abby–type column in the *Wisconsin State Journal*. In the May 12, 1940, issue of the newspaper she answers a letter from "Walter Meditating," who inquired about the men she loved. Here, in part, is her response:

> Dear Walter Meditating,
>   On the men I love I find [many] have been gentlemen for whom I worked. When I think of the bosses I feel a sharp twinge of nostalgia and a deep realization that these are the boys who helped me get along and who paid the salary.

Gypsy on the Streets of Paris. *The New York Times* also covered Gypsy's appearance at The World's Fair in the August 30, 1940, issue. A photograph of Gypsy was captioned: *Gypsy Rose Lee, the deciduous damsel now appearing in the* Streets of Paris *at the World's Fair.*

"PIC" Gypsy. *"PIC"* magazine loved Gypsy. She graced the cover of the August 6, 1940, issue of the magazine that purported to cover "The Entire Field of Entertainment."

Gypsy and the Police. Gypsy appeared on the cover of the August-September 1940 issue of the *National Police Gazette*, which included the article "An Unusual Strip-Tease—Gypsy Rose Lee Is First to Do a 'Talking' Strip."

Backstage with Gypsy. Gypsy was featured in the November 1940 issue of *Stage* magazine with a photo of her in costume for the Cole Porter musical *DuBarry Was a Lady,* which was playing at the Royale Theatre in New York City.

Gypsy: Victim of Prudery. The November 1, 1940, issue of Florida's *Panama City News* included an article describing Gypsy's reception by Hollywood.

> Gypsy Rose Lee would be a great comedienne but once she was under contract ... her bosses ... nervously restored her name of Louise Hovick. They dressed her in high-necked black outfits and wouldn't allow her to remove even a fur ... or a pair of old gloves and they slashed her roles to such sparkling lines as "How d'you do" and "I'll want the big car this afternoon." Gypsy remained a victim of Hollywood's peculiar prudery....

• 1941 •

Letters from Gypsy. Between January 4, 1941, and August 28, 1941, Gypsy wrote thirteen letters to her friends Lee Wright and Charlotte Seitlin at Inner Sanctum Mysteries, regarding her work on *The G-string Murders.*

The original letters were donated, by Gypsy, to Princeton University. The collection is missing one letter. However, the editor of Inner Sanctum Mysteries printed a pamphlet containing all thirteen letters. The letters were heavily edited for the pamphlet. The pamphlet begins with the following:

A note from the publishers of

THE G-STRING MURDERS*
By Gypsy Rose Lee

For the past six months, The Inner Sanctum has been enjoying a new recipe for laughter. The explanation is simple: somebody has just received a new letter from Gypsy Rose Lee.

We (Lee Wright, editor of Inner Sanctum Mysteries, and Charlotte Seitlin, Essandess Publicity Director) started corresponding with Miss Lee back in January when Janet Flanner tipped us off that The Belle of the Bistros was writing a mystery story. As can be seen at a glance, the correspondence began on an extremely polite and formal plane. Like Miss Lee's celebrated specialty, however, it gradually built up to a stunning climax.

These letters have given us (not to mention all our friends who have seen them) such fun that we consider it only fair to share them by reprinting them here. The contents of this booklet represent the extracts from as gamey a correspondence as a publisher is likely to receive.

To all the skeptics who are constantly coming to us with: "Say, I hear you're doing a book by Gypsy Rose Lee. Off the record — who's the ghost?" we say: "Read these letters." If, after doing so, you still think that Gypsy doesn't know from writing (Gypsy's accent is rubbing off on us), we will stake you a diamond-studded, plush-lined G-String — complete with a grouch bag.

Lee Wright,
Editor of Inner Sanctum Mysteries

See the unedited letters in Appendix A.

Music and Rhythm. Gypsy appeared on the cover of the February 1941 issue of *Music and Rhythm* wearing an outfit she wore in Mike Todd's *Streets of Paris* with the headline "Music Slays Me."

Inside *Music and Rhythm* "Gypsy Rose Lee Talks About Music and Musicians" in an interview with Don Manning. When Manning asked her about hot jazz fans Gypsy said, "I married one!" Gypsy's first husband, Robert Mizzy, had a record collection, based on Gypsy's estimate, of 1,200 [78rpm] records.

Gypsy had cataloged her husband's records about which she said, "By the time I got through with that job

She dislikes the "abruptness of his crescendos" and says she prefers Beethoven because "the listener is better prepared for the climaxes." Gypsy also likes hot music, but thinks collectors take the art too seriously.

I knew about Bix Beiderbecke, Louis Armstrong, Bing Crosby (when he was with the Rhythm Boys), Jimmie Lunceford, Duke Ellington, Benny Goodman, Gene Krupa, and a whole lot of bands whose names I can't even remember."

At the time of the *Music and Rhythm* interview Gypsy was divorcing Mizzy. The couple had been married since August of 1937. Manning reports, "She laughs at the idea that Mizzy's interest in hot jazz had anything to do with it. 'That sort of thing's no more a cause for divorce than not liking the way a man squeezes toothpaste out of a tube or objecting to his taste in ties.'"

Gypsy then discusses some of the classical music she likes, and composers such as; Shostakovitch, Borodin, and Beethoven. She especially enjoys Debussy's *La Mer* and *Nuages*.

Gypsy reveals her philosophy concerning music: "Music is something free. It belongs to everyone in the world. If you let it go by you're missing something. I wouldn't want to do that, and I haven't."

Gypsy told Manning the type of classical music she liked best were the pieces where she could identify a theme. Dvorak's *New World* symphony was at one time a particular favorite of hers. Now it no longer appealed to her, and the Phillip Morris ads ruined the Ferde Grofé composition *Grand Canyon Suite*. She still enjoyed the "lovely unpretentiousness" of the *Peer Gynt Suite* by Grieg. She also listened with pleasure to Prokofiev's *Lieutenant Kije* and *Peter and the Wolf.*

Gypsy's figure is a sight to behold, yet she modestly affirms, "This form divine stuff is the bunk!" On her own wedding night she visited the Open Door in Hollywood and Louis Prima and his boys played a hot version of the "Wedding March" for her.

Manning describes her as "earthy and honest." She tells him with honesty that she does not understand "the great contrapuntalist," Johann Sebastian Bach, and never went any further than his *Toccata and Fugue in D Minor*. When she appeared on the radio program *Musical I.Q.* listeners felt she made the show easy to listen to; however, many felt her criticisms were "too heretical for conservative listeners."

She told Manning that friends sometimes found her pretentious while discussing music. Gypsy said this was not true and that she made no claim to be a music expert, stating: "Any simple mind can appreciate the *Scheherazade Suite, The Carnival of Animals*, or Debussy." She also felt that listeners should explore music and perhaps find something with greater satisfaction. She did so and found that, like old furniture and modern art, music fulfilled a need for her.

Gypsy was an enthusiastic shopper, especially when it came to New York's secondhand stores. It was there that she found many of the old records in her collection. She discovered that refugees from Europe often bought and discarded records when they found out they had no monetary value, and so she was able to find rare labels and varied music.

However, the bulk of the music she took with her on trips was American. She had a special fondness for "My Gigi from the Fiji Isles" because she had performed it on stage. Other favorites included "Hello Central," "Dardenella," "Mr. Gallagher and Mr. Sheen" and "The Bells of St. Mary's." The latter had a spoken piece in the middle announcing that "The Bells of St. Mary's will now continue." She found humor in tunes like "I Want to Be a Monkey in a Zoo," "Let's Bury the Hatchet in the Kaiser's Head" and "Black Bottom."

The interview ends with a mention of Gypsy's time in Hollywood (1937–38). When she had a longing to hear hot jazz she often got around the rule that a woman could not go into clubs unescorted by asking a waiter to accompany her. That way she got to hear Louis Prima at the Open Door and Louis Armstrong at The Plantation (of all places).

A Peek at Gypsy. Gypsy was featured in the May 1941 issue of *Peek Magazine*.

Gypsy Burns Bridges. The feud between Gypsy and the infamous Harry Bridges was seen in numerous newspapers on Tuesday, June 24, 1941. The following excerpt is from the *Jefferson City Post-Tribune*, Missouri.

> Gypsy Rose Lee, daughter of a sea captain, gave Harry Bridges a piece of her mind on patriotism last night ... the president of the Union took it with a very red face. The strip tease dancer, wearing blue slacks and a bright red coat, was invited to speak before 200 members of the United Service Organization Drive.

On June 25, 1941, *The New York Times* reported on the squabble between Gypsy and Harry Bridges of the International Longshore and Warehouse Union. The headline read, "BRIDGES HALTS USO GIFT: Longshoremen's Leader Deaf to Plea by Gypsy Rose Lee."

Gypsy's Parade. *Pix Parade* magazine of July 1941 featured a glamorous Miss Lee.

G-String Gypsy. The July 15, 1941, issue of the *Jefferson City Post-Tribune* announced:

> Gypsy Rose Lee the well known strip dancer will see her new mystery *The G-String Murders* published shortly. The strippers are all going in for curricular activities. Most of them pine for the legitimate stage. Georgia Southern [*sic*], Ann Corio, Margie Hart all are essaying the sterner demands of dramatic acting.

Gypsy Exposed. The article "Gypsy Rose Lee Exposed in Attempt to Cover Herself with Literary Laurels" by Tom Wolf was published in the *Daily Capital News* (Jefferson City, Missouri) on August 19, 1941.

Gypsy Barred. *The New York Times* ran the headline "Providence Bars Gypsy Rose Lee" on September 1, 1941.

Bedlam for Gypsy. On September 7, 1941, *The New York Times* reported that Mike Todd had "collected" the stars for a new musical called *And So to Bedlam*. The musical had first been known as *Viva McKeever*. In addition to Gypsy, Mr. Todd had signed on Carrie Finnell, Jed Prouty, Ned Sparks and the Nonchalants. The show was never produced.

***It* Magazine.** According to the November 1941 issue of *It* magazine, "Gypsy Rose Lee Knows All About "It."

> Louise Hovick ("*Gypsy Rose Lee" to you*), is an example to *IT* in many different forms, embracing physical, photogenic and dramatic.
>
> Gypsy has grace in the grand manner as she artfully trips across the stage in pantomimic posturizations while giving free rein to a reckless abandonment of apparel. This so impressed the Shuberts that they took this "IT" girl from Irving Place and featured her in their production of the Ziegfeld Follies.
>
> Hollywood began to take notice and it was not a great while before Gypsy Rose Lee was transplanted, and transformed into Louise Hovick of the cinema. Let it be said to her credit that Miss Hovick looked positively radiant and displayed dominant, dramatic determination that could have been developed into stellar possibilities. But, it is presumed, the Hays Office was not at all assured that the public could be made to forget the former specialty of abundant appeal, and Miss Louise Hovick, became once more, Gypsy Rose Lee.
>
> Subsequently, Miss Lee was starred in Michael Todd's "Streets of Paris" which had an extended run at the World's Fair. She also appeared in "DuBarry Was a Lady" and has been a feature of other Broadway productions.
>
> Gypsy has glorious eyes, a lithe figure, an integrating smile, a resonant vocal insistence, a pleasing persuasiveness, and a particular personality. She has ability, and definitely has *IT*.

Music and Rhythm. Gypsy appeared again in *Music and Rhythm* in November 1941. In this issue she was shown backstage writing *The G-String Murders* wearing pigtails and glasses, looking like a serious author. The caption for this picture said that she was 28, but she was actually 30. A second photo shows Gypsy with her tiny dog, Candy. The article accompanying the photos was entitled "Strawinsky to Minsky," and named after a poem, written by Gypsy, that she planned to use in an upcoming Broadway show.

The G-String Murders. Gypsy's first book, *The G-String Murders*, was published by Simon and Schuster in 1941 and was an instant critical and commercial success.

CHAPTER FIVE

Who Done It?

• 1942 •

Mother Finds a Body. Gypsy's second murder mystery also enjoyed popular success. However, it was not received as well as *The G-String Murders*. It was widely reported that Gypsy worked with a ghost writer on *Mother Finds a Body*. The writer was said to be Craig Rice, a talented author who specialized in murder mysteries. Craig Rice was, in fact, a pseudonym of Georgiana Ann Randolph Craig, who wrote mysteries with a comedic flair and was known as the Queen of the Screwball Mystery.

Gypsy at Liberty. The February 13, 1942, issue of *Liberty Magazine* featured "*Mother Finds a Body*— the novel by Gypsy Rose Lee — abridged to a reading time of one evening," prefaced with the following introduction.

> WHAT HAPPENS ON A HONEYMOON?— When mother finds a body? Anything can happen when Gypsy Rose Lee "makes with the typewriter" to tell a story. A year ago Gypsy Rose clicked off the best selling mystery, *The G-String Murders*. Now she has taken time off from strip-teasing, movie acting, and top billing in a Broadway musical hit, to "play a revival"— another best selling whirlwind mystery that won't turn you loose until you've read the last word.

Surely You Jest. *Jest* magazine, one of the many men's magazines that were precursors to Hugh Hefner's *Playboy*, claimed to be "The Zest of Life." The February 1942 issue features the stripper Zorita in an article titled "The Spice of Light." Gypsy appeared on the last page of the magazine. Accompanying her lovely form is a letter from the editors of *Jest*.

> Dear Selectee:
>
> If you happen to be one of those who did not receive a photo of GYPSY ROSE LEE please accept our apology. We were completely snowed under by your requests and in a short time we had sent out all the photos available.
>
> As more photos of Miss Lee arrive we shall send them out to those who have made prompt requests. In the meantime we hope you will find some small measure of consolation in this full page reproduction.

Another Look at Gypsy. The March 10, 1942, issue of *Look* featured a six page photo essay "How America Is Escaping War Nerves." Numerous Broadway and Hollywood stars were shown entertaining wartime audiences, including Danny Kaye, Eve Arden, Bob Hope, Eddie Cantor, Dinah Shore, and Arturo Toscanini. A photo of Gypsy was accompanied by

Gypsy graces the cover of the May 1942 issue of *Argosy*.

the following caption: *A STORY SESSION on a new murder mystery, "Mother Finds a Body," is held by the author, Gypsy Rose Lee (right) and three book-publishing editors (l. to r.), Jerome Weidman, Charlotte Seitin and Lee Wright. First issue "who-dun-its" usually total about 5,000 sales. Gypsy Rose Lee's first book, "The G-String Murders," broke all records with a 24,000 copy sale.*

Gypsy's Gazette. The April 13, 1942, issue of *Time* ran an article, "Expectant Publisher," which described Gypsy's interest in acquiring the *Police Gazette*—she decided the $20,000 price tag was a bit steep.

> Ecdysiast Gypsy ... almost achieved a literary ambition ... all but bought the *Police Gazette*. ("Everything ... appeals to me ... the name ... the pink cover ... meat & potatoes Americana it prints.")

Gypsy Sparkles. In the May 1942 issue of *Spark Magazine* ran a one page photo spread entitled "Gypsy Teaches the Stripsy." One photo shows her with the legendary comedy team of Abbott & Costello. In another she is seen with comedian Billy "Sneeze" Gilbert.

> Again, as Gypsy Rose Lee opens her "School for Strip Teasers" on the Atlantic City Steel Pier, Billy "Sneeze" Gilbert, film comedian, along with Abbott and Costello, enroll for the new semester. SPARK's photographer peeked in on the private session — hoping to sneak a lesson — but Gypsy made him pay — and how!

Gypsy's Murder. The May 1942 issue of the popular *Argosy* published the first of four installments of Gypsy's best-seller *The G-String Murders*. While *Argosy* takes four issues to cover the book, later in the year *Detective Book Magazine* will offer the entire book in one installment.

Star and Garter. Hot on the heels of their triumph with the *Streets of Paris* at the 1940 New York World's Fair, Gypsy and Mike Todd opened a new show on Broadway. *Star and Garter* combined the raunchiness of burlesque with the opulent extravagance of the *Ziegfeld Follies*. Opening night was June 16, 1942, at the Music Box Theatre. The show closed on December 4, 1943, after it was performed six-hundred and nine times.

As the star of *Star and Garter* Gypsy had her work cut out for her. She sang the title song and appeared in five burlesque scenes: Jennie Windsor in "That Merry Wife of Windsor," as The Lady Known, as "Lou" in "In the Malamute Saloon," as "The Girl on the Police Gazette," as Gloria Pinkee in "Aired in Court," and as the Nurse in "Crazy House." She also had a solo turn, in which she stripped

GYPSY ROSE LEE

Her particular gift was once described by a famous writing man in the following: "Sublimating nudity into an aesthetic abstraction by singing detachedly of frustration, psychoanalysis, philosophy and vitality."

Gypsy and Mike Todd continued their association as star and producer. This time Mike Todd created *Star and Garter* for his paramour. This photograph is from page 3 of the program.

Theatre program cover

while reciting the monologue "I Can't Strip to Brahms." Adele Jergens and Gypsy's longtime friend and fellow stripper, Georgia Sothern, were in the show as well.

Stanwyck Strips. On July 16, 1942, it was announced that Barbara Stanwyck was signed by Hunt Stromberg to play the lead character in the screen adaptation of Gypsy's bestseller *The G-String Murders*. *The New York Times* published the news the next day.

The star of *Star and Garter* is seen here as "The Girl on the Police Gazette."

Gypsy and the Bronx Chorus Girl. Anita Arden, a chorus girl from Billy Rose's Casino de Paris Theatre, met and became friends with Gypsy during a stage production of Jumbo. True to his reputation as a producer of spectacles, not unlike Mike Todd, Billy Rose had a live elephant on stage.

When *Star and Garter* went into production, Gypsy cast Anita as a Southern Belle in one of the show's spectacular production numbers. In Liz Goldwyn's *Pretty Things: The Last*

Generation of American Burlesque Queens, Anita remembered how Gypsy would sew Anita's costume on her, and then cut her out of the costume after the performance. This was something Gypsy did with all of the girls who appeared with her in venues from nightclubs to the tours she made across America and Europe.

Anita remembers Gypsy as a perfectionist, a producer who paid attention to every detail, no matter how small. Each and every sequin had to placed just so. Anita was with Gypsy when *Star and Garter* toured the United States. Anita's mother went along on this tour, employed as Gypsy's dresser. Erik, Gypsy's son by Otto Preminger, traveled with Gypsy (as he had done since the age of 6 months). Anita accompanied Gypsy on a tour of Europe, where they performed for troops fighting in World War II.

In *Pretty Things* Anita recalls a Chicago production called The Frolics, in which Gypsy and her girls would perform the routine known as Gypsy's reverse strip. The girls came on stage in skimpy burlesque costumes, and Gypsy would proceed to dress them. Anita describes Gypsy's 10-foot-long sable cape, the blue jeans and golden high heeled sandals she wore with the cape and how Gypsy would toss the sable on the floor as a bed for her dog, and concludes, "Now, that's style!"

Anita also appeared in two more Broadway musicals; *Strip for Action* (1942–1943) and *Mexican Hayride* (1944–1945), a musical in which Gypsy's sister, June Havoc, was featured. Havoc played a character named Montana. Coincidentally, the show was produced by Gypsy's paramour, Mike Todd. It also starred Gypsy's *Star and Garter* co-star, burlesque comic Bobby Clark. Anita also appeared in Gypsy's 1952 film *Babes in Baghdad.*

Liz Goldwyn calls Gypsy "The most famous burlesque queen…" and notes how Gypsy was influenced by her exposure to Ziegfeld style and flair, and made it a point to create an act that appealed to, and entertained, both sexes. Goldwyn emphasizes that with *Star and Garter,* Gypsy, who received no credit as the show's co-producer, brought the world of burlesque from the tawdry burlesque theatres to Broadway with its "mainstream" audiences.

Gypsy on Sunday. To promote *Star and Garter* Gypsy appeared on the cover of the August 30, 1942, issue of the *Sunday News: New York's Picture Magazine.* The color photo showed Gypsy at her alluring best in her first act finale costume.

Life of the Wedding. The September 14, 1942, issue of *Life* featured a photo essay of the marriage of Gypsy Rose Lee and Alexander Kirkland. *Life's* coverage of the wedding ran three pages, and included seven photographs. The photos show the bride and groom with their mothers (Gypsy's mother is identified as Mrs. Thompson), the maid of honor (Lee Wright, the mystery editor at Simon & Schuster), the best man ("Litterateur" Carl Van Doren, a 1939 Pulitzer Prize–winner), Gypsy's fellow stripper Georgia Sothern and German-born surrealist painter Max Ernst. Here's an excerpt from the article, "Hovick-Kirkland — Gypsy Rose Lee, author, weds Broadway actor":

> Fully dressed and in her right mind, Gypsy Rose Lee (nee Hovick), author of *The G-String Murders* (25,000 copies to date) who is well known as a stripteaser, married William Alexander Kirkland, an actor, on Sunday, Aug. 30, just as the hands of her press agent's wristwatch pointed to midnight…. The jittery bride, who was making her second start in the matrimonial sweepstakes, wore a tight-fitting black-silk dress, black shoes and black stockings…. By nightfall the wedding guests began arriving and the imported champagne flowed impartially down tough and tender throats. The bride announced she felt like "an Aztec virgin being prepared for the sacrifice." … The Rev. J. A. Lazell married them beneath Modernist Darrel Austin's painting of a nude mother and child. Gypsy, trembling, twice muffed her lines. But no one

minded. In fact, just before she started bawling, Georgia [Sothern] said, "My Gawd, what a performance!"

Gypsy Strikes Out. Softball teams comprised of the casts of Broadway shows, usually musicals, have been a long-running tradition. In 1941 Gypsy had her own team, as did Lowell Thomas, Robert R. Ripley and Danny Kaye. The teams joined up to play a series of games benefiting the USO. The games took place at Mamaroneck's Arbor Island Park. A headline in the September 24, 1942, issue of *The New York Times* read: "Umpires Decision Costs Shirt, Coat, Too, but It's All for USO; Losing Girls' Softball Team Strips...." It was reported that the townsfolk had never seen anything like it before.

"PIC" Shows Gypsy's Girls. The September 29, 1942, issue of *"PIC"* magazine included an article "Four Understudies of Gypsy Rose Lee," which described the challenge they faced. "So complex are Miss Lee's duties that impresario Mike Todd has engaged four understudies, each of whom is prepared to continue where the other takes off."

Gypsy's G-String. The fall issue (Volume 4, No. 1) of *Detective Book Magazine* featured the entire text of Gypsy's first book *The G-String Murders*, which was presented with the following tease:

> Behind the gay, gaudy backdrops of the Old Opera Burlesque glittered a four-a-day world of strip teasers, line girls, comics and stagehands — happy despite professional jealousies and little hates. Then death, sinister and stealthy, raised the curtain on a hideous pageant of murder, claiming two of the strip-queens with a sparkling strand. And when Gypsy Rose Lee at last discovered the killer — his hands, dangling the flashing G string, were at her throat!

The story was also prefaced with this from the editor:

> We consider ourselves exceedingly fortunate in securing Miss Lee's bestseller (published in book form for $2.00) for our readers. Due to its length — and we know you wouldn't want it cut — we are unable to include the usual number of shorter stories. "The G-String Murders" is the liveliest, most thrilling murder-mystery ever published. It has already out-sold every mystery novel of the past ten years.

Something Wrong with Strippin'? "Say, what's going on around here, anyway?" was the opening line of *The New York Times* theatre critic Brooks Atkinson's September 13, 1942, article, "HIGH COST OF RESPECTABILITY: 'Star and Garter' Illustrates the Law of Increasing Returns in Burlesque at Cultured Prices — Gifted GRL," which highlighted the irony of New York's Mayor La Guardia's refusal to renew the licenses for the city's burlesque theatres boosting business for *Star and Garter*.

Gypsy's Dead Body. *The New York Times* printed a review of Gypsy's second murder mystery, *Mother Finds a Body* on October 25, 1942.

Gypsy on the Spot. *"Spot* Attends — The Wedding of Gypsy Rose Lee." The four-page photo spread ran in the November 1942 issue of *Spot Magazine* (Vol. 3, No. 3).

> It was no ordinary wedding in the first place. The reception ran through the late afternoon and evening and the ceremony was at midnight. This gave Gypsy, well gartered star of "Star & Garter," and the groom, Alexander "Bill" Kirkland of "Junior Miss," an opportunity to make merry with friends, neighbors and two chimpanzees who attended.
>
> The wedding took place at the country home of Miss Lee in Highland Mills, N.Y. It was

held on a Saturday night since that was the only free evening the acting participants had; the date was determined by the fact that it was the birth date of Mrs. Rose Evangeline Thompson, Gypsy's mother; and the hour was prompted by certain astrological calculations of the bride.

Gypsy, ordinarily the acme of aplomb under all circumstances, was cat-nervous as she approached the minister (see the full-length on the next page) and broke down immediately after the ceremony as she turned to be felicitated by Best Man Carl Van Doren, providing the superb photograph on the opposite page.

The guest list, as mixed as it was carefully selected, included Pulitzer Prize–winning writer Van Doren, Matron-of-Honor Lee Wright of Simon & Schuster, publishers of Gypsy's best-selling "The G-String Murders"; and her impending "Mother Finds a Body," the bride's sister-in-strip, Georgia Sothern; associated representatives of the literati and press, and Herman and Henrietta, Gil Maison's chimpanzees from "Star & Garter." It was Herman who goes berserk eight times a week in the revue when Mr. Maison mentions the name of "Frank Buck," whom Herman classes with the contaminated clam. Nobody mentioned F____ B___ and all was quiet.

The couple honeymooned "until their gas ran out," were back at their respective theatres within 24 hours.

Gypsy Close-Up. In the December 14, 1942, issue of *Life* Richard Lauterbach examined Gypsy's life in an article "CLOSE-UP: GYPSY ROSE LEE," which begins:

> Gypsy Rose Lee is a classic paradox: an intellectual strip-teaser. Her purely physical accomplishments have helped her to become in the last decade one of America's most famous women. She has built up a huge personal following which is as fanatical as Aimee Semple MacPherson's, as faithful as Shirley Temple's, and as argumentative as Eleanor Roosevelt's. She has this huge following because she is probably the only woman in the world with a public body and a private mind, both equally exciting.

• 1943 •

The Strip-Tease Murders. *The G-String Murders* was a success in England where it was retitled *The Strip-Tease Murders* and published by John Lane.

Guggenheim Gypsy. In January of 1943, world-renowned art collector Peggy Guggenheim showcased works of art created by women. The show was called "Exhibition by 31 Women" and opened on January 5, 1943. Some of the artists included were Djuna Barnes, Carrienton, Buffie Johnson, Kahlo, Gypsy Rose Lee (who submitted a self-portrait), Louise Nevelson, Meret Oppenheim, I. Rice Pereira, Kay Sage, Hedda Sterne, Dorothea Tanning, and Sophie Taeuber-Arp.

Strip for Action. The following appeared in *The New Yorker* on January 2, 1943: "*STRIP FOR ACTION*: A pleasant and spirited comedy, by Howard Lindsay and Russel Crouse ... and a high-class parody of burlesque, with Bobby Clark and Gypsy Rose Lee."

Cover Girl. Gypsy graced the cover of the February 10, 1943, issue of *The Complete Photographer Magazine* dressed in her costume from *Star and Garter*.

Gypsy in the War of the Wolves. The March 1943 issue of *Mademoiselle* featured Gypsy's story "What's New in War-Wolves."

Lady of Burlesque. Talented movie star Barbara Stanwyck starred in the film adaptation of *The G-String Murders*. Others in the cast of the 1943 film included: Michael O'Shea, Charles Dingle, Iris Adrian and Pink Lee.

Lady of Burlesque was filmed in black and white, and was ninety minutes long. It was directed by William A. Wellman. His film credits include *A Star Is Born* (1937), *The Ox-Bow Incident* (1942), *Roxie Hart* (1942) and *The High and the Mighty* (1954). The film's score was created by Academy Award Nominee, Arthur Lange. Film critic Leonard Maltin gives *Lady of Burlesque* three stars. Maltin writes, "Stanwyck attempts to uncover — no pun intended — killer of strippers in this amusing adaptation of Gypsy Rose Lee's *G-String Murders*."

Tower Books released a "tie-in" edition of *G-String Murders* to promote the movie. The front cover featured a photo of Barbara Stanwyck in an appropriately risqué costume.

Mama Rose Is Knighted. Gypsy's story "Mother and the Knights of Pythias" appeared in the April 10, 1943, issue of *The New Yorker*.

Gypsy at Home. On April 12, 1943, *The New York Times* divulged that "Mrs. Orme Campbell, national director of Bundles for America, and Gypsy bought Dwellings in the Sixties...."

Gypsy's Lack of Decency. "Legion of Decency Bans 'Lady of Burlesque' as Film on Gypsy Rose Lee Book Opens Here" ran the headline in *The New York Times* of May 14, 1943. The film received a "Class C" rating, "C" stood for "condemned." The condemnation came from The National Legion of Decency on the day the film premiered in New York. A month later, on June 17, 1943, *The New York Times* announced: "Ban on Film Is Lifted: Legion of Decency Puts 'Lady of Burlesque' in 'B' Category." The rating of "B" meant that the legion found the picture "objectionable in part."

Mama's Man. "Mother and a Man Named Gordon" was Gypsy's second story in a year to appear in *The New Yorker*. It was featured in the May 20, 1943, issue.

Gypsy the Mechanic. Gypsy Rose Lee was, in all probability, the only stripper ever to appear in *Mechanix Illustrated*. The article "The Mechanix of Gypsy Rose Lee" by Louis Hochman appeared in the June 1943 issue and went into great mechanical detail as to how the huge sets of *Star and Garter* were moved, and began with an account of an accident.

> "Look out!" yelled a stagehand, and four men and a girl scrambled for their lives as 400 pounds of wood and steel came crashing into the spot they'd been occupying just a split second before. The four men were stagehands, engaged in the task of hoisting a 400 pound prop stairway into the air to get it off the floor, when the cable parted and the piece came crashing down. The girl was Gypsy Rose Lee!

The article included one photo of Gypsy accompanied by the following caption:

> *Gypsy Rose Lee, above, is well built, but not strong enough to withstand the impact of 400 pound prop stairway, right arrow, which nearly fell on her when a cable snapped backstage.*

A Gypsy in the Family. The cover of the June 18, 1943, issue of *The Family Circle* showcased a photograph of Barbara Stanwyck, headlined as "... the 'Lady of Burlesque' in the movie made from *The G-String Murders* by that eminent lady of burlesque, Gypsy Rose Lee." Here's an excerpt from the review.

Gypsy returned to Hollywood in 1943 to do a censored version of her famous strip in the film *Stage Door Canteen*. She was one of many stars to appear in this morale booster filmed for the brave U.S. soldiers fighting in World War II. This was just one of the many patriotic activities Gypsy participated in during the war.

"Lady of Burlesque"

Wriggling precariously through Hays Office restrictions, this is the first full-fledged feature about the old "burleycue wheel" to reach the screen. It's a faithful enough adaptation of Gypsy Rose Lee's novel "The G-String Murders," which by a calculated use of not quite *double entendres* and an avoidance of complete undress manages to skirt the offensive and at the same time convey the flavorsome spirit of its behind-the-scenes setting. Those in the know will recognize in its lively unfolding a great deal to remind them of that atmosphere of blubbery nostalgia which hung like a smoke haze above the old burlesque houses. They will find themselves chuckling (or maybe wiping away a beery tear) as much over what is left out as over what is actually shown.

Gypsy at War. The June 21, 1943, issue of *Life* ran an article called "Show Business at War," which included coverage of the 1943 film *Stage Door Canteen*. Gypsy made an appearance in the film, which featured a number of stars including Helen Hayes, Tallulah Bankhead, Katharine Hepburn, Ethel Merman, Ray Bolger, Benny Goodman and Peggy Lee.

It appears that the director (Frank Borzage) of *Stage Door Canteen* is demonstrating just how much leg Gypsy can show. From this film forward she was billed as Gypsy Rose Lee.

Third Time's a Charm. Gypsy was back in the pages of *The New Yorker*. Her story "Just Like Children Leading Normal Lives" appeared in the magazine's July 3, 1943 issue.

Gypsy Solves Another Murder. In the Fall of 1943 issue of *Detective Book Magazine* followed their prior publication of *The G-String Murders* with the complete text of *Mother Finds a Body*. The cover announced: "Gypsy Rose Lee Presents Her Thrilling Sequel to *The G-String Murders—Mother Finds a Body—* A New Mystery Novel Complete and Uncut." The internal tease read:

She found it at the trailer camp. Never mind exactly where. Never mind what she did with it, either. At all costs Gypsy must be protected — whether she is guilty or not. Somebody was throwing all those knives — and putting heroin in her Mother's asthma powder. Clues pointed Gypsy-ward and Mother suddenly felt maternal. And so the trail was obscured as it wound its winsome way through perjury, arson, and ordinary murder.

Gypsy's Gold Rush. Newspapers around the country published the following tidbit on September 4, 1943: "William Goetz announced today that the first picture to be produced by his newly-organized International Picture Corporation will be "The Belle of the Yukon," a musical of the Gold Rush. The film will star Gypsy Rose Lee...."

Gypsy's Genius. Meanwhile, it was reported in *The New York Times* on September 18, 1943, that Gypsy's play *The Naked Genius* would open in New York on October 15, after concluding its run in Boston, from where it would move on to Baltimore, and finally Broadway.

Gypsy's New Ziegfeld Man. The October 2, 1943, issue of *Liberty Magazine* ran a lengthy article on Gypsy's producer, and rumored paramour, Mike Todd by venerable journalist Earl Wilson entitled "The New Ziegfeld":

> The remarkable success of *Star and Garter* proved Mike's analysis of audience was correct. But Mike had done more than just give them what they wanted. He had squandered. In one number alone he had spent $180 to dress each girl — to dress her so that she looked undressed. For $180 he got one chastity belt, one necklace, one hat as big as possible, and one brassiere as small as possible. He picked all the girls for looks. When asked how he had found so many pretty girls, he replied, "I don't pick mine in the dark like so many producers do."

The article went on to describe how Todd produced the musical *Something for the Boys*, a show he bought sight unseen for $75,000 simply because it had been written for Broadway legend Ethel Merman. He then proceeded to invest his profits from *Star and Garter* into the new Cole Porter show to the tune of $62,500.

The Naked Genius. Gypsy's play *The Naked Genius* had a short run on Broadway. It ran from October 21, 1943, to November 20, 1943. This was another Mike Todd production backed by Gypsy. She would have been better off with another producer. Fate stepped in when Hollywood actress Joan Blondell was cast in the leading role of stripper Honey Bee Carroll. Blondell and Todd fell in love, and eventually married.

Gypsy Bids on Modern Art. During the Broadway opening of *The Naked Genius,* according to the October 21, 1943, issue of *The New York Times* Gypsy was among the bidders at an auction at the Parke-Bernet Galleries, where New York society bought $61,740 worth of modern art collected by Frank Crowninshield, whose collection included oil and watercolor paintings, sculptures, drawings and prints.

Gypsy a Clothed Genius. On November 7, 1943, *The New York Times* traced the history of *The Naked Genius* in an article headlined "GENIUS WITH ITS CLOTHES ON; Being the Incredible Saga of How Miss Lee's Drama Got at Last to Its Present Spot on Broadway."

Gypsy in *Time*. The following excerpt is from the article "Todd's in His Heaven, which appeared in the November 8, 1943, issue of *Time*.

It was less a Broadway opening than a kind of $5.50 question. On its road tryout Gypsy Rose Lee's maiden effort at playwriting, *THE NAKED GENIUS,* had become the script-tease of the season. Two days after it went into rehearsal, it was sold to 20th Century–Fox on a sliding-scale basis for a maximum $365,000. In Boston, Baltimore, Pittsburgh, it packed them in — but kept stalling off its Broadway opening. Then Producer Michael Todd (*Star & Garter, Something for the Boys*) boldly announced he would open the show there over the violent protests of Gypsy and Director George S. Kaufman, who wanted it buried. As a final flip of the G-string, Todd took advance ads in Manhattan papers reading: "Guaranteed not to win the Pulitzer Prize." There is no doubt whatever about the justice of this comment. The play is frightful.

The article goes on to say the New York theatre critics showed no mercy in their reviews. However, thanks to Mike Todd's ingenious ads and Gypsy's name the public showed up in droves; among them men in the military and laborers such as plumbers and welders. The article closes with this exchange between director George S. Kaufman and producer Mike Todd, when Kaufman called after the second night:

> Todd chuckled: "We had 14 standees." Snapped Kaufman: "Say that slowly. I know you must be hysterical." Said Todd slowly: "Fourteen standees." "Send me the statement, verified," barked Kaufman. "And if what you say is true, then I'll quit show business."

A single black and white photo accompanied the article. It shows Gypsy and director George S. Kaufman sitting in the empty theatre; Gypsy is wearing a huge pair of bedroom slippers.

Naked in *Life*. The November 15, 1943, issue of *Life* revealed "The Naked Genius: Gypsy Rose Lee's play is a hit despite unfavorable reviews," which it was quick to verify:

> *The Naked Genius* is [Gypsy's] first try at a play. Bumbling and unsatisfactory, it proves that she has stretched and parodied her experiences to the breaking point. Employing the services of Joan Blondell, a cast of 43, seven dogs, one rooster and one monkey, *The Naked Genius* is the saga of a burlesque queen who has a lot in common with Gypsy Rose Lee. Concerning the monkey, whose name is Herman, New Yorker's crabby Wolcott Gibbs said: "Only the monkey seemed to have much confidence in the script."

At Home with Gypsy. The December 1943 issue of *House & Garden* included an article written by Gypsy, entitled "My Home." The following excerpts from the article were printed in the catalog that was created by Sotheby, Parke-Bernet Los Angeles when Gypsy's estate went up for auction following her death.

> On matinee days I took most of the hand sewing to the theater and stitched away as my maid dressed me for my performance. The needlepoint and the lampshades were all made during these costume changes....
> But my "French Provincial" library is too much. A Directoire daybed! Modern chairs! Queen Anne! Italian commodes! A student lamp! Surrealist painting! A twelve-dollar typist chair! It is just about as "French Provincial" as the back line of a Minsky chorus....
> ... A year ago I would have settled for an Aubusson rug the size of a bathmat and now I find it hard to believe that the big one in the drawing room is mine to walk on! Not that I would, of course, unless I took off my shoes....

• 1944 •

Gypsy in Alabama. On January 28 of 1944 Gypsy brought her show to Gunter Field in Alabama. Gypsy performed at numerous military bases to boost the morale of the men in uniform.

Ever the patriot, Gypsy signs the cast of one happy soldier. 1944.

Gypsy the Patriotic Trouper. The February 2, 1944, issue of *The Joplin Globe* (Joplin, Missouri) reported that Gypsy showed up for an army camp visit despite the fact that she was in pain, and "… rush dental work" was needed.

The Gypsy Rose of Texas. Gypsy performed at Bergstrom Fields in Austin, Texas, on February 6, 1944.

Gypsy at Home. *Home Was Never Like This*, a World War II patriotic magazine, published Gypsy's wartime story "They Need It for BULLETS!" which follows in full.

For three weeks I had been searching for a certain type pin. It had to be a long pin with a heavy, white head. I use that type only in my specialty. The small, wire-like pins become lost in the folds of my costume, and to a strip-teaser a lost pin can mean the difference between success and failure. A theatre full of people can be unsympathetic about a misplaced pin.

In a ten-cent store, I found the pins, a whole counter full of them. Delighted, I scooped up every package on the counter and began counting them carefully. The sales girl appeared, and I asked if there were more cards of pins. "Behind the counter, perhaps," I suggested, leaning way over to see for myself.

"No, there aren't," she said unpleasantly, "and put *those* right back where you found them."

"Oh, no," I said, all personality. "I have been looking for pins like these all my life, and I intend buying every card you have in the store."

"Only one to a customer," she said. She ignored the ragged five-dollar bill I offered with a trembling hand.

"One card *a day*," she added. "Priorities, you know."

"Priorities on pins!" I gasped. "It's impossible. They can't do this to me. I can't perform without my pins. How can I get my dress off? How can I make a living if I can't get off my dress?"

By then a small crowd had gathered, and as the sales girl slapped the pins from my hands they giggled. One cheerful woman stopped laughing long enough to say, "You still have a type-writer, haven't you?"

I didn't know what she was driving at until she explained that she had read my book and had liked it. I naturally forgot about the pins. Writing a book does that to a person. On the way back to the theatre with my one precious package of pins I began to wonder what the other women in my particular field of endeavor were doing about priorities.

Take fan dancing. Some of my best friends are fan dancers; so I don't want to give the wrong impression about this, but, of all the careers available to a healthy woman and normal enough young woman, why should she choose fan dancing? It certainly isn't easy work. It may look easy, but those fans weigh something. The strain on the arm muscles is terrific, and after wav-ing those fans four or five times a day, for ten years, you're apt to end up with shoulder devel-opment like Errol Flynn, which is lovely on him but extreme for a girl. There are occasional hazards too. Draughty theatres. Picking up a tack in the foot. What if you suddenly develop and allergy to feathers? It's happened before. You never know what you're allergic to until you get behind a dusty fan. Then you have that dark-blue spotlight to worry about. If it's too dark you may fall into the orchestra pit. If it isn't dark enough you have a dark cell and a policeman in a dark uniform waiting for you.

My fellow-artiste Lulu La Zonga, anxious to get away from her fans (I mean, strictly the ostrich-plume variety), took up the new art of balloon dancing. She didn't exactly change her career; the step from fan to balloon is a short one, but enough to give her a whole new set of headaches. Even before the war and the priority on rubber, the balloons were hard to get and very expensive besides. They had to be made of a certain translucent rubber. Not that I know anything about them other than what Lulu told me. She was visiting me one night in my dressing-room. I had met her before but we hadn't much to talk about then. This night was different. Lulu was thinking of doing a new act. When I saw her looking, rather wistfully I thought, at my costumes hanging on the wall, I knew something was on her mind. "It must be interesting," she said, with a sigh, "to wear so many things. My goodness, there isn't one thing in your wardrobe that you have to worry about. No priorities, I mean. My balloons, you know? Well, they're out. I can get them, of course, but I think it's unpatriotic. Don't you?"

I watched her nervously snap her fingernails. They were dry, without polish, and the cuticle was brittle. Little flecks of white body paint were buried under the flesh of her fingers.

"I had to give it up," she said.

"Your balloon routine?"

"No, honey, the body paint. I really had to. Look what it's done to my hands. So drying! But it wasn't easy. They tell me that you can't tell the difference from the audience, but the first time I went out without it, I thought I'd die! I felt so … so *naked*. Really, I'd rather be caught without my fans. But it's just as well. The Government needs it."

"Needs what, Lulu?"

"The body paint. Something in the stuff they use for bullets or something."

The talk drifted back to balloons. With Lulu you never know how you get around to talking about her and her career, but you just suddenly get there.

"They cost me sixteen-seventy each," Lulu said. There was a worried frown between her eyebrows. "That's in hundred job lots, too. Then I play a town like Hartford, and those little brats sit in the front rows and flick pins at them."

Naturally I went tch, tch, because it was expected of me. The tomboy in me made me feel a sneaking sympathy for the brats. It must be a great temptation to flick a bent pin at such an important balloon.

"So help me, Gyp," Lulu said, thumping my dressing-table. "One of these days I'm going to have a baby and give it all up."

An hour after Lulu left my dressing-room, Zuleika, the snake dancer, dropped in. It really was old-home week down there in Miami. Zuleika, I was pleased to notice, was minus her snake.

"It died," she said, with an angry toss of her head. "I paid seventy-five for it, too. Me, who's never paid more than six or seven bucks for a snake in my life, let that guy talk me into a seventy-five-buck python. He was so heavy I could hardly work with him."

"I'm so sorry you lost him," I said. Having read Zuleika's press notices, I knew snakes were almost like children to her. Once, to show how affectionate a snake could be, she had picked up Joe (he was a seven-dollar boa) and kissed him on the nose. It made a wonderful picture. "But don't you still have Joe?"

"Joe's passed on, too," said Zuleika, mournfully. "He was getting old, Gyp. You can always tell, their eyes get glazed-like. Anyway here I am making an overnight jump to Chicago, and I have to fly. They won't fly animals or snakes or things unless you have them crated, you know. Well, there I am. Two snakes that don't know each other and only one crate. I was stuck, believe me, but good. So I rolled the old guy, Joe, around my waist, and put on a coat. He curled around me and was just sweet and quiet. The new one, that seventy-five-buck one, I put him in the crate. The minute I get on the plane, I go to sleep, and don't wake up until we land in Chicago.

I have a cup of coffee, and when I unfasten the seat belt I'm careful not to disturb Joe. He was being such a lambie boy…. Then I get off the plane, open up the coat, and what do you think?"

I was afraid to think.

"Dead!" said Zuleika, dramatically. "He was stiff he was so dead. And there was me, sleeping all night with him like that. Can you imagine, Gyp?"

I took a glass of water, then asked her what she was doing in Florida.

"Trying to get a new snake," she said. "This war is making it awfully tough to get a good one."

So there you are. I thought about the troubles of Princess Wanda, the flame dancer. Without even going into the details of her act, you can imagine the danger. She dances on her toes, to make it more difficult, around a lighted candle that stands center stage. She is naturally dressed as a moth. She naturally dances too close to the candle and burns off the costume. Naturally. And Wanda rather enjoys telling people about the number of times the costume has burned too close for comfort.

"Only last month I was working at an outdoor fair," she told me. "There was a wind, and instead of blowing the flame away from me — well, just look at my back! I thought I was going to be scarred for life."

Now, with the war, there is a doubt that Wanda can even get the necessary material for the wings. It is something called "flash paper," and I hear they need it for bullets. Or something.

Well, I'm glad I got my typewriter before there was a priority on them. Guess I'm pretty lucky to be making with the words. In my old career — take the beads for a G-string — for instance. Can't get them. Can't get my pins. My lacy stockings couldn't be more valuable if they were spun from gold, instead of rubber and silk. I have one pair left and am saving them for state occasions. Even my garter belt is on the list!

Girls, my advice, if you are entertaining ideas of taking up fan, balloon, flame, or snake dancing, is to forget it. Get a good, sturdy pair of dungarees and learn to dissect a motor. Learn how to fly a plane or drive a taxicab. Anything but the career of nude, or semi-nude, dancing.

You just can't get the merchandise.

Gypsy's All a-Titter. Billed as America's Merriest Magazine, *Titter* featured photos of young ladies attired in lingerie and less — the less the better — and ran articles with titles like "An Amazon Beauty," "Just a Robin Hood-lum" and "Hi-Jinx." The February 1944 issue of *Titter* presented a photograph of Gypsy to supplement the article "Life Begins at Midnight." She wore the costume from the finale of *Star and Garter* and the caption read:

> *All we can say about the beauty of this lovely charmer is that it must be the Gypsy in her (Yeah — its Gypsy Rose Lee, kiddies, as if you didn't nude!)*

Gypsy Is a Yank. *Yank—The Army Weekly* featured a photo of Gypsy in its March 17, 1944, issue. Found on page nineteen the photo shows Gypsy with a very unique line of chorus "girls." The caption explains all:

> *GYPSY'S "GIRLS." Gypsy Rose Lee, authoress and teaser, leads a chorus of GI "beauties" at Bergstrom Field, Austin, Tex., where she stopped on a tour of Army camps. Backing her up are Cpl. Charles Burgh, Pvt. Calvin Benell, S/Sgt. John Plewacki, S/Sgt. Olin Elliott, Sgt. Keith W. Clark and Sgt. Victor Solimine.*

Gypsy for One Shilling. *Lilliput* was a humor magazine from the UK. It cost one shilling. Gypsy appeared in the April 1944 issue. The photo shows a sailor in the British Navy gazing at a photo of Gypsy from *Star and Garter*. The caption reads: *Gypsy Rose Lee entertains the Navy.*

Belle of the Yukon. The *Stars and Stripes* newspaper dated Monday, July 3, 1944, ran a photo of Gypsy, where the glamorous star of the forthcoming film *Belle of the Yukon* was being cinched into a corset. The caption read: *It's a tough struggle, but Gypsy Rose Lee, dressing up more than usual for a scene in "The Belle of the Yukon" will achieve that 17-inch waistline or else.*

This photograph of Gypsy and her beautiful "Girls" appeared in the March 1944 issue of *Yank* magazine. Gypsy toured many military bases, performing for thrilled U.S. soldiers.

The original studio caption of this production still read: *"SHE'S THE DANCE HALL QUEEN!"* So says *"Honest John" Calhoun (center) (Randolph Scott) when he introduces Belle DeValle (Gypsy Rose Lee) to Sam Slade (Bob Burns) shortly after her arrival in Malemute, roaring Alaskan boomtown.... Belle apparently has Calhoun under her control as he succumbed to her whim and is carrying "Hercules," the lady's one-pound shivering Chihuahua.* The shrewd businesswoman, Gypsy, made certain Hercules was paid for his services. She happily collected his pay and her own.

After an absence of six years, Gypsy returned to Hollywood. For the first time she was allowed to use her stage name. She was given a splashy Technicolor production starring alongside one of Hollywood's best loved cowboys, Randolph Scott. Gypsy played the title role of Belle DeValle. Film critic Leonard Maltin wrote this in his book *2002 Movie & Video Guide*: "... saloon owner Scott going straight at the insistence (Lee); fast-moving, forgettable. Technicolor is film's best feature."

One of Gypsy's co-stars was a very young Dinah Shore. Dinah sings the Oscar-nominated song "Sleighride in July" by the celebrated song writing team of Sonny Burke and Jimmy Van Heusen.

When *Belle of the Yukon* played in Holland a special six page program was distributed. The title, in Dutch, was *Alaska Dronning*.

Motion Picture. Gypsy was seen in the September 1944 issue of *Motion Picture*. Other stars in the magazine were Lucille Ball, Clark Gable, Susan Hayward, Rosalind Russell and

Gypsy made another trip to Hollywood to appear in the 1944 RKO movie *Belle of the Yukon.* Her leading man was the handsome western hero Randolph Scott and a very young Dinah Shore (left) also starred.

Frank Sinatra. Katharine Hepburn, dressed and made-up for her role in *The Good Earth,* is on the cover.

Hello Reno, Goodbye Husband. On September 6, 1944, newspapers nationwide announced:

"A Reno friend of Gypsy Rose Lee who admits she is in Nevada to establish [the] necessary six weeks residence for divorce proceedings ... said the dancer expects a baby in January. The friend said Miss Lee stated she was to have custody of the child under a verbal agreement with her husband, Alexander Kirkland."

Look at the Belle of the Yukon. A full page ad for *Belle of the Yukon* appeared in the October 31, 1944, issue of *Look.* The legendary Bob Hope was on the cover.

A Romantic Gypsy. A color photo of Gypsy graced the cover of the November 1944 issue of *Personal Romances Magazine,* which featured the article "The Things I Want: A husband—a baby—a home, don't all women want them?" The piece was "revealed" to writer Gladys Hall by Gypsy and begins, "I want the baby I'm to have and the husband I may soon be divorcing."

This photograph of Gypsy and her son, Erik Lee Preminger, appeared in the May 24, 1945, issue of *Liberty* magazine.

After that attention grabber Gypsy goes on to say that she wants to keep all the things that life has given. Gypsy the collector expresses her wish for a cluttered house with little room to move. A house where a ghost would be hard pressed to find elbow room, let alone Gypsy and her visitors.

Like most people Gypsy wants money. This means that she had to excel as a business woman. While reading the script for *Belle of the Yukon* Gypsy felt that her character, dance hall hostess Belle DeValle, was the kind of woman who would have a small dog. Gypsy mentioned this to director William Seiter and soon Hercules became a member of the cast. His proud owner didn't mind collecting his salary.

She claims that she wants to stay married to her second husband, Bill Kirkland. Unfortunately, the union seems to be over. Gypsy places the blame on her career and overdoing her role as a housewife. She finds that she must be "all-consuming, all-out," with everything she does.

Gypsy's Bouncing Baby Boy. Erik Lee Preminger was born on December 11, 1944. On December 13, 1944, readers saw the bold headline "GYPSY ROSE LEE GIVES BIRTH TO A SON." Erik's birth was reported in newspapers nationwide. The following excerpt is from the *Moberly Monitor*, Missouri:

> Gypsy Rose Lee former burlesque performer and author of the *G-String Murders* gave birth to a five and one-half pound son yesterday, the day after her divorced husband was expected to marry. Miss Lee, born Louise Hovick, was reported to be in just fine condition by a nurse in the office of her physician Dr. Morris.

• 1945 •

Movie Story **Magazine — January 1945.** This issue of *Movie Story* ran an article describing the plot of Gypsy's film *Belle of the Yukon* and supplemented it with three photos of Gypsy.

Mama Gypsy in *Life*. The March 19, 1945, issue of *Life* had a full-page photo of new mother Gypsy with her son Erik. The caption simply read: *A newly maternal Gypsy Rose Lee pins up her son Eric* [sic].

Artists Engagement Contract. A contract obtained by the author from eBay shows that Gypsy was represented by M.C.A. Artists Limited (Music Corporation of America). She was booked into the Fox Theatre in Atlanta, Georgia. Her opening night was to be March 29, 1945. She played the theatre for one week. Under the area designated for the artist's salary the section reads: "Five thousand dollars net ($5,000 net) plus 25% net split of gross box office receipts (in excess of thirty thousand dollars ($30,000)." Under "Special Instructions" the following is typewritten: "To appear in conjunction with Tommy Tucker & His Orchestra. Tommy Tucker does not assume any responsibility herein and acts herein only on behalf of the theatre specified. Rider attached hereto is hereby made a part of this contract. Kindly initial same. Artist is to receive split headline billing with Tommy Tucker in the same size and type with her name appearing second to Tucker. It is further understood and agreed that in the event the artist misses any shows due to the later arrival of her train no deduction is to be made from her compensation." The contract was signed by Gypsy and dated March 13, 1945. Gypsy, ever the shrewd businesswoman, had all of her bases covered.

Gypsy Frolics. Chicago was a busy town during the months of March and April 1945. The Chicago Stagebill included ads for the following plays: *Windy Hill* starring Kay Francis, *Laughing Room Only* with the comic team Olsen & Johnson, Nancy Walker in *On the Town*, and *The Late George Apley* starring Leo G. Carroll.

Swank nightclubs like the Boulevard Room, the Empire Room, Ricketts and the Glass Hat at Chicago's Congress Hotel were filled nightly. Over at the Frolics Theatre Restaurant

Chico Marx, of the famous Marx Brothers, opened on April 4th and played for two weeks. On April 18th a new show opened at Frolics: *Gypsy Rose Lee and Her Girls!*

Go Have Sex. "Good, Wholesome Sex" was the name of an article by Gypsy published in the May 1945 issue of *Go* magazine.

Gypsy's Zoo. On June 14, 1945, Gypsy attended the annual garden party hosted by the New York Zoological Society.

Gypsy's Shampoo. In an ad for Mar-o-Oil shampoo in the August 1945 issue of *Movie Stars Parade* Gypsy showed off the same elaborate hairstyle she wore in *Belle of the Yukon*, and announced, "My search for the perfect shampoo ended when I found Mar-o-Oil. It's grand!"

Doll Face. Never one to let a creative idea go to waste, Gypsy overhauled the script of *The Naked Genius* and came up with the screenplay for the 1945 film *Doll Face*.

A young Vivian Blaine played the role of Mary Elizabeth "Doll Face" Carroll, the character known as Honey Bee Carroll in *The Naked Genius*. Blaine was a fresh talent, not yet known for her trademark performance as Adelaide in the Broadway musical *Guys and Dolls*, which opened on November 24, 1950.

Other new talents in *Doll Face* included the vivacious, wacky, one-of-kind bombshell Carmen Miranda and a very smooth, romantic singer named Perry Como who sang the Jimmy McHugh and Harold Adamson song "Dig You Later (A Hubba-Hubba-Hubba)."

Three other songs included: "Somebody's Walking in My Dream" sung by Vivian Blaine (later sung and danced by Martha Stewart in the finale), "Red Hot and Beautiful" sung by Perry Como and danced by chorus girls (later sung by Vivian Blaine and a male quartet) and "Here Comes Heaven Again" also sung by Como (later sung by Como and Blaine in the finale).

Gypsy Gets Swanky. Gypsy published an article "Kathleen, Dear" in the September 1945 issue of *Swank*.

Gypsy & Minsky II. On April 5, 1945, Leonard Lyons' column, as seen in the *Amarillo Daily News*, included this tidbit: "… Gypsy Rose Lee, who retired from burlesque to tour in legit, is working at the St. Charles Theatre in New Orleans, where it was discovered that she's still working for Minsky: the house manager is Harold Minsky, son of the burlesque producer … Miss Lee's routine now includes singing, 'I have modulation in my voices,' she reports, 'modulation should not go good with undulation.'"

• 1946 •

The Unconventional Gypsy Rose Lee. The April 1946 issue of *Reader's Digest* includes a section with the title "Talkfest — II Unconventionally Speaking." The magazine describes the special feature as follows:

> This is the second in a series of experiments in Recorded Conversations. Five well-known persons were invited by The Reader's Digest to gather round a table and bandy words on the subject of unconventionality. The following is a condensation of their remarks as reproduced by a General Electric wire recorder.

The conversationalists were: Bennett Cerf, publisher, columnist, and author of *Try and Stop Me*; John Erskine, novelist and lecturer; Gypsy Rose Lee, premiere striptease of burlesque, and author of *The G-String Murders*; Roland Young, star of stage, screen and radio; Henry Morton Robinson, roving editor of The Reader's Digest.

The actual conversation went as follows:

Robinson: Gypsy, shall we assume that everyone knows what Unconventionality means — and take off at once?

Gypsy Rose Lee: Let's not be in such a hurry to take off anything. With all the amateurs at it, how do you expect a girl like me to make a living?

Cerf: Gypsy's right — let's slow down for a few definitions. I've always thought that Lewis Carroll's little stanza from the "Hunting of Snark" said volumes about the nature of conventionality. It runs: "*What's the good of Mercator's North Poles and Equators, Tropics, Zones and Meridian Lines?*" So the Bellman would cry: and the crew would reply, "*They are merely conventional signs!*"

Young: Clever chap, Carroll. Putting it that way, the conventions are nothing more than a set of zoning laws that give us our longitude and latitude.

Lee (under her breath)*:* But never enough latitude!

Cerf: You're in high company there, Gypsy. The navigator who discovered the New World paid no attention to zoning laws, either real or imaginary. As Goldsmith says, "Great minds are bravely unconventional; they scorn the beaten track."

Erskine: I would amend that word unconventional to read "original" or "sincere." Truly great lives have a creative originality that mustn't be confused with undisciplined morals or merely startling behavior.

Robinson: Amendment gratefully accepted. What we're talking about then is originality in the art of living. Such originality needn't be world-shaking; even a small trace of it adds savor to life, zest to the day's experience. Any examples from your book of Zesterdays, Mr. Young?

Young: Offhand, I think of the old lady in Philadelphia — a Biddle, I believe, who never bothered to mail her letters. She just threw them out the window of her hotel. Someone always picked them up and dropped them into a mailbox for her.

Robinson: Here we've talked for two minutes about original characters and no one has mentioned Alexander Woollcott.

Cerf: I'm afraid that Woollcott's unconventionality was often marred by rudeness. You all know the story of his visit to Moss Hart. When leaving he wrote in the guestbook: "I, A. Woollcott, have just had the most unpleasant week-end of my life." Hart said to George Kaufman: "Thank God, Woollcott has gone. Can you imagine how terrible it would be if he had broken his leg and had to stay all summer?" At this point the two playwrights looked at each other, unleashed their typewriters and didn't stop till they'd written *The Man Who Came to Dinner.*

Robinson: A much kindlier original was Clarence Day, the housebound invalid who wrote the *Life with Father* stories. Day had a charming method of handling his overflow of correspondence. When he fell behind in answering his friends' letters, he would stuff the electric bill or some cigar bands into an envelope and mail it to them. I still treasure a watch-repair ticket he sent me.

Young: Why don't more people do imaginative things like that?

Cerf: Because most people think that the only "correct" way of communicating with friends is on note paper. Emerson wasn't talking through his sideburns when he said: "The virtue most in request is conformity."

Erskine: And rightly so. The truly unconventional person may have had many daring or creative *ideas* as he pleases — but his *manners* should be as good as, or better than, those of the people around him. I think that is the secret of great originality.

Lee: I know a lot of screwballs who don't rub up any Town Hall ideas — but they're fun to have around. Take Harpo Marx. I once had lunch with him, a big lunch with terrapin and pitchers of Rhinestone wine. When he got the bill he studied it like a bank examiner, added it up three or four times — then sprinkled it with sugar and ate it!

Cerf: John Barrymore's life, too, was a saga of unconventionality. One night when he was playing Hamlet, an epidemic of coughing swept the audience. Barrymore stood it as long as he could, then pulled a sea bass from his doublet and threw it at them. "Here, you walruses," he cried, "busy yourselves with this while the cast gets on with the libretto."

Young: His biographer, Gene Fowler, is in the same tradition. Late one evening Gene called on Leo McCarey. McCarey was in bed reading, when his little daughter came up and said, "Daddy, Mr. Fowler is downstairs and wants to see you." Leo asked, "Is he drunk?" "I don't know, Daddy," said the little girl, "but he's wearing the uniform of the New York Giants."

Cerf: One thing has never been quite clear to me: where does originality end, and eccentricity begin? I give you the case of Harry Lehr, playboy of New York's "400." When he handcuffed himself to Mrs. August Belmont and swallowed the key — was he being unconventional or eccentric?

Young: You must remember that Lehr was a wine-salesman, which is merely another word for "press-agent."

Robinson: I'm always fascinated by stories about people who land jobs or sell goods by unconventional methods. The best one I've heard is about a brick manufacturer who sent carrier pigeons to prospective customers. "Attach your order, and release pigeon from nearest window," read the tab on the bird's ankle. One pigeon flew home with an order for 600,000 bricks. Pretty quaint, eh?

Lee: How much quainter it would be if the pigeon *delivered* the bricks!

Cerf: Hey, you're cribbing Oscar Wilde's stuff, Gypsy. When Wilde came to America, a delegation of proudful citizens showed him Niagara Falls and asked his comment. Wilde surveyed the awesome waters. "Marvelous!" he murmured, then added: "But, gentlemen, think how much more marvelous it would be if the water ran the other way!"

Young: Wilde's charm has always eluded me. Personally, I prefer my originals to be somewhat less bizarre, more constructive. Like the two young friends of mine who wanted terribly to get married, but couldn't find an apartment in any section of Manhattan that their conventional friends or families thought "desirable." So they went down to Avenue B, deep into the cold-water, no-heat district, found two rooms there, fixed them up and lived...

Lee (eagerly): Happily ever after?

Young (dry but not bitter): Well, as happily as most couples who live in conventional apartments.

Robinson: Which gets us back to our muttons: the art of unconventional living. I suppose you've all heard of the famous experiment in that line made by a fellow named Thoreau?

Lee: Thoreau, Thoreau! Everyone's always making with double-talk about Thoreau. Why, I can't get my hair curled without the hairdresser bending my ear about him. What did the guy have?

Erskine (eyeing Robinson): You tell her. (To group): Robby's and old student of mine and I want to see if he remembers his stuff.

Robinson (in an A-for-effort voice): Henry David Thoreau built a hut for $28.76 on the shores of Walden Pond near Concord, Mass., and lived there for two years in solitude. His express purpose was "to drive life into a corner, in order to find out whether it was a mean or noble thing." Wild creatures were his only companions; he charmed the lake trout with his flute and practiced catching mink with his bare hands.

Lee: Now there's a man I could go for! What the American home needs is more good mink-catchers.

Young: I had no idea you were an authority on home matters, Gypsy. If only you could cook...

Lee: But I can cook. You boys don't realize how unconventional I really am. I do all my own laundry, then turn around and whip up quite a flock of tasty dishes.

Young (cautiously): Er... ah... What do you cook, Gypsy?

Lee: What do you like, darling? I will cook whatever you like best.

Robinson: Now that Young's wolf-call has been hushed I'd like to ask, Gypsy, what you think of Bernard Shaw's epigram: "Men like conventions because men made them"?

Cerf (interrupting): I wouldn't quarrel with Shaw — he's one of my most quotable sources. But if men really like conventions, why are they so eager to break them?

Lee (sweetly): Not eager enough, if you ask me. If men knew what women were really interested in you'd have to make a new set of zoning laws to handle the traffic!

Young: Gypsy, you say that because you're still in the flush of youth. When fatigue sets in with the years you'll be glad to retreat with the rest of us into havens of conventionality.

Erskine: I can't agree with that point of view. In my experience I've found that most young people haven't the imagination or the authority to be original — and don't acquire these qualities until they're older. Beethoven, Dante, Goethe — to mention three great originals that come first to mind — were fully matured before they displayed in their art or lives the unconventionality we call genius.

Robinson: Which is probably what Browning was thinking about when he wrote that wonderful line, so hard to believe when one is young and conventional: "Grow old along with me — the best is yet to be."

Gypsy Goes Fishing. Lew Morrison, sports editor of the *Milwaukee Sentinel*, went fishing with America's favorite stripper and caught more than fish when his hook snagged Gypsy's dress, he reported in June of 1946.

Gypsy and June Circle Manhattan. Gypsy and sister June Havoc took a trip around Manhattan on the famous Circle Line cruises, circa 1946.

Gypsy & Erik. On August 4, 1946, the cameras of International New Photos caught Gypsy as she and her son Erik arrived in Chicago:

Authoress-Strip queen arrives in Windy City Chicago, Ill.... Gypsy Rose Lee, strip-teaser queen now gaining fame as an authoress, fairly drips with sables on her arrival in Chicago with her 16-month-old son, Erik Lee Kirkland. Gypsy has a contract to appear in a prominent Loop nite spot.

Gypsy's Big Catch. A photograph dated August 19, 1946, shows a very proud Gypsy holding up a huge musky. The caption reads:

Gypsy's Musky — Gypsy Rose Lee, strip-tease-artist-playwright-author vacationing at Sturgeon Bay, Wis. Apparently used the right bait when she went fishing over the weekend. At any rate she landed the whopping musky.

The photo ran in numerous magazines to promote tourism in Wisconsin.

• 1947 •

National Trailer Stores News. The ever frugal Gypsy had been traveling with her trailer for years, which meant she didn't have to pay for a hotel and she could cook her own meals. A February 1, 1947, front page article in the *National Trailer Stores News* circular is headlined "Gypsy Rose Lee Is 'Real Trailerite': Joins Trailer Association in Florida: Gypsy Rose Lee, the world famous striptease, now in Florida for night club engagements is doing her traveling and living in a deluxe specially-built trailer coach."

Suzie N. Short, writing of the membership ceremony in *Trailer News*, humorously recounted how she and President Cox of the UTA met Miss Lee.

We stood in a semi-circle in front of Miss Lee's swanky custom-built coach and spoke in hushed tones. Any moment now she might emerge. Suddenly the door swung open. Mr. Cox who was carelessly watching developments through his magnifying glass took one look — and fainted dead away. We were able to revive him rather quickly by explaining that he had not seen Miss Lee emerge from the door. As a matter of fact, it was her colored maid who had appeared.

In the middle of the excitement the door opened again and a tall, attractive young lady attired in culottes, blouse, sandals and about a half-ton of assorted jewelry stood in the doorway.

With his customary suavity President Cox stepped forward and presented Miss Lee with a membership card in the United Trailerites Association as the flash bulbs popped.

For our money, Miss Gypsy Rose Lee is a good showman, a good sport, and a good trailerite. Oh yes. For the information of our readers who don't happen to make $5,000 a week, there are some very nice people who do.

Parisian Belle. A stunning color photo of actress Maureen O'Hara graced the cover of the December 2, 1947, issue of French movie magazine *Cinémonde*. The back cover had an equally stunning photograph of Gypsy showing lots of leg, all decked out in her costume from *Belle of the Yukon*. The caption read: *Le charme aggressive de Gypsy Rose Lee dans le décor désuet de Belle of the Yukon*. (The aggressive charm of Gypsy Rose Lee in period costume for *Belle of the Yukon*.)

• 1948 •

Gypsy's Lingerie. "SALES EXCELLENT AT LINGERIE SHOW: 110 Producers Display Their Lines — Gypsy Rose Lee Stars in Revue," announced a headline in the January 20, 1948, issue of *The New York Times*. The event drew several thousand visitors.

Gypsy's on First. Gypsy performed at Atlantic City's Steel Pier with Abbott and Costello in July of 1948.

Gypsy marries Julio de Diego. She married Julio de Diego, a talented and well-known artist, in 1948. Julio was eleven years older than Gypsy. Both de Diego and Lee loved to cook and both were blessed with artistic temperaments.

The Cosmopolitan Gypsy. For the July 1948 issue of *Cosmopolitan*, Gypsy's longtime friend the incomparable Fanny Brice wrote a piece entitled "I Knew Gypsy Rose Lee When." In the following excerpt she recalls meeting Gypsy.

When I first met Gypsy Rose Lee she was a newsboy.

That's right, a news*boy*. In regulation boy's knickers and a tweed cap. Eleven years old at the time, she was one of the chorus members of a vaudeville act called "Dainty June and Her Newsboy Songsters."

The management of the Orpheum Theatre in San Francisco wanted me to put on a dramatic skit that I did occasionally — a tear jerker in which I gave motherly advice to a teen-age girl who was staying out all night and getting in trouble with the police. The manager said, "There's a new kid in this newsboy act called Rose Louise Hovick. Let's try her."

That afternoon the "newsboy" came to my dressing room. It was Gypsy, all right — but nobody could have guessed that here was a future queen of burlesque.

We practiced the skit, and before the first matinee performance Gypsy climbed into one of my evening dresses. It was a spectacular outfit of flaming orange feathers, with the skirt hanging low in the back but up to the knees in front. For a girl of eleven, Gypsy did all right in it.

Gypsy Rose Lee and pilot-guide stand on Norseman float with proof that fishing is good in Minnesota's Arrowhead Lake.

The trouble was, she looked scared to death. "I can't wear this in front of an audience," she said. "It isn't modest."

"Look, kid," I said. "You can't be too modest in this business."

Seeing Gypsy. Gypsy was seen in the July 1948 issue of *See* magazine.

Flying Gypsy. Gypsy appeared on the cover of the July 1948 issue of *Flying* magazine. She is proudly holding her catch of four huge fish caught in Minnesota's Arrowhead Lake.

Looking in on Gypsy. The September 28, 1948, issue of *Look* featured thirteen photos of Gypsy, alone, with her son, her mother, in *Star and Garter*, in a lush evening gown designed by Charles James, and with all three of her husbands: Robert Mizzy, Alexander Kirkland, and Julio De Diego. There is also a photo of Gypsy's younger sister, June Havoc.

An excerpt of the accompanying article, "The New Gypsy Rose Lee — Dynamo Without Direction," reads: "That's the new Gypsy — a belligerent intellectual. Yet in all her phases — her burlesque-with-class days, her literary-tea period, and her successes on Broadway and in Hollywood — she remains her tough, sentimental self."

Gypsy Vanishes in *Time*. "The Vanishing Stripteaser" appeared in the October 4, 1948, issue of *Time*.

> Last week, television preserved … decencies just in time by shutting its eyes. True to the old code, it apologized by explaining that it was a cinder....
>
> The occasion was an Air Force Association reunion … the TV camera dwelt fondly on a long succession of … celebrities: Jimmy Stewart, Bob Hope, Marlene Dietrich, and Lena Horne.
>
> … Cinemactors Margaret O'Brien and Walter Pidgeon were announced, the camera gazed … elsewhere … M-G-M contracts, which forbid their appearance on TV.
>
> Then who should appear on the stage … tall, bouncy Gypsy Rose Lee. She had given up stripteasing for authorship — but you could never be sure, with Gypsy. The camera gave her a nervous glance. … As she got well into her song, Psychology of a Stripteaser, she began to pluck at her shoulder. That was enough: the picture wavered … vanished in a hysterical band of jiggling lines.
>
> … televiewers found themselves staring at nothing but the initials CBS … in the background, Gypsy's voice trilled on … enthusiastic Air Force veterans shouted … "Take it off! Take it off!"
>
> At the end of Gypsy's number, CBS got the cinder out of its eye … the rest of the show (including a parody striptease by Bob Hope) was perfectly clear.

The following morning CBS denied that it had attempted to censor Gypsy's appearance. It seems that technical difficulties were to blame. Gypsy's response: "It was nearly midnight. Surely the kiddies aren't watching at that hour!"

The New York Times covered the incident on October 27, 1948, in the article "Radio and Television: Incident on Air Forces Unit Video Show Saturday Proves 'Comedy of Errors.'" Gypsy's appearance was referred to as "… a minor cause célèbre for the television industry."

Gypsy and the Windy Cave. On November 30, 1948, the television station WNBT broadcast a one-time only "tryout" performance of a program entitled "Cave of the Winds." The experimental show featured Gypsy, Ben Grauer, Henry Morgan, Basil Davenport and author James Michener. *The New York Times* mentioned the show in the November 27, 1948, issue, calling it "a conversation piece" with guests discussing a variety of topics. Ben Grauer was the moderator.

Gypsy's a Mile High. In November of 1948 Gypsy performed at Denver's Artist's Repertory Theatre.

CHAPTER SIX

On the Road Again

• 1949 •

Gypsy Thinks Fast. *Think Fast* was an early television game show. It ran on ABC from March 26, 1949, through October 8, 1950. There were five panelists, three of them regulars and two weekly guest panelists. The competition was to see which of the panelists had the most to say about a given subject. The subjects were decided by the host. If a panelist could outtalk the others he, or she, got the chance to sit on the "King's" throne. This must have been a dream job for a fast thinking, non-stop talker like Gypsy. She was the host, a first for a woman in the early days of television. She took over when the original host, Mason Gross, left after the few first episodes. Perhaps she talked him off the air.

The front cover of the Royal American Carnival program.

Gypsy's One Ring Circus. In her January 13, 1949, column, "The Voice of Broadway," Dorothy Kilgallen reported the following: "Gypsy Rose Lee is in Florida — in the vicinity of Tampa — inspecting a small one-ring circus. She may buy the show and tour the nation as its top attraction."

Gypsy spent the bulk of 1949 — ten months — touring with the Royal American Carnival. Even with this lengthy commitment, Gypsy still managed to do her usual myriad of creative projects and managed to do what she did best — keep her name in print. The majority of the newspaper items were publicity for the carnival and her show in it. Promoting the carnival meant more customers; more customers meant more money.

Gypsy Is the Best Entertainment. "Gypsy Rose Lee will get $180,000 this year for taking off her clothes on the carnival circuit. Remember when Hollywood was selling the public on "Motion Pictures Are Your Best Entertainment"

The front cover of the Royal American Carnival program (with flap open).

and Gypsy paused in the middle of her act, winked and said, "Motion pictures are your second best entertainment." This quip appeared in Erskine Johnson's "Man-About Hollywood" column in various newspapers on January 20, 1949.

Gypsy was mentioned again on January 28, 1949, by Dorothy Kilgallen, who wrote, "Harold Minsky is planning an independent film biography of the famous Minsky's and their careers in burlesque. Gypsy Rose Lee is being talked about for the leading feminine role...."

Unfortunately, this film never came to be. There was, however, a film made in 1968 titled *The Night They Raided Minsky's*. Leonard Maltin gives the film three stars and writes that Britt Ekland, "... gets involved with burlesque comic ... and accidentally invents the striptease...." The cast included Jason Robards, Forrest Tucker, Denholm Elliott, Elliott Gould, and the legendary Burt Lahr in his last film appearance. Lahr, like Gypsy, began his career in vaudeville and burlesque. He and Gypsy co-starred on Broadway in *DuBarry Was a Lady* in 1939–1940, the same year Lahr played the Cowardly Lion in *The Wizard of Oz*.

Earl Wilson also noted Gypsy's upcoming tour in his "It Happened Last Night" column. She was in his WHAT'S HOT section: "Gypsy Rose Lee is joining the 'carny' people. She leaves Saturday on a 10-month tour...." The blurb appeared on February 4, 1949.

And so it went throughout the carnival tour with a succession of short articles commenting on Gypsy's carny exploits in newspapers from coast to coast. Here are a few of the more interesting items by date and newspaper.

"The things that go on in a strip teaser's mind, would give you no end of surprise. But if you're really interested, there's more to see than meets the eye."

"For an example, I'm wondering if the composer was thinking of me when he wrote, 'Don't Fence Me In'."

"Do you think I was the inspiration for that song, 'BUTTONS & BOWS'?"

"Who else could he be thinking of when he wrote, 'I'll Be Seeing You'?"

"I don't care how much it may storm. . . . I've got my Bank Book to keep me warm."

"Oh Boys—I can't take THAT off! I'd catch cold."

Instead of taking it off, *Gypsy* is going to cover it up . . . A sort of strip-tease in reverse.

This gown is designed to bring out her best points.

Gypsy says clothes make the man but girls make more without them.

A fantastically articulate stripper Miss Lee came to the studio in a sable coat with a sable hand-bag in which there was a sable change-purse. And under all that sable she wore a little costume, put together with pins, that she had made herself. . . . *Vogue Magazine*

A shape, some tape, two yards of crepe . . . and the girls have been *Draped.*

March 1, 1949 — *The Democrat and Leader.* In his "In Hollywood" column Jimmie Fidler wrote, "A local columnist who received a letter from Gypsy Rose Lee the other day, setting forth of the carnival contract recently signed by our No. 1 strip teaser. Gypsy, for artfully peeling of her duds from 10 to 12 times per diem, while paying costumers stare, is to receive $10,000 a week plus a percentage of the popcorn, soda water and candy sales...."

March 9, 1949 — *The Abilene Reporter.* Gypsy's pal Walter Winchell offered this to readers, "Gypsy Rose Lee (touring the country on a percentage deal) does 14 shows daily. When stars are asked to do a 5th show in the theatre they throw tantrums. It all depends on how early in life you want to retire."

March 25, 1949 — *Wisconsin State Journal.* "We just slid up to the bar at the old absinthe house and ordered an absinthe frappe, when in came Bradley Smith of *Holiday* magazine.... He told us something new has been added to strip-teasing hereabouts, which'll be of interest to Gypsy Rose Lee, Georgia Sothern, et al. Grandmother's are now strip-teasing here." So wrote Earl Wilson in his "It Happened Last Night" column.

May 31, 1949 — *The Rhineland Daily News.* Correspondent Clark Porteous wrote of Gypsy's life in her trailer. The following is an excerpt from the article, titled "Gypsy Rose Lee Is Rover — She 'Camps' in Plush Trailer."

When Gypsy Rose Lee decided to live like a real gypsy, she didn't.

She's traveling around the country in a swank trailer, towed by a swankier Cadillac. Her four-year-old-son goes by train accompanied by two nurses joining his mother only when she stops. No self-respecting gypsy would sanction a scheme like that.

Nevertheless, Gypsy Rose Lee, the erudite ecdysiast — smart stripper, in runway talk — is being about as gypsyish as she can be. Miss Lee is on the carnival circuit, taking it off from coast to coast. While the rest of the troupe travels on a show train, she and her husband hit the road in their trailer.

Her husband is Julio de Diego, a Spaniard turned modernist painter and metal smith. While Mrs. de Diego tours with "Gypsy Rose Lee and Her Royal American Beauties," Julio has his own show. It's called "What Are Your Dreams?" and is slightly on the surrealistic side....

Gypsy and Julio took to the open road because they like trailer camp life. They registered quietly at a trailer park here, as Mr. and Mrs. de Diego. After all, that's correct, but nobody recognized Gypsy.

She did the family wash in a 25-cents-a-throw automatic laundry at the camp. She saved an additional quarter by hanging the clothes on a line instead of using the automatic drier.

Her long career (she started when she was three) in vaudeville, burlesque, the stage, movies and literature has enabled her to become the owner of a big mansion in New York, which she left to tour with the carnival. She's drawing a salary that runs into four figures a week.

She and Julio, happy in their trailer, will stay with it and the carnival until late fall, when the engagement ends. They will drive about in their new Cadillac, wagging their trailer behind them throughout the United States portion of the itinerary. When the carnival goes to Canada, they'll place the car and trailer on a show train flat car, because the jumps there are too lengthy. But they still live in it.

Traveling with the de Diegos, who've been married about a year, are Gypsy's French poodle, Georgette, and her son by a previous marriage to playwright Alexander Kirkland, Erik Lee. And two nurses.

Trailer life hasn't changed Gypsy. She's still the same gal who was once included in the list of "America's 10 worst-dressed women." Around the trailer park she went in for denim skirts and jeans and such.

The Lima News— June 2, 1949. Newspaperman Ben Smith wrote an article bearing the title "Gypsy Hits Carnival Trail," which read:

Gypsy Rose Lee likes big girls in her shows, but that doesn't mean she thinks there is a new trend toward outsize showgirls. "I'm big and I like them my size," the five foot 9½ stripper explained. Then she broke out in a grin and added "it has a practical advantage, too. Ten big ones fill the stage better than ten little ones, and they all cost the same. You don't have to pay them by the pound you know."

HER TWO BIGGEST? girls are even six footers. The smallest is five feet 8½. Filling up the stage means more to Miss Lee this year than ever before. For the first time she is hitting the carnival trail, making a six month tour of the United States and Canada with the Royal American shows.

Her outdoor stage is roughly six times the size of the average nightclub space she has been used to, Miss Lee said.

"That big stage is really wonderful," she said. "Now we can make a good swing line without falling all over each other."

THE TOUGHEST part of the show is getting used to the short amount of time allowed for the act — half an hour.

"That doesn't give us much time to warm up the audience," she said. "Usually takes 10 or 12 minutes to get people feeling right for a show, but here we have cut it down as much as possible."

"There's no special theme to the act, a little dancing and a choice display of the human form." Gypsy Rose likes this new kind of life.

"IT'S FUN — even when you have to go on before a crowd and have to look glamorous with dirt in your fingernails and sand between your toes. Even when you get waked up in the morning by the roar of a portable power plant — it's good to know you'll have your lights."

The stage and screen star lives in a comfortable trailer, on the road and during stops. When the show is traveling, the flatcar carrying the trailer is between two cars full of animals.

Just why that is, no one seems to know.

MISS LEE reported just one serious worry. How is she going to feel in mid-summer weighed down by her costume masterpiece — a strapless gown so heavy trimmed with rhinestones it tips the scales at 70 pounds?

Life Magazine — June 6, 1949. "Gypsy Joins the 'Carny': She Goes on Junket with a Girlie Show."

"I'm probably the highest paid outdoor entertainer since Cleopatra," announced Gypsy Rose Lee recently, "and I don't have to stand for some of the stuff she had to." Confidently taking her place among history's great ladies, Gypsy has for the first time in her life gone outdoors professionally. At Memphis, Tenn. last month she began a six months' tour with the world's largest carnival, *The Royal American Shows*. For a minimum guarantee of $10,000 a week, plus a fat percentage of the gross above that, Gypsy will do her celebrated strip tease on the "carny" route all across the country to Saskatoon, Saskatchewan. Her salary is not all gravy because she must pay for the roustabout, musicians and girlie line that work in her 40-minute show. But giving 8 to 15 performances a day in a 1,400-seat tent at one dollar admission, Gypsy Rose Lee is doing all right.

As "carny" performers go, Gypsy has it soft. She lives in her own trailer with her third husband, the noted Spanish painter, Julio de Diego. With them is her 4-year-old son Erik with his nurse. Julio, who loves to cook, sets up a stove behind their trailer and does a wonderful job on fish, and fried chicken. Gypsy, who loves to fish, carries an elaborate angler's kit, and whenever the show plays near a river, goes out and hooks fish as ably as she does customers.

Gypsy Wows 'Em in Minnesota. The official program for the 1949 Minnesota State Fair Centennial, which ran from August 27th to September 5th, featured a glamorous photo of Gypsy. Below her name the caption read: *Outstanding Attraction of the Royal American Shows at the 1949 Centennial Minnesota State Fair.*

Gypsy and the Art Professor. "Art Professor Turned Side Show Barker Finds It's 'Quite a Thrill'" ran a headline in the September 16, 1949, issue of the *Indiana Evening Gazette*. The article, excerpted below, told how Professor Alonzo Hauser, formerly the head of the art department at McAlister College, gave Gypsy's husband a sabbatical.

Old Friend of the Gypsy

An old friend of Gypsy Rose Lee — he once carved a portrait of her — Hauser went to see her revue when it hit Minneapolis on the State Fair circuit. There he met Gypsy's artist husband, Julio de Diego. De Diego, making the circuit with Gypsy, had his own show, a gallery of surrealist, dream-like pictures using live models.

But with some painting and a couple of one-man exhibitions awaiting him, de Diego wanted to return to New York. He asked Hauser to take over as barker and manager for the show's remaining two months on the road.

Gypsy's Union. Victor Riesel often included blurbs about Gypsy in his "Inside Labor" column. This news appeared in the September 20, 1949, issue of the *Chester Times*:

Talking about active labor leaders, please note that Gypsy Rose Lee is back in union politics, having won hands down (that's all at this time) a three-year term on the National Board of the American Guild of Variety Artists. All board members have to sign "loyalty pledges" saying they're non–Commie....

Gypsy in Soapsuds. In the September 29, 1949, issue of the *Wisconsin State Journal* Earl Wilson wrote of the rumors about Gypsy's marriage.

A rumor that Gypsy Rose Lee had separated from her husband, Julio de Diego, the artist zipped around Broadway.

I telegraphed Gypsy, who was in Tulsa, Okla., stripteasing with the huge carnival, Royal American Shows, asking her to phone me.

"Telephone?" she wired back. "We don't even have bathtubs. We live in a tented world and if it's not canvas, we don't have it."

Then came the letter — and a picture of Gypsy, practically nude, in a collapsible bathtub out on the circus lot. All she was wearing was some soapsuds.

"The report about Julio is completely untrue and unfounded," she said.

"Julio left to prepare for an exhibition in Chicago. I was fooling about the bathtub. I have a lovely one with four exposures — five including mine."

I found Julio at his studio at 65th W. 56th St. He was framing his paintings ... and would creep back into Gypsy's tent in Shreveport, La. shortly.

Knock, Knock. Gypsy was in Victor Reisel's column "Labor Comments" again on December 20, 1949. Here, in the *Oakland Tribune*, he shared a story about the ever-joking Gypsy:

NOT DRESSED

Such interesting things department: In the full line of duty the other day I telephoned striptease artist Gypsy Rose Lee to ask for an interview, now that she has become an active union leader of the American Guild of Variety Artists.... As we talked on the phone some one apparently knocked on her door. "Just a moment," she yelled. "Who is it?" Some one answered. "My heavens, don't you dare come in," she shouted. "I'm only half dressed."

• 1950 •

Gypsy, Parlez Vous Français? In France, Gypsy's book *Mort aux femmes nues!* aka *The G-String Murders* was a hit. *Mother Finds a Body* was also published in France the same year with the title *Madame Mère et le macchabée*.

Gypsy's Picture Show. The January 1950 issue of *Picture Show* magazine inquired "Sex for the World's Fair?" and featured photos of sexy attractions of past World's Fairs, including the bathing beauties of Billy Rose's famous Aquacade, Sally Rand at her Nude Ranch, and Gypsy's carnival escapades: *Versatile Gypsy Rose Lee proved the power of pulchritude for Fair, recently wowed them at carnivals thru U.S. Appearing as star of Mike Todd's "Star and Garter," gyrating, glamorous Gypsy kept World's Fair theatre packed.*

Gypsy Whispers. *Whisper* is a typical men's magazine with cheesecake photos of scantily clad dames. The January 1950 issue ran articles entitled, "Cult of the Leopard Men," "Can Science Switch Sexes?" and featured a homo-erotic photo spread of Male Cheesecake. Gypsy was mentioned in an article called "Hi Priced Teasin'," which confirmed that Gypsy was paid $10,000 for her carnival tour.

Gypsy's Tavern. Gypsy made a guest appearance on the popular television show *Duffy's Tavern*. The show began on radio where it had a huge listening audience. Gypsy's appearance was filmed on February 17, 1950, and broadcast on April 6, 1950.

Gypsy Heads West. The March 1950 issue of *See* magazine featured an article written by Gypsy's former boss, Harold Minsky. The title was "Striptease Goes West — Road Tours Beckon Big-Name Peelers." Gypsy is mentioned just briefly: "Incomparable Gypsy was touring in carnivals." The one photo of Gypsy was accompanied by the following caption: *Most illustrious name in striptease, Gypsy Rose Lee toured carnivals with her own act last year, started 1950 with a $7,500-a-week salary plus cut in profits.*

Gypsy's Financial Killing. On March 19, 1950, Hollywood's queen of gossip, Hedda Hopper, mentioned that Gypsy had made a "financial killing with a circus last season...."

Gypsy's Virgin Strip. "GYPSY ROSE LEE BARES PAST" was the headline of an article by syndicated columnist Earl Wilson that ran in April 1950. Mr. Wilson wrote, "Gypsy Rose Lee has made a living doing what comes naturally to a girl — taking off her clothes." He also revealed the place where "It all started...." The journalist wrote that Gypsy's first strip was at the Gaiety Theatre in Kansas City on "... that day in 1930 when Gypsy then known as Rose gave an audience a couple of peeks at her snowy white beauty...."

Gypsy's Carnival Flair. The June 1950 issue of *Flair* magazine included an inserted booklet entitled *I Was with It*, which *Flair* describes as Gypsy's "rainbow-colored reminiscences of her own carnival life." The booklet is illustrated by Gypsy's third husband, Julio de Diego, whose accomplishments *Flair* itemizes.

> De Diego's career included various stints as a Madrid opera scene painter, movie actor, soldier, Left Bank Paris painter and American fashion illustrator. In 1926 he gave up all commercial work to concentrate on serious painting; his work has since won honors in Madrid, San Francisco, the Chicago Art Institute, New York's Nierendorf Gallaries and Museum of Modern Art.

The table of contents featured a photo of Gypsy cooking in her trailer with Julio.

Flair also is quick to applaud the accomplishments of Gypsy.

When famed ex-burlesque stripper Gypsy Rose Lee is asked for the secret of her success, she points to her forehead. There have been hundreds of strippers, she says, who never get anything but whistles and catcalls because they lack her kind of "versatile mentality." Miss Lee's versatile talents have enabled her to write two best-selling mystery novels, a play, two motion-picture stories, and articles for *The New Yorker* and other magazines, and have her scrivenings enclosed in the Rockefeller Center time capsule.

I Was with It
By Gypsy Rose Lee

Before I joined one the word carnival had always been magical to me. It meant Ferris wheels, merry-go-rounds, candied apples on a stick, music, lights and gaiety. I never thought much about where the carnival came from or where it went when the fair was over. It never occurred to me that the day before the show hit town the midway was a barren lot. My only experience with outdoor show business was a season at the World's Fair in New York and a fast three days in Syracuse for an agricultural exhibition where I was in the grandstand show with a race track between me and the customers. The stage was in the open air, and it rained for the entire engagement. My dressing room was a tent where during the day they curried the horses.

"This is my last state fair," I said with firmness. "They can have their mud operas, from now on I'll take my jobs in a nice warm saloon."

But I forgot all about that when I saw the Royal American Carnival. They had four Ferris wheels. Seventy all-steel Pullman cars to transport the twelve hundred people on the show. They trouped their own neon shop, welding shop, carpenter

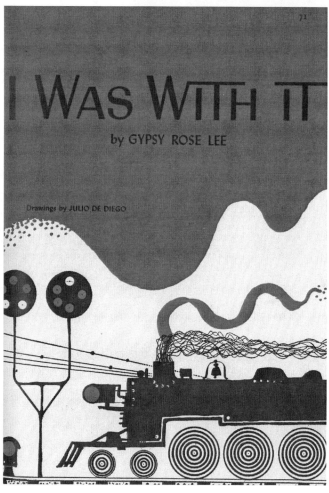

I WAS WITH IT

by GYPSY ROSE LEE

Drawings by JULIO DE DIEGO

In 1949 Gypsy and her third husband, artist Julio de Diego, traveled with the Royal American Carnival for six months. Gypsy's four-year-old son trouped with his mother as he had done since he was six months old. For the June 1950 issue of *Flair* magazine, now considered a collector's item, Gypsy wrote "I Was with It," telling the story of her carnival adventures. Julio de Diego did the artwork seen above.

shop, even a cook tent just for the show people. My company, if I joined the show, would have its own private car. The wagon which was to be my dressing room was paneled in full length mirrors, with built-in wardrobe closets, sliding doors to the dressing alcove, and draperies of heavy green silk. Besides all this I was to get ten thousand dollars a week plus a percentage. It seemed almost too wonderful to be true. Of course, we were to do twelve to fourteen shows a day and out of the ten thousand I was to pay the salaries for two vaudeville acts, twelve show girls, and supply all the costumes. I was too excited to read the small print in the contract.

I bought blue jeans, rubber hip boots, lanterns, buckets, shovels, a heating stove, electric fan and a thing that looked a doughnut and when you dropped it in a bucket of water it heated the water to bathing temperature. I already owned a trailer I had trouped in for a couple of years and a brand-new Cadillac convertible. Erik, my four-year-old son, had trouped with me since he was six months old. I had no worries about how he'd take the trip. What were fourteen shows a day to me? A new town every week? So what? I didn't get the name Gypsy for nothing.

Opening day in Memphis, we did nine shows in five hours. At about ten-thirty that night it started to rain. We were set up at the bottom of a steep hill, and the rain gushed down the tent aisles like a river on the rampage. The customers stood up on the benches so they wouldn't get their feet wet and held umbrellas over their heads while they watched the show. Carl, our head canvasman, tried to explain to me that our tent wasn't exactly leaking. That the rain pouring through the top in bucket loads was seepage.

I just looked at him with the rain dripping from my false eyelashes. "Sort of like osmosis, huh?"

"Yeah," he agreed after a slight pause. "Best thing that coulda happened to us. The rain'll shrink up the canvas, and when it dries out it'll be tighter'n a drum." I believed him. What did I know about canvas?

On the eighth show my voice went dead. Nothing came out but a croak. Fortunately, my artistic endeavor doesn't depend completely on my voice, but I did have a couple of music cues I had to give the orchestra. The leader couldn't catch them. In desperation I decided to go into my strip. Voice or no voice, I figured I could find enough energy to walk across the stage and drop my garter belt into the tuba. I was halfway across when I felt the platform sway. Before I could avoid getting the heel of my shoe caught in it, a split two inches wide appeared in the stage floor. The rush of rain down the aisles had loosened the platform supports, and two of the stage sections had separated. I struggled to get my heel free, and then decided that this was as good a time as any to take off my rhinestone dress. I found the zipper key and pulled gently. Nothing happened. After tugging at it from sixteen bars of music the stage manager closed in the front traveler on me standing there completely dressed. Six customers demanded a refund on their tickets while I waded back to my dressing room wagon. It was after eleven. The storm seemed to be getting worse. The wind whipped the canvas side walls making an angry snapping noise. The stage creaked and swayed, and my wagon pitched from side to side like an unseaworthy vessel. With my last bit of courage I began pulling off the false eyelashes. I heard Duke's voice.

"Bally, girls! Everyone on the bally stand."

I struggled to my feet and clutching the sides of the wagon I made my way to the stage. Duke, our talker, wearing a Uneeda Biscuit raincoat with a hat to match, was all smiles.

"They're mobbing me out there," he said happily. "Can't sell tickets fast enough."

"Do you mean to tell me that you expect us to go out there at this hour and do another show?" I put all the dignity I had into the speech. "Do you expect those girls to stand out there on the bally stand in that wind and rain?"

Duke stopped smiling. He thought it over for a minute. "Yeah, I guess it is kinda rough," he admitted. "It'd sure as hell ruin the costumes." Then he yelled into the girls' wagon, "Hey girls, wear your bathing suits for the next bally!"

Three days and thirty-eight shows later the sun came out. Tear-down night Duke came backstage with the box office statements. He had changed to a chartreuse sports jacket, maroon slacks and a lime green tie.

"Thirty-three thousand, six hundred and seventy-two dollars and forty-seven cents," he announced, as though he had just printed up the bills himself.

I did a little quick arithmetic on my portable adding machine. Six hundred and twelve bucks on the souvenir programs, two hundred and twenty-seven on the Coca-Colas, fifty-fifty with the boss on the box office gross. As I added up the take my enthusiasm for the carnival came back to me. I began looking forward to the run into St. Louis.

The trains were right back of our tent. The girls in my company had worked all week making their car cozy and comfortable. They made cretonne draperies for the windows with bedspreads to match and had painted the woodwork and hung pictures on the walls. There were three girls to a stateroom for seven dollars a week each — a little crowded, but the season was new. They trouped with buckets to bathe in and a community icebox. The owner of the show had two cars for his family and himself. But the freak show car was the nicest of all. Not that it was any better than the others, but they had it fixed up more. Besides Prucilla the Monkey Girl, and Emmett her husband who was the Crocodile Man, there were Joan the Armless Girl and her two children, the Alligator, Anato the Stomachless Man, the Frog Girl and many others. They had lace curtains and potted plants in their windows, a canary bird and rugs in the corridor. It was very homelike and cheerful.

The concessionaires and front-end people had four cars, and there were other cars with just uppers and lowers for the crew and roughies. Besides the pie car, the others had flat cars. That's where I traveled. My car and trailer took up an entire flat, which was between Terril Jacob's wild-animal circus and the wagons for the Ferris wheels.

After Duke left I pinned my money to my underwear and drove the trailer to the loading ramp, where the train crew was waiting. The flats are loaded in sections of eight cars. Tractors pull the wagons off the midway and to the loading ramp where they are poled into position by boys who have not only the strength but the agility for the job. They guide the wagons with long detachable tongues. If the wheels should hit a rock or take a swerve the tongue could fly and toss the poler twenty feet. It is especially dangerous when they are unloading the wagons.

"Don't they get hurt?" I asked Red, foreman of the train crew.

"Yep." He couldn't have been more unconcerned. "Couple guys got killed last season." Then he pointed to the ramp ahead of me. It was a steep incline made with two planks braced against the end of the car. "Straighten out your wheels," he said. "And turn off your headlights." Then he turned on his flashlight. He walked over and stood between the railroad tracks, his head just clearing the flatcar.

"Follow my flashlight," he yelled up at me. "When I say 'Hi!' stop and stop fast."

The planks were no more than a foot wide each. I could barely see the gleam of Red's light. I looked at Erik and the dogs asleep in the back seat of the car, then I called to a roughy standing near by. Rolling Erik in a blanket, I asked the roughy to hold him. As a second thought, I handed him the dogs on their leads. Then I got back in the car and started the motor. The front wheels skidded on the wet planks, and I shifted into low.

"Give 'er the gun!" someone yelled. My foot trembled on the gas pedal, and I could feel the car move jerkily ahead. Suddenly, the tires made traction, and with a rush of power I was over the first plank.

"Hi!" four voices shouted out in a chorus. I slammed on the brakes with such force my leg ached. Red and the crew moved out the planks about three inches on each side. The car was wider then the trailer, and at each section the planks had to be moved in and out. At the end of the eighth section the crew chalked down the wheels by shoving wedges under them which were riveted to the flats. Then they pulled chains through the wheelbase of the car and trailer and fastened them tightly.

"That oughtta hold 'er on," Red said. "Unless we hit a bump," he laughed.

There was less than six inches between the side of the trailer and the edge of the flat car. Getting out of my car I hung onto the side as I inched my way to the trailer door. It had started to rain again, and inside the trailer was cold and damp. I turned on the butane-gas lights and heater, then I reached over and took Erik from the roughy. The dogs jumped into the trailer and snuggled down in bed beside Erik.

I bathed with rubbing alcohol, then I took off my stage make-up and stretched out on the sofa with a book. The rain fell softly on the tin roof of the trailer, and the flickering butane light cast strange shadows on the walls. I lit a cigarette and poured a cup of coffee from the thermos. I was doing a good job of pretending to myself that I wasn't frightened when with a screeching of wheels and a grinding crash, the train started to move. The dishes slammed against the shelf wall and the water can slid across the floor. The coffee spilled down my chest, and both dogs barked hysterically as an end table went flying toward them. I jumped from the sofa and made a dash for Erik's bed. I could have saved myself the trouble. With another lurch the bed came to me. A can of olive oil crashed off the shelf and the oven door flew open. A cabinet drawer opened and banged shut as if by magic. Then suddenly the train stopped. I pushed Erik's bed back into the bedroom and looked around at the chaos. Groceries were strewn on the floor, a pound bag of coffee had burst when it hit, the closet door hung on one hinge. The dogs looked up at me with a big question in their eyes.

"We're going bye-bye," I heard myself say. "Bye-bye on the choo-choo."

I crawled through the mess and fell into bed. To put myself to sleep, I invented a game called "What I'll do with my ten thousand a week when this season is over?"

At dawn, I learned the train was going out in three sections. I was on the Flying Squadron. That's the first section and carries the most important parts of the rides, the seven diesel engines and light towers, platforms and the canvas. And, of course, the roughies who set it up.

The roughy travels under the wagons. He rolls himself in a blanket and uses his suitcase or a paper bag with a clean shirt in it for a pillow. A flashlight, a water can and a bottle of rye, and he's ready for the run. A fancy guy sometimes hangs up a strip of canvas to cut with wind, but it marks him as a dude and he won't last long. A foreman like Carl, or Ace who had the diesels and towers, travels in his wagon with the equipment. Runs are anywhere from twelve to forty-six or -eight hours.

Eating is a problem. The roughies crawl alongside the wagons to reach the pie car which is in the middle of the train. When they reach the coupling between cars they jump. The pie car isn't like an ordinary diner with waiters and a guy announcing "Dinner is now being served." The food is cheap, the service negligible. At four in the morning the menu might consist of pot roast and vegetables with Jell-O and coffee for sixty-five cents. Or corned beef and cabbage for a half a buck. At breakfast, a bowl of chili is a quarter.

The pie car is open day and night. It closes only when the show is on and all hands are at work. A long counter runs almost the length of the car, a section of it cut off to make room for a card table. Directly opposite is a nickel slot machine.

Flatcar manners dictate the exact moment when one is allowed to dump the garbage. As Ace explained to me, it's dangerous to wait for the train to get up to full speed, but you must wait until you have cleared the depot or settlement. With the cans handy and the door open, I hung onto the side of the trailer and waited for my cue. Looking ahead, I could see the cars stretched out on the tracks for what looked to me like a mile or so. The engine had made a curve, and for a moment I forgot all about the garbage cans while I admired the wagons. They were painted red, blue and green with the lettering, ROYAL AMERICAN SHOWS, in lurid contrasting colors. Some of them had paintings of lions and tigers on the side. Others had wild men and baboons. Four of them had my picture painted on them.

"It's like a tinsel village that's been folded up and packed away," I said to Ace. "A magical city that will appear overnight."

Ace didn't say anything. He had that faraway, sort of superior look in his eyes all carnies have when a May talks about the show. We had slowed down to go through a town. The townfolk crowded about the platform to watch the train go by. They pointed at the wagons and waved at us. The kids jumped up and down and clapped their hands in delight. When we really stopped to check the cars the roughies would jump down from the train and refill their water cans. The town folk weren't quite so smiling then. They stood way back, giving us lots of room. They hung onto the children's hands and eyed the carnies closely. Ace told me that was because they were afraid we'd kidnap the kids or lift their wallets. I don't know where civilians get the idea that show people lift things. We may take a few hotel towels and forks or maybe milk cans and stuff, but nothing that's nailed down.

I waved back at the town marks as we passed by, then I saw roughies emerge from under their wagons. They leaned over the side of the car holding buckets and cans in their hands. Ace shouted, "Okay, Gyp, let 'em go!" and just as I emptied the cans, eight or ten roughies emptied theirs. The wind almost dragged the cans from my hand, and I pulled myself back into the trailer and slammed the door. I was very pleased with myself.

We hit town at 5 A.M. the following morning. Getting the trailer off the flats was easier than getting on. I arrived at the fair grounds to find the midway under two feet of mud. Each show staked off for the footage it needs, but I couldn't find the stakes. Then I saw Carl. He and about twenty roughies, eight or ten of them local gazoonies, were waiting in the mud up to their knees for the wagons. Carl knew the grounds so well he didn't need stakes.

"Straighten the trailer out along this ridge," he shouted, using his lantern as a guide light. "Keep 'er in low gear or you'll never pull it through the mud."

Low gear and all, I got stuck twice. The wagons were rolling on the midway by then so I knew I was on my own. Pulling up my hip boots I piled out of the car and threw a section of rope with knots in it under the rear wheels for traction. A few feet further on I'd pile out and go through the same act all over again.

It took me an hour to get alongside the ridge. What I wanted at that moment was an electric outlet to get the heating stove and Frigidaire working. I wanted a real electric light, not the flickering butane lamp. I wanted a bath too, but I knew that was a luxury beyond a carny.

With three hundred feet of outdoor electric cable I started out toward a gleam of light in the distance. It turned out to be the public restrooms, and by unscrewing a light bulb I managed to plug in my cord. Holding up the rest of the wire I started back.

"Well," I thought, as I pulled one foot then the other out of the mud, "this is going to be real cozy."

Balancing the cord and the flashlight I knelt down to plug in the wire to the trailer socket. Blue lights danced in front of my eyes, then nothing. I came to flat on my back in the mud. One of the roughies helped me to my feet.

"Got a shock, didn't ya," he said cheerfully as he led me to the trailer. He had plugged in the lights. Ace carried Erik and put him to bed, the dogs were following behind, holding up their heads to keep from drowning. I let my sticky wet clothes fall in a heap and piled into bed.

Through the rest of the night I could hear Carl barking out orders. "Hey, you, get a hold on that pole. Don't let that canvas hit the mud! Pick up them benches!" The tractors chugged through the mud, dragging the midget-show wagon into position. The Motordrome frame was going up, I could tell from the hammering. One of the tower lights went on, and I knew Ace was on the job. There was a faint aroma of coffee in the air which meant the cook tent was up and open. Carl yelled, "Get that lead line out, the towers have got juice." Gradually as the midway lights went on the lanterns were put out.

At noon the show was open. Clean white shavings covered the mud, the merry-go-round music was playing, the trained monkeys were on their bally stand and the freaks were doing their first show. The snake show was next to our tent, and I woke up hearing the talker's pitch.

"Here they are folks! Brought from the four corners of the earth! It's educational! It's the greatest show you've ever seen! See the Bombay Bone crusher! The Mandalay man mauler! The Congo cobra, thirty-nine feet long and capable of swallowing a man alive!"

Down the midway I could hear Mush, the talker on the side show. "Right this way, folks, it's all free! The most amazing collection of human oddities the world has ever known! Prucilla the Monkey girl! The man with three legs! The Turtle Girl! It's free, folks! Absolutely free and without any charge whatever!"

Over the insistent voices of the talkers on the back end I could hear the front-end guys pitching the ball games, the string joint, the mouse game. "Test your skill," they'd yell, and another would take up, "If I don't guess your weight within three pounds you take your pick of these beautiful plaster dolls!" The girls with their hair lacquered stiff and piled high on their heads held out a red-fingernailed hand with a trio of balls in it. "Knock down a milk bottle and win a Navaho blanket!" Older women stood in the entrance to the mitt camp. "Like to have your palm read?"

The roughies were selling tickets, Cokes and programs, pulling curtains, working spotlights. They had worked all night setting up the show. Then they had washed up in buckets back of the tent. It wasn't until the last show was over that they would roll back in their blankets and go to sleep on the stage or in the aisles of the tent. Some of them had cots, but most slept on the ground. The next day, unless we had an early call, they'd find a Lend-a-Hand joint or a Y and take a bath for a quarter.

The average pay for a roughie is thirty a week, with a five-dollar-a-week bonus if he finishes the season. He doesn't get extra pay for working the spotlights or pulling the curtains, but he can add to his weekly by getting a percentage on the Cokes or the souvenir programs he sells. Filling the backstage water buckets is good for five-spot a week in tips. Selling tickets is the best job of all. There are no grifters allowed on Royal American, and each carny has his orders: "No beefs. If a town mark squawks, right or wrong, give him back the money!" But if a mark walks away and leaves his change, that isn't the ticket-seller's fault, is it? The "walkaways" is his. If a ticket-seller learns how to slow up on shoving back the change he can pick up thirty-five to fifty a week, and all strictly legitimate.

The real money is made by the carnies on the front end, with their games of "chance" and "skill." They are the ones who live in the fancy hotels with the jacked up prices, they drive Buick cars and drink imported V.O. The carnies who run and work the shows on the back end live on the train. If they have someplace to go they walk and if they have time to drink they go for a quart of Petri's. The front-end guy has his worries, of course. No carny has life really easy. Maybe the local fuzz won't let him spring. Maybe he has to spring only for stock, or perhaps the fix costs more than the take. But he doesn't have salaries to pay, livestock to feed all winter and scenery and costumes to buy. His investment is small. He buys the slum by the gross; the show furnishes the canvas and the booth. He runs the games himself with his wife helping out on the big days or an assistant who works on a percentage basis. The back end is the prestige of a carnival, but it's the front end that pulls the show out of a still date in Davenport when it has rained for the eighth night.

The class distinction between the front end and the back is obvious, but when trouble hits the show they're all carnies together. When my dog bit a town mark in Shreveport they didn't make me fight it out by myself. Three carnies who had been on the other end of the midway when it happened swore they saw the mark kick my dog. When some local busybody wrote to a magazine protesting Erik's being on the show, the mag was flooded with outraged answers from the carnies. When you're with it, the carnies are with you. Right down the line. If a carny gets sick he doesn't go to a charity ward. The show chips in and gives him the best. It might mean a ding or two, but the carnies take care of their own.

When the cyclone hit the show in Saskatoon and bent the eighty-foot light tower into pretzels, tore down the fronts of the shows and ripped the canvas into ribbons, no one sent for outside help. The first gust hit the show at one-thirty in the morning. I was having a couple of beers with the comics in my show when it hit. The beer bottles went flying off the table, and a second later we heard the first light tower crash. The tent poles were dancing a foot off the ground when I ran out of my wagon to see if Erik was all right in the trailer.

"He's okay," Carl yelled to me. "Your awning's ripped to hell and gone, but the boy's sound asleep."

The snake-show front was down. A popcorn stand rolled clumsily down the midway. Dust and shavings stung my face as I clung to the guy lines of the big tent. The water wagon drove madly past, and Emmett the Crocodile Man ran behind it with a bucket of water.

"Fire!" he yelled.

The fire was in the brush back of the Ferris wheels. It lighted up the sky and the big wheels looked delicate against the flames and smoke as they swayed back and forth in the wind. The ride boys were stripping the seats, alert for the first sign of collapse. Gazoonies, talkers, showgirls and freaks, front-end guys in their pale gray suits with lavender shirts, actors and roughies grabbed up extinguishers and bucket and ran to the fire.

Carnies who had been in town when the wind hit were piling out of cabs, rolling up their sleeves as they ran. The boss, who had been sleeping in his train miles from the fair grounds, was there in less than ten minutes. The water wagon rolled madly back down the midway. Someone yelled, "Fire out?"

"Nope," the driver shouted. "Goddam water wagon's empty."

An hour later the fire was out. It took the rest of the night to patch up the fronts and get some of the canvas back over the shows, but by dawn if a mark had walked down the midway with a buck in his hand he wouldn't have seen a show or a joint not ready to spring. The towers bent over like wilting tulips, the side show had lost the top half of its front, torn canvas was piled up high in back of the tents where the customers couldn't see it, but if you didn't know how beautiful the midway was before the cyclone hit, it would still look okay to you.

The boss with his arm in a sling and his face smudged and singed looked over the damage. "Good thing it hit us at night with no customers on the midway," he said. He turned to Carl, who was sewing up a large tear in his canvas. "Anybody send for the fire department?"

"Hell no," Carl grinned up at him. "We'd a never put the fire out with them local gazoonies gettin' in our way."

For those readers not up on their carnival lingo Gypsy included the following Glossary of Carnival Terms:

Back end End of the carnival where shows are located.

Bally Show in front of a show.

Bally girl Girl who doesn't appear in Girl Show, only for bally.

Bally stand Platform in front of a show where free performance is given.

Blow off End a grandstand show, or featured freak of side show.

Blow the date Not open the show.

Brass Used for money on a show when no salaries are paid. Good only in pie cars and trains.

Canvasman One who sets up and tears down tent.

Carny One who works for the carnival.

Ding A plea for money.

Dishpans Reflectors on top of light towers.

Floss joint Candy floss stand.

Front Entrance of show, including photographs and bally stands signs.

Front end Part of carnival where all games of chance are located.

Front traveler A curtain that works on a pulley in front of the stage.

Fuzz Police.

Gazoony Worthless character.

Gilly Small, cheap carnival.

Girls, girls, girls Usually the show inside tent — big show on the midway.

Grab joint Hot dog stand.

Grifter A sharper.

Grist To cheat.

"I'm with it." Expression used to tell other carnies you are part of the show.

Independent One operating a grab joint not connected with the carnival.

Load the flats Put show wagons on show owned joints.

May, First of May Novice worker — derives from the fact that most shows open the season about that time.

Miler or **Forty Miler** Owner of a small concession who never goes farther than forty miles from his home base.

Mitt camp Fortuneteller booth.

Mugg joint Photographer's booth.

Pie car Diner on train.

Pitch Speech given by talker.

Poler One who "poles" the wagons on and off the flatcars of a train.

Posing show One to four or six girls who pose "artistically."

Gypsy's Red Again! A dozen years after her encounter with the Dies Committee, Gypsy was once again labeled a "Red." Evidently, someone in government had it in for Gypsy. They were still trying to link her to the Communist Party.

This time it was the Illinois Department of the American Legion who made the slanderous claim. *The New York Times* ran an article on September 13, 1950, entitled "NETWORK REJECTS PROTEST BY LEGION; A.B.C. Refuses to Cancel New Gypsy Rose Lee Program...." ABC challenged the legion, unless they could prove that Gypsy had communist sympathies, the show would go on as planned.

The Illinois Department of American Legion responded the following day. The September 14, 1950, headline in *The New York Times* read, in part, "LEGION WON'T BACK LEE CASE CHARGES; Says 'Red Channels' Must Prove Dancer Is Red Sympathizer...." The "American" Legion officer who made the claim that Gypsy was pro–Communist said it was up to the publishers of "Red Channels" to prove the allegations were true.

Gypsy's woes made front page in newspapers across America. On Wednesday, September 13, 1950, in Missouri's *Jefferson City Post-Tribune,* the headline said it all: "Gypsy Rose

Lee Is Commie," which it "retracted" the next day: "Gypsy Rose Lee Strips Down Charges of Red Channels."

Gypsy's Son Loves Sunday School. On November 6, 1950, a line in the *Los Angeles Times* read, "… Gypsy Rose Lee's young son Erik has discovered Sunday School and loves it.…"

Gypsy's All a Titter. Gypsy appeared again in *Titter, America's Merriest Magazine* in the December 1950 issue. She is called "The Champ of Oomph" and "Beautiful — But Not So Dumb" by Art Owens.

> Beautiful but not so dumb — that's Gypsy. Albert Einstein hasn't revealed how much help he got from this gorgeous babe in formulating his new Field Theory of General Relativity, but it wouldn't be surprising if she got credit for an assist.

Gypsy Gets Dressed for Radio. "GYPSY ROSE LEE, M.C.; Ex-'Ecdysiac' Now Runs a Radio Quiz Show" read a headline in the December 24, 1950, issue of *The New York Times*, which broached, "It's a fairly safe bet that Gypsy Rose Lee is the only woman in radio who buys a new dress for each broadcast." Gypsy countered, "Maybe radio isn't visual, honey, but that studio audience sure is.…" The program was called *What Makes You Tick?* Gypsy was the hostess from September 23, 1950, to March 31, 1951.

• 1951 •

Gypsy's Big Show. A contract from January 21, 1951, shows that Gypsy signed a Single Engagement Agreement to appear on NBC's *The Big Show*. The famous radio show, the last of its breed, was hosted by the legendary Tallulah Bankhead. The show Gypsy performed on was broadcast on January 21. Her salary was $1,500. Aside from Gypsy, the other guests that night were Eddie Cantor (her co-star in *Ali Baba Goes to Town*), Judy Holliday, Vaughn Monroe, Patrice Munsel, Fred Allen (her co-star in the film *Sally, Irene and Mary*) and Portland Hoffa.

Looking at Mike Todd. The February 27, 1951, issue of *Look* profiled the one and only Mike Todd. The article, "The unpredictable MR. TODD," began: "In a period that abounds with tea-table-polite producers, Mike Todd stands almost alone as a shirt-sleeves showman. His colorful antics and unpredictability, in the tradition of an earlier generation, have made him one of the most talked-about operators on Broadway."

In the requisite Gypsy photograph she is flinging her slip aside, one hand clutching the curtain in her customary fashion. The caption bragged on her behalf: *When burlesque was banned in N.Y., Todd signed Gypsy Rose Lee for a tamer version,* Star and Garter *('42), which grossed $2,000,000.*

Gypsy's Art. The March 1951 issue of *HIT!* asked, "Is Modern Art Crazy?" in an article accompanied by photos of various artists with their paintings and sculptures. Artist Gypsy pointed to her painting: a depiction of a frying pan with eggs, in which the yolks of the eggs were eyeballs, and a pair of spectacles floated in space to the left of the pan. The caption read: *Gypsy Rose Lee proves that she can paint too by submitting this canvas to a collection by amateur artists. She called the painting "Adam and Eve."*

Gypsy in Greenwich. In March of 1951 Gypsy attended a meeting of the Greenwich Village Humane League.

Gypsy and Ken. *The Ken Murray Show*: Gypsy was Ken Murray's guest on episode 42 of the 2nd season which aired April 28, 1951. Other guests included The Mary Kaye Trio, Robert Q. Lewis, Constance Moore, Phil Silvers, Don Ameche, Dagmar and Frank Sinatra.

"All Aboard!" Gypsy Catches the White Springs Special. Gypsy, her son Erik and Col. Elliot White Springs attended the dedication ceremony for the Lancaster & Chester Railway Terminal on June 2, 1951. Col. Elliot White Springs was the founder of Springmaid Sheets. Shortly after, Gypsy began to appear in Springmaid ads.

SS Gypsy. On June 10, 1951, Gypsy set sail on the S.S. *Degrasse* accompanied by her son, Erik.

A Quick Peep of Gypsy. Gypsy appeared in the July 2, 1951, issue of *Quick* magazine. President Franklin Roosevelt graced the cover.

Gypsy Abroad. In August and September of 1951 Gypsy and Erik took a trip to the British Isles. They visited England, Scotland and Ireland where Gypsy was seen kissing the Blarney Stone.

Everybody's Gypsy. The British publication *Everybody's Magazine* dated August 25, 1951, ran the following article.

"Just a Joke to Gypsy!"
by Charles Graves.

Gypsy Rose Lee is a phenomenon — a best-seller of thrillers, a well-known portrait painter, a strong trade-unionist, a successful playwright, a high-priced script-writer, a working editor, and ex-screen villainess, a contributor to famous American magazines, and an expert angler.

She is also a beautiful woman with the following measurements: bust, 36 in.; waist, 24 in.; hips, 39 in.; 5 ft. 9 1/2 in.; weight 8 st. 11 lb.

She is best known, of course, as Queen of the Strip-Teasers, the exploitation of which has brought her anything from 800 to 3,000 a week, for over twenty years. At present she is on a short tour of the provincial music halls, accompanied by a number of American 'lovelies' and her six-year-old son, Erik.

USUALLY IN THE WAY

Sister to the film star, June Havoc, she first appeared on the stage at the age of three, then performed in an act called "Dainty June and her Newsboy Songsters." Like all children backstage, she and her sister were usually in the way, but not with the circus acts. They learnt to know and love them, because when they went to the theatre at ten every morning for their school classes, the circus acts were always there rehearsing. Gypsy Rose Lee and June soon learned to work revolving ladders, to eat bananas under water, to ride bareback, and so on.

When Gypsy — they called her Gypsy because she was always telling fortunes — was fifteen her shoulder strap broke while she was doing a song-and-dance act in Kansas City. The manager invited her to stay on another week and change her act to a strip-tease. There were at least eleven other strip-teasers on the halls at the time — coy, fast, slow, and slinky, but nobody did it with humour.

So young Gypsy did a little bit of all of them, guying each of them but stripping very little herself. "That was the basic idea," says Gypsy, "satire."

But audiences which had never seen the real thing did not realise that it was satirical. They just thought to themselves, "this is it." Whereupon, Gypsy decided that if that was what they wanted to think, they could get on with it. It gave her a nice living. Actually, she appeared only thirty-six weeks in burlesque in the whole of her life, but this fantasy which has been attached to her has been most profitable.

"It has given me a generous living for years," she says. "The only drawback has been the difficulty of getting sponsors for my commercial television programme in New York, although I have two registered psycho-analysts to support me."

As she spoke, she dabbed a spot of cold cream on to her completely unmade-up face. Only Marlene Dietrich of all the established stars I have met, has the poise, unaffectedness, and confidence in her looks — call it what you will — to make up completely from scratch in front of me. In private life, she talks fast and her conversation shows that she is a good psychologist. "You can't get a laugh out of showing a naked woman, and it is always the women members of the audience who have to start the laughs, not the men. ... Do I play outdoor games? Certainly not. They give you muscles in the wrong places. But I'm crazy about fishing."

PLAYED TOUGH PARTS

When she first broke into pictures she had to play tough female parts bundled up to the nose in clothes, bitter to the end of the picture and never getting her man.

She claims that her secret of stage success lies in the sophistication on which her act is based. There are four show-girls besides herself, wearing (to start with) tights which cover them about as well as a modern bathing-suit. Gypsy Rose Lee herself wears four complete sets of clothes over a specially designed costume. The to the accompaniment of the orchestra and her own patter, she takes off her four sets of clothes and puts them on the show-girls. As she says, "It's a satire on the normally accepted strip-tease act."

American critics rave about her. One described her as "sublimating nudity into an aesthetic abstraction by singing detachedly of frustration, psycho-analysis, philosophy and vitality." Another said, "Gypsy Rose Lee projects as much rare, gracious femininity by face, timing and voice as Katherine [sic] Hepburn projects the opposite with the same means."

LITERARY ACHIEVEMENT

She has also been called the Diva of Divest, Premiere Stripteuse, and — after she had written "The G-String Murders"— the Leggy Literatease.

"The G-String Murders" her first best-seller, was translated into Japanese as well as Spanish and French.

It was a lurid, witty and highly competent detective story. The plot involved the murder of two strip-teaser queens and the dialogue was so peppered with show-business vocabulary plus stage-door gags, that serious American book critics described it as a social document, as well as being a first-class thriller.

Gypsy Rose Lee takes much more pride in her literary achievement than in her stage successes. "I would never think of saying that I had given a swell performance when I come off stage," Gypsy Rose Lee told a reporter. "But when I finish a piece of writing I read it over and say to myself—'Say! that's a swell hunk of writing!' ..."

In 1942 she very nearly bought the Police Gazette, but the selling price was two hundred thousand dollars — a trifle more than what she had bargained for. Today, she is the editor in chief of "Agva," the trade organ for members of the vaudeville profession in the United States. Not only does she write editorials and dictate policy, but she writes most of the contents under assumed names.

She first gate-crashed highbrow American literary circles by taking the side of Franco's opponents in the Spanish Civil War, and undressed on their behalf at a charity performance. This ultimately led to her being denounced years later — in 1950 — as "an entertainer reported to be a dear and close associate of the traitor in our country."

NEVER A "RED"

Gypsy Rose Lee retorted smartly that entertainers are always being asked to help causes which all sound quite innocuous:—"Must we wire our Congressmen before doing a benefit?"

she demanded, adding that she was never a "Red" and never would be one. This statement was immediately accepted by the vast U.S. public, who have a very soft place in their hearts for any beautiful woman who is also intelligent.

It is no secret that she has over five thousand books at her house in the country and has read most of them. The usually skeptical American public is quite satisfied that she writes her own books, her own plays and her own films, and dresses her own show-girls. As for her patriotism — besides having taken off her clothes for the enemies of Franco, she took off her clothes during World War II for France, Britain and the aluminum drive....

Her first husband was a dental supply manufacturer called Robert Mizzy whom she described to me as her only "civilian" husband. To Gypsy, a civilian is somebody not in show business. She divorced him on the ground of his having "knocked her down twice." Her second husband was Robert Kirkland, a film director, who she divorced on the grounds of "mental cruelty" whilst expecting her first baby.

Her present husband is Julio de Diego, a contemporary Spanish painter who was formerly a bull fighter, and who also danced in Diaghilev's Russian Ballet — whereby hangs a charming fact. Julio de Diego is by no means a rich man. So, although Gypsy stays in the smartest hotels and leads the opulent life expected by her public when her theatrical engagements keep her away from him, she always stays at the most inexpensive places when she is with him to suit his purse.

JOURNEY ON COAL BOAT

Thus, when she has finished her tour of English music halls she is going happily off on a coal boat from Barcelona to Cadiz with only three other passengers, stepping off at various dingy little ports, on a voyage which lasts ten days, as opposed to going by a modern, streamlined luxury ship taking thirty-six hours. This is not what you would expect of the star of "Star and Garter," a musical comedy which ran for a year and a half on Broadway. Nor again of the leading lady in "Carnival," for which she was paid three thousand pounds a week.

Some may recall her playing the title role in "Belle of the Yukon." In those days she wore "bangs," — a cluster of curls cascading from the top of her head down on to her forehead. They became the bane of her life. Whenever she changed her appearance, the cash customers complained.

It was not until her first appearance on television that she was allowed to brush her hair straight back as an experiment. The experiment was a success. Now everyone tells her that of course she should have done it long ago. It makes her so much more attractive.

Gypsy at the Palladium. Gypsy and six-year-old Erik traveled to London where Gypsy performed at the world famous Palladium theatre in September 1951.

• 1952 •

When in Spain. Gypsy celebrated New Year's Eve in style in Barcelona, Spain, and toured Spain in the beginning of 1952. Her Scandinavian tour continued with a visit to Sweden. In May 1952, Gypsy and her girls made an appearance at the China Theatre in Stockholm.

Moulin Gypsy. On February 10, 1952, Gypsy and Julio attended the New York premiere of the film *Moulin Rouge*. A film directed by John Houston and starring Jose Ferrer, Zsa Zsa Gabor, Christopher Lee and Peter Cushing.

Gypsy in Bagdad? *Babes in Bagdad* was released in 1952. Gypsy suffered the biggest film flop of her career in this ill-advised movie, but she and Paulette Goddard did look great in their Harem costumes. Gypsy was cast as Zohara.

Gypsy and Julio de Diego arrive at New York's Capitol Theatre to see the premiere of *Moulin Rouge*.

Looking at Gypsy. In her "Looking at Hollywood" column of March 4, 1952, Hollywood gadfly Hedda Hopper mentioned that Gypsy had returned to Spain.

Gypsy was in Hopper's column again on May 1, 1952, when Hedda described Gypsy's role in *Babes in Baghdad*, "Gypsy Rose Lee had the part of a faithful wife...."

Get Dressed, Gypsy! On August 1, 1952, the *Corpus Christi Caller Times* ran the following story.

Gypsy Rose Lee Ordered to Be Dressed by January
by Graham Miller

LONDON, August 1. The London County Council has given Gypsy Rose Lee from now until next January to put her clothes back on.

The mean old council has outlawed strip-teasing, right smack in the middle of a series of skin shows by Gypsy.

But the council is acting pretty much like the gentleman who, when his privacy was invaded by an uninvited woman guest, said, "I'll give you six hours to get out of here." The ban on bare bodies does not go into effect until next January, which gives the girls plenty of time to get dressed.

Meanwhile, Gypsy sat around in a couple of leaves yesterday and said she wasn't bolstered at all even if she was being stripped of her rights, for a change.

A COMEDIENNE

"I'm not a stripteaser, anyway; I'm a comedienne," said Gypsy, who'll say almost anything for a laugh.

Gypsy was waiting for her spirit gum to dry, which takes a long time, in this wet country, and maybe that has something to do with the county council's attitude. Spirit gum keeps the leaves stuck to Gypsy's figure where there isn't much else on it. When she first got to England, she didn't give the gum much time to dry. The leaves were strictly from autumn the first couple of times, until the county council caught on and Gypsy took a little more time with the spirit gum.

That was 18 months ago, when Gypsy arrived here for what was supposed to be a three week tour. She's been packing them in with this comedienne act ever since.

Today 2,000 people jammed the Finsbury Empire Theatre in North London, where she was undressing — for laughs.

ONCE WROTE BOOK

"A stripteaser," continues the scholarly Miss Lee, who once wrote a book and even was reported on another occasion to have read one, "is a woman who puts on an exotic sexual spectacle. My act is straight comedy and boy, they love it."

Gypsy's Empire. Gypsy performed at Moss Empire Theatre in Liverpool August 11, 1952.

Gypsy on the Isle of Man. Gypsy and Erik were spotted at Ronaldsway Airport on August 17, 1952.

Gypsy's Rolls. In September of 1952 Gypsy purchased her Rolls Royce from Hoffman's Garage in Halifax, England.

No Vacation for June. June Hovac had planned to travel to Europe for a two-month vacation with Gypsy and Erik in September of 1952. After touring in *Sadie Thompson* for eight-weeks she needed a rest. June took all of the inoculations necessary, but when a new play beckoned, she liked it enough to cancel her vacation.

"Gypsy's New Leaf." This article appeared in *People Today* magazine of September 24, 1952.

"Vows Gypsy: 'My Act Is Straight Comedy'"

Gypsy Rose Lee has four months in which to get dressed. The London County Council put the finger on Gypsy smack in the middle of a record-breaking series of performances, issued an order banning strip acts. But the Council, an understanding body of lawmakers, apparently made allowance for the difficulty of obtaining a full wardrobe in austerity-ridden England. Their edict does not take effect until January.

A trouper as always, Gypsy took the order philosophically, stopped playing with her son

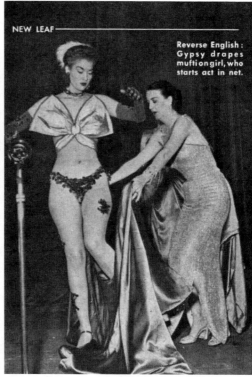

From *People Today* magazine September 24, 1952. These photographs are from an appearance Gypsy made in London. The photo-essay was titled "Gypsy's New Leaf."

Erick [sic], 6, who's accompanying her on the tour, long enough to comment: "Why should I worry about my clothes? I have my bank book to keep me warm."

Gypsy's act, which has been leaving English audiences goggled-eyed for almost 2 years, includes 4 U.S. lasses who can toss more curves than Yogi Berra will ever be called upon to handle.

The girls come out on stage covered with fishnet costumes tastefully decorated with colored sequins in a few strategic spots. Gypsy starts the act wearing enough clothes to stock a Fifth Avenue dress shop. Piece by piece, she carefully removes the garments, drapes them on the girls. The act ends with the girls completely clad and Gypsy almost in the altogether, wearing only some scattered leaves which had the autumnal tendency to fall until the London County Council issued its ban. Since then, Gypsy has been more painstaking in applying the spirit gum which keeps the leaves from slipping.

• 1953 •

Not Interested in Sex? Dorothy Kilgallen's column appeared in newspapers across the U.S. This quote from Gypsy was seen in the *Mansfield News Journal* on March 2, 1953: "The Scotch aren't interested in sex, but they like comedy." Kilgallen wrote parenthetically, "Oh, come on now Gypsy!"

The legendary Gypsy Rose Lee poses with the legendary Marlene Dietrich at the Ringling Brothers Circus.

Gypsy Does the Math. Leonard Lyons, in his "Lyons Den" column on March 23, 1953, in the *Post-Standard,* Syracuse:

> "The Education: Gypsy Rose Lee recently returned from a long European tour, on which her 8-year-old son, Eric [sic], had accompanied her. Miss Lee enrolled the boy at the Professional Children's School, and now devotes her evenings to help him with homework." "I'm learning

long division," said Miss Lee, whose year in Europe netted her $500,000 and a new Rolls Royce car. "Until now I never thought arithmetic important. I always hired people to do it for me."

Gypsy and the Ringling Brothers. Gypsy and Marlene Dietrich performed at the opening show of the Ringling Brothers Circus on April 2, 1953.

Easter Fashion Show. Gypsy, June Havoc and Mr. John, who designed Gypsy's hats, joined the elite of New York at the Easter Fashion Show. The event was held at the Plaza Hotel.

Gypsy Goes Latin. Gypsy is seen at the legendary New York nightclub The Latin Quarter. Ever the patriot, she takes the time to have her picture taken with a Korean War POW.

Oh, Canada! Gypsy and her Royal American Beauties perform at Montreal's Gayety Theatre.

Gypsy's Boston Tea Party. May 15, 1953, finds Gypsy on stage at a Boston nightclub.

United Jewish Appeal Auction. Gypsy does her part to raise money for the United Jewish Appeal Auction benefit.

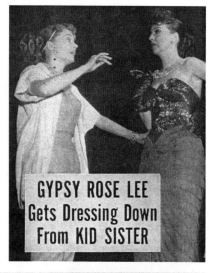

GYPSY ROSE LEE
Gets Dressing Down
From KID SISTER

Someone's in the Kitchen with Gypsy. *Kay's Kitchen* was a popular cooking show broadcast from Syracuse, New York; Gypsy joined the fun on the show in October 1953.

• 1954 •

Gypsy's There, Come Hell or High Water. Gypsy attends the premiere of *Hell or High Wate*r on January 30, 1954.

Focus on Gypsy. The February 3, 1954, issue of the tiny ten-cent *Focus* magazine ran a photo-essay entitled "Gypsy Rose Lee Gets Dressing Down from Kid Sister." The eight photographs show Gypsy and June rehearsing for a production of Claire Boothe Luce's play *The Women*. Other cast members included the daughters of Joan Bennett, Federal Judge Tom Murphy and Connecticut Governor John Lodge.

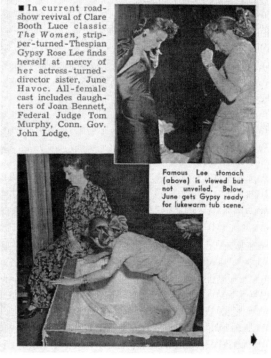

■ In current road-show revival of Clare Booth Luce classic *The Women*, stripper-turned-Thespian Gypsy Rose Lee finds herself at mercy of her actress-turned-director sister, June Havoc. All-female cast includes daughters of Joan Bennett, Federal Judge Tom Murphy, Conn. Gov. John Lodge.

Famous Lee stomach (above) is viewed but not unveiled. Below, June gets Gypsy ready for lukewarm tub scene.

Gypsy's Back in Burlesque. The March 1954 issue of the magazine *Cavalcade of Burlesque* included one black and white photo of her at the end of the magazine. This photo had been used before, especially to promote her appearance with the Royal American Carnival. She is seen in a black "Merry Widow" corset with a phone in her hand.

Gypsy's Naked. In March of 1954 Gypsy acts in her original play *The Naked Genius* at the Bermuda Theatre in Bermuda.

Gypsy's Naked Again. June Havoc directs her older sister in a production of *The Naked Genius*. The play is seen at the Court Square Theatre in Springfield, Massachusetts, and the Parsons Theatre in Hartford, Connecticut. These productions took place in March and April of 1954.

They Can't Kill Burlesque. A photo of Gypsy appeared in the April 1954 issue of *Point Magazine*, yet another of the popular mini-magazines of the 1950s. The photo shows Gypsy in a classic early 1940s pose. She is just about to do her trademark move of pulling the curtain in front of her as she finishes her strip. The accompanying article was titled "Why Don't They Bury Burlesque?" Shelley Winters graced the cover of *Point*, which offered the following headline, "Is Hate a Sex Drive?"

The Women. Gypsy appeared in *The Women* by Clare Boothe Luce during July of 1954. She was seen in performances at the Norwich Summer Theatre in Greenwich, Connecticut. Her fellow actresses included Catherine Doucet and Rosemary Murphy.

Darling, Darling. Gypsy brought playwright Anita Loos' adaptation of a new French play *Darling, Darling* to the Westport County Playhouse in Connecticut, and the Pocono Playhouse in Mounthome in Pennsylvania. The cast included: Tom Tyron, Florence Sundstrom, Jill Kraft, and James Nolan. This engagement was in the late summer of 1954.

Casino Royal. During August and September of 1954 Gypsy entertained at the Casino Royal in Washington, D.C.

Gypsy Goes Green. In 1954 she joined forces with her neighbors on East Sixty-third Street to oppose the widening of the street. *The New York Times* covered the story on October 9, 1950. In part, the article read: "Edward L. Bernays, publicist, Gypsy Rose Lee and other residents ... joined yesterday in protesting ... widening of the street would strip it of its old and beautiful trees...."

Gypsy's French Act. Gypsy appeared at Montreal's Chez Paree nightclub in late 1954.

Gypsy Goes Down Under. Gypsy and Erik traveled to Sydney, Australia, in October 1954. They watched sheep being sheared and Erik tried his hand at the boomerang. Later Gypsy performed at the Palladium Stage Theatre.

***Xclusive* on Gypsy.** The October 1954 issue of the mini-magazine *Xclusive* ran a six page article entitled "Gypsy Rose Lee: The Naked Genius."

The article describes a day Gypsy spent in court defending her friend from vaudeville, singer Gus Van. The sixty-seven-year-old headliner had been a member of the singing team of Van and Schenck. At the time he was being sued by a thirty-eight-year-old musician who claimed that Van had beaten him up.

The case was heard in a Superior Court where Gypsy, claiming to be a bump specialist, was called upon to explain the difference between assault and a bump.

Gypsy testified that the fight was "a push, a bump...." She then added, "I should know." Due to her status as a great strip-artist and her success as an accomplished writer and playwright, her testimony was taken seriously. Furthermore, the article states that Gypsy "is a mother" to her younger sister, screen star June Havoc. The article's unknown author states that "in America, a mother deserves to be heard."

June is given due credit as an accomplished singer, dancer and as an actress who can play drama and comedy.

Gypsy stated that Gus Van was innocent. She claimed that he did not hit musician Ross on his head, nor did he throw the younger man ten feet. Ross said his injuries caused him to be hospitalized for ten days.

The court ordered Van to pay five hundred dollars for punching Ross. Luckily for Van he didn't have to pay the full fifty thousand he was sued for.

Unfortunately, the jury accused Gypsy of lying when she said that Van didn't "clobber" Ross. This, the article states, made Gypsy a "revaricatrix." *Xclusive*'s readers were also reminded of another time when Gypsy herself had been on trial.

This was when the manager of a nightclub called La Martinique accused Gypsy of "becoming demure and refusing to strip." She then walked out on the club's opening, taking the costumes of forty chorus girls. Gypsy lost her cool and made the response that she'd been fired and hadn't been paid. She was not reimbursed for the chorine's costumes, which she had created.

Her walking out of La Martinique was over money; it had nothing to do with modesty. "Modesty is a four letter word," she said.

The judge in the Gus Van case told his jurors that they had the advantage over other juries because they "heard the testimony of Gypsy Rose Lee, who is an expert on bumps and grinds, twists and twirls...."

At the close of the article it is stated that the judged favored Gypsy, "the Naked Genius who outstrips them all!"

Gypsy's All Woman. Gypsy's and June's production of *The Women* opened at the Astor Theatre in Syracuse, New York, in October of 1953. In July of 1954 the company moved to the Norwich Summer Theatre in Connecticut.

• 1955 •

The March of Dimes. Gypsy modeled a dress designed by Charles James at the March of Dimes Annual Fashion Show. The fundraiser took place at New York's famous Waldorf-Astoria in the beginning of 1955.

Gypsy's Point. The cover of *Point* magazine dated January 1955 showcased a photograph of the popular MGM star Cyd Charisse with the headline "The Psychology of Striptease." The article included a photo of Gypsy next to a photo of Margie Hart with the following caption: *Margie Hart and Gypsy Rose Lee, two earlier strippers who made the act pay off.*

Gypsy's Garbage. On January 26, 1955, Earl Wilson's column posted a provocative piece about Gypsy's garbage. It began:

> Here in the biggest, weirdest city in America, you can get many things you can't find else-where — including troubles.
>
> Miss Gypsy Rose Lee has just paid a $15 fine for not having her garbage can covered....
>
> "At 9 in the morning a man came to the door," Gypsy related.
>
> "I got my caretaker to accept it as soon as I saw it was a summons. I'd had about 10 garbage can covers stolen. You can't keep them — you know that!
>
> "My caretaker paid the fine down on 2nd Ave. Later I walked down the street to buy a garbage can cover.
>
> "Well," snorted Gypsy. "I counted 18 cans in the block that weren't covered."
>
> "Then I tried to buy a garbage can cover. Did you ever try to buy a garbage can cover?"
>
> I admitted I had never been so favored.
>
> "'You have to buy the whole garbage can, Miss,' they say. I said I didn't want a whole can. I just wanted to cover my garbage can up. Well!"
>
> Finally, Miss Lee spent $8.95 on a garbage can with a cover chained to it.
>
> "It seems a little ironic," she said, "that Gypsy Rose Lee should have the only garbage can on the block that's covered up! After all my years of not being covered.

***Jet* Magazine.** The popular *Jet*, another 1950s mini-magazine, cost only fifteen cents. The February 3, 1955, issue included a photo of Gypsy with Charlie McCarthy, Edgar Bergen and Duke Ellington. The four showbiz vets were photographed at the Waldorf-Astoria where they appeared on Bergen's popular radio show. The caption to the photo read: *Dangerous Curves: Offering a restraining hand, band leader Duke Ellington cautions Edgar Bergen's brainchild Charlie McCarthy to beware of the charms of the ex-stripteaser Gypsy Rose Lee. The foursome got together for Bergen's radio show at New York's Waldorf-Astoria.*

Gypsy in Vancouver. Gypsy was photographed , with her paint brush in hand, during a May 1955 visit to Vancouver.

Gypsy at Ciro's. Gypsy worked at Ciro's, the famous Los Angeles nightclub, in June of 1955.

Gypsy's Life Is a Cabaret. Marilyn Monroe appeared in a bubble bath on the cover of the July 1955 issue of *Cabaret* magazine. The headlines promised "The World's Most Exciting Body," "The Cleanest Women on Earth" and "Strip Tease Intellectual," an article about Gypsy prefaced with the comment: "Gypsy Rose Lee survives rigors of time to become oldest stripper in business by giving customers palaver instead of pulchritude."

> "Strip Tease Intellectual"
> by Eugene Pawley
>
> A woman's figure, being somewhat perishable and ephemeral as a thing of beauty, the career of a strip teaser is necessarily limited to a span of years when she can still be termed whistle-bait. There comes a moment when the rigors of time take their toll and as the veteran director of the Follies Bergere, Michel Gyarmathy, has put it: "Alas, the breasts, after a time, they fall." But one stripper has defied the passing years and still responds to the familiar call of "Take it off" after more than 25 years in a G-string. She is celebrated Gypsy Rose Lee, now in her 40's but still displaying liberal expanses of flesh in stripperies around the nation.
>
> Gypsy is no superwoman; she shows the wear and tear of time under the revealing glare of spotlights. But the oldest stripper in the business today has been able to stay in the business by substituting her brains for her body, by giving customers palaver instead of pulchritude and

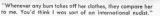

"Whenever any bum takes off her clothes, they compare her to me. You'd think I was sort of an international nudist."

Peeling herself, Gypsy jibes at the modern bustline. "This blouse! It's all right for a country girl, but I've been abroad."

"I wonder if the composer was thinking of me when he wrote, 'I'll Be Seeing You.'" Gypsy speculates at curtain.

Gypsy shows why she is the Queen of the Strip-Tease. These photographs appeared in the July 1955 issue of *Cabaret*.

making them like it. Now admittedly on her sixth farewell tour, Gypsy will probably be making her farewell for years to come simply because she can talk as well as walk.

Early in her career, Gypsy learned that the customers out front get a kick out of a girl who is articulate as well as well-stacked. She spent long hours in longhair books and amazed her audiences with her intellectual repartee. Soon she became known as the striptease intellectual and reviews of her performances were to be found in such egghead publications as the New Republic and New Yorker. One voluble critic acclaimed her for "sublimating nudity into an aesthetic abstraction by singing detachedly of frustrations, psychoanalysis, philosophy and vitality."

Today Gypsy is still going strong by virtue of her talents in puns and patter which she delivers with polish while either taking off her own satins and bows or else removing the assorted accoutrements of four stripping apprentices who have hit the road with her. Most of her own stripping is done behind a screen so that she is silhouetted while delivering some of her risqué lines.

In her younger years, however, she gave the gents out front a full measure of flesh for their money — but always with an additional bonus of some clever banter. In the 30's striptease routines were divided into two categories: sweet and hot. Gypsy was the foremost proponent of the sweet tease.

She would emerge bundled to the ears in a big, white fur coat with large buttons and glide across the stage as though bound for the opera, while the orchestra played a restrained tune. On her way back to the wings she twitched her coat open with a negligent gesture, disclosing a low-cut evening gown, and immediately the audience screamed for the greater expanse of Gypsy's skin. Then she came out and played with the pins and snaps of a specially designed dress, revealing a bit more of her epidermis. On the next chorus the house lights went down and a baby blue spotlight showed Gypsy minus either the top or bottom of her dress. Then she walked and skipped sweetly across the stage shedding the rest of her costume as she exited to the wings.

Whistles, shouts, thunderous applause found the Gypsy generally peering from the wings and giving tongue to a standard line: "Darlings, please don't ask me to take off any more. I'll catch cold. No, please, I'm embarrassed. No, honestly, I can't. I'm almost shivering now."

But in the end she yielded to the clamor of conoscenti [sic] and came out once more with her dress thrown so loosely about her that it slipped off as she reached stage center. Just before the blackout, she plucked off her brassiere and for one swift second she stood completely nude except for a small beaded G-string that satisfied most city fathers.

To say that bedlam broke loose after such a performance is putting it mildly. When Billy

Gypsy has running commentary as she undrapes beauties: "Clothes may make the man, but girls make more without them."

"With these costumes, it's the little things that count. The littler they are, the more they count."

"The things that go on in a stripper's mind would surprise you. If you're interested, there's more than meets the eye."

"I've taken a few apprentices under my wing. It's up to you customers who will inherit my old G-string."

Gypsy in action. These photographs also ran in the July 1955 issue of *Cabaret* magazine. The cover girl for the magazine is a young actress named Marilyn Monroe. She is in a bubble bath promoting her new movie *The Seven-Year Itch*.

Minsky introduced the lady to New York in 1931 in the city's largest burlesque house at $1,000 per week, she was an overnight sensation. By the time she put on a modified version of her famous act for the 1940's World's Fair, Gypsy was a national institution. By then her intellectual accomplishments had begun to win fame, too.

After writing a guest column for Walter Winchell, she got the literary urge, dashed off the outline of a mystery story and sold the idea to a publisher. Her "G-String Murder Mystery" sold thousands of copies. In between her stripping stints, she also wrote articles for the *American Mercury* and *Harper's Bazaar*.

She performed her striptease routine with a fat chunk of culture. While undressing, she tossed French phrases into the gapping mouths of her admirers; and she recited smutty Dwight Fiske monologues like "Virgin Sturgeon" imported from Café Society's plusher amusement parlors. Her tough audiences took readily to this tonier entertainment, although it was believed that many burlesque patrons can neither read nor write.

When H.L. Mencken used the word "ecdysiast" to displace the term "stripteaser," Miss Lee found it most fitting to argue the matter in the press.

"The man is an intellectual snob," she screamed. "Ecdysiast he calls me!" And when a reporter, innocent of her literary leanings, asked whether she had ever read Mencken, Gypsy replied heatedly, "Certainly, I've read his stuff— in my youth."

Actually most of her youth was spent on the stage. Her real name was Rose Louise Hovick and she was born on January 9, 1914, in Seattle, Wash. Her father, a Norwegian, was a newspaper man; her mother, of German descent, has traveled with Gypsy most of her life, later becoming a talent scout for Earl Carroll. At the age of six, Gypsy was first exposed to the glare of the footlights, with her sister June (later known as June Havoc), and wore male attire so often in this child act that she was referred to by stagehands as Baby June's kid brother. Later the act was called "Rose Louise and Her Hollywood Blonds," and barnstormed all over the country, rarely playing more than two days in one town. Gypsy never attended school while trouping, but used to spend her allowance on books.

When vaudeville took a nosedive, Gypsy was reduced to playing second-rate night clubs, she booked part of her troupe into a burlesque show. It was then that Rose Louise Hovick became Gypsy Rose Lee. She changed her name because her mother feared that Gypsy's grandfather would be shocked to have his kin cavorting about in burlesque.

The birth of her striptease is a saga in the burly world. One night as she did her turn singing and dancing (even today she is pretty terrible at both these pursuits), she coyly allowed the shoulder strap of her gown to slip down. A generous expanse of milky white bosom was thereby exposed, and a great career was launched. The vision wowed the audience and they screamed for more. But Gypsy held out in the teaser's tradition. The next night she repeated this subtle gesture and by the end of the week her salary was upped to $75. Four weeks later she was established as a first-rate stripteaser drawing $350 weekly.

"I guess I wasn't used to so much money," Gypsy says today, "because the more I got, the more ambitious I became to land on Broadway."

She credits Walter Winchell for helping her achieve this ambition. He induced the late Florenz Ziegfeld to catch her act at Minsky's. As a result she dropped a big paying job for a minor role in the chorus of "Hot-Cha," the last Ziegfeld production. After "Hot-Cha" she returned to burlesque. It was at this stage in her progress that she added the refined touches of French and Fiske. She then resided in a snooty Gramercy Park penthouse, the theatre where she displayed her arts being only a few blocks away.

It was Gyp's habit to walk to work attired in a diaphanous nightgown over which she wore an expensive mink coat. Sometimes she veered over to Union Square, where she stopped to hear the Communist soapboxers. She says they used to sneer at her.

"They probably didn't realize," she explains now, "that my five turns a day were tougher than standing on a soapbox talking."

When Hollywood beckoned in the person of Daryl F. Zanuck, 4,000 highly moral letters of protest immediately poured down on producer Daryl Zanuck. Mr. Zanuck issued reassurances:

henceforth Gypsy would be known as Louise Hovick, and she would no longer indulge in the striptease.

"She is a dramatic actress," said he, "and will be exploited as such."

The news came as a kind of surprise to Gypsy, but she decided to try. If she failed, it was for no lack of trying. Before exposing her to the cameras, Hollywood straightened her front teeth, raised her eyebrows, changed the shape of her mouth and corrected her walk, which had an excessive slink.

"They made me look like a Park Avenue debutante," said Miss Hovick proudly.

She remained in Hollywood almost two years, at $2,000 a week, appearing in "You Can't Have Everything," and "Last Year's Kiss," but the drama in her just wouldn't come out. With its accustomed perversity Hollywood gave the lady the two things she needed least — a new name and at least twelve changes of clothing in every picture. Unfortunately the changes were made beyond the range of camera and the pictures flopped miserably just about everywhere in the country.

In the cinema capital, however, Miss Lee achieved fame for class consciousness. Among other things she became chairman of the clothing division of a relief committee for the Spanish Loyalists. The committee places advertisements graced with a seductively stripped Gypsy asserting: "Clothes? Any New Clothes, Old Clothes? Gypsy Rose Lee appeals for Clothing for Spanish Refugees ... and she is not teasing!"

She began appearing at meetings, her name always a good come-on for any cause. But she disappointed the audiences with some such remark as, "I've come here not to lift my skirt but to help lift the embargo."

As a result of this behavior, Miss Lee tangled with the Dies Committee. She tried to brush aside the subpoena with the comment, "With my act and Dies' publicity we could bring back vaudeville." She denied vehemently that she was a Communist or even a fellow-traveler. The Dies inquiry was dropped.

Actually, her vices are few and chiefly include smoking two packs of cigarettes a day and a firm devotion to brandy depending on her mood. She tried smoking marijuana a couple of times but claims she found it revolting.

When it was the fashion in sophisticated circles to sniff cocaine, she sampled it once, but spilled her helping on the rug.

Otherwise she is a perfectly normal, voluptuous five feet ten and 130 pounds of cosily-distributed curves.

Gypsy insists that she prefers the simple life. Most of her amusement in the evenings takes place in her own home — when she is at home — a sort of little thinkers' salon. The festivities often wind up with Gypsy showing her guests several reels of "blue" movies, the kind favored at stag parties. She boasts that she has over 160,000 feet of such film, one of the most torrid collections in the country. Gypsy also talks about music. Her remarks sound a lot like Deems Taylor annotations on a national radio hookup. In fact, she once had a hot discussion with Deems on modern music in one of her rare visits to the Stork Club.

She was on firmer ground when she discussed the merits of White Orpingtons or Rhode Island Reds. She had 300 pedigreed hens on her Highland Hills farm. When her mother served some for dinner, Gypsy grew nervous and got rid of them all.

In her 14-room Colonial country home, "Witchwood Manor," she has installed an elaborate heating system so she can enjoy the simple life in the winter too, when she so desires. Pets roam all over this plantation, including three monkeys, two sheep, two turkeys, three dogs. Her favorite monkey is Rufus-Veronica II, whose exact sex is something of a puzzle. Of this little pet Winchell once cracked in his column, "Where did Gypsy Rose Lee's monkey bite her?" Gypsy won't tell.

Gypsy's interest in art, as manifested by the décor of her apartment, is rather one-sided. Her living room, on the socially correct East Side, is full of ornate Louis XV furniture and penciled on the walls are some startling female nudes by a French artist. In her bedroom stands a four-poster bed with wooden parrots perched on the posts, the canopy having been removed. On the wall at the head of the bed is a large, lascivious pastel of two nude women. On the other walls are additional esoteric gems, but almost all nude females in erotic moods. Gypsy gushes that she simply adores French modernists, naming Jules Pascin, the noted painter of nudes, and Marc Chagall. Her own portrait, painted by Henry Major, was hung in the Marie Harriman Galleries before the war.

On the literary side, Miss Lee is more versatile. Her taste runs the entire gamut from ten-cent and quarter astrology magazines to Marcel Proust. Of the latter she says simply, "He's marvelous." The pages of only one of his volumes on her shelves were cut. She reads the two New York tabloids, the News and the Mirror, but snubs papers of larger format. She cannot sleep without a gander at Winchell's column, her substitute for Ovaltine.

To explain her failure in Hollywood, Gypsy noted: "I loused myself up," she says, "by play-ing with people from the wrong side of the tracks, inviting grips and electricians to dinner at my house."

But when Hollywood's columnar cynics badgered her into admitting her acting talent was nil, Gypsy explained, "I guess my Fourteenth Street burlesque technique wasn't so good. There never was any Stanislavsky in my methods. I just got up and said my lines." Anyhow, as she puts it, "I came back with a swell collection of autographs."

Despite her sad experiences, Miss Lee is still eager for a career on the legitimate stage. She toured the summer theatres playing the lead in "Burlesque," and then she did the principal role in a minor offering called "I Must Love Someone." She, also, took over Ethel Merman's part in the bawdy musical "DuBarry Was a Lady." Her big success included starring roles in Mike Todd's "Streets of Paris" and "Star and Garter," which was her longest Broadway run, over a year. She penned "The Naked Genius," which was presented by Mike Todd at the Plymouth Theatre in New York. Her first marriage, in 1942, to writer Alexander Kirkland lasted about a year. In 1943, Gypsy had a separation and gave birth to a baby about the time her ex was mar-rying socialite Phyllis Adams. The newspapers made a bit of a splash about that but Miss Lee's comment for the benefit of the press was just about her newborn.

Aside from unchallenged status as the only striptease intellectual in America's theatre, she has without doubt been a stripper longer than any other burlesque queen. Of course, today she no longer appears in places like Minsky's, but rather at first nighteries in Las Vegas, Hollywood and Miami. Her press agent may not be too far off when he claims that Gypsy is the "most publicized woman in the world, as she has been interviewed, painted and photographed more often then any other woman alive."

Note: Gypsy's first husband was Robert Mizzy. Alexander Kirkland was her second. Also, there is no evidence that Gypsy appeared in the movie *Last Year's Kiss.*

Gypsy's All-New Summer Revue. The July 2, 1955, issue of the *Reno Evening Gazette* ran the headline "Gypsy Rose Lee in Mapes Skyroom."

The famous Minsky Follies starring Gypsy Rose Lee, the stripeuse, headlines the all-new Sum-mer revue in the world-famous Sky Room of Hotel Mapes.

Gypsy Rose Lee is a vibrant personality in a teasing, satirical strip routine, and a handsome figure she cuts indeed as she presents her four femme aides billed as the Royal American Beau-ties, who admittedly can't sing or dance or cook but they certainly look good as enticing man-nequins in Gypsy's big drape scenes.... She is a fine show-woman, and tosses off recitations guaranteed to tease the risibilities of the most hardened audience.

Tea Time with Gypsy. Magazines including *The American Weekly* featured Gypsy's 1955 ad for Springmaid Sheets.

Gypsy Strikes a Pose. In September 1955 *Pose* magazine offered a special issue tribute to the "World's Sexiest Girls," including Marilyn Monroe, Sophia Loren, Janet Leigh, Kim

Mrs. Julio de Diego, charming collector of modern art, and one of the ten best dressed women in New York, entertains the Debutante Committee for the coming Colonial Ball at Madison Square Garden to raise funds for the restoration of George Washington's Distillery.

Joan Smith will represent Massachusetts, Georgia Washington will represent Virginia, Jeannette Lafitte, Louisiana, and Andrea Jackson, South Carolina, in the tableau depicting their ancestors.

Herself a relative of the Colonial hero who gave his name to Fort Lee, Mrs. de Diego is a playwright and author of distinction, whose works have been translated into many languages and dialects, including the Southern, and she has traveled widely.

Mrs. de Diego says, "I always carry my own linens with me, and on my last world tour I took only Springmaids. They are everywhere considered the best example of Ameri-

can superiority. In Calicut a Nabob forced his way into my bedroom and I was terribly frightened until I found he only wanted to unravel a sheet to see how the smooth yarns were spun. In Yokohama a pillowcase was stolen off my bed by a Japanese spy so they could try to copy the lustre of the finish.

"The Bey of Algiers is now wearing a fitted sheet as a dinner coat, and the Sultana of Sarawak has made quite a riotous romper out of a purple percale pillowcase.

"In Monte Carlo they used one of my green sheets to cover a casino table, which inspired the Duchess von Bourbon who is an exchambermaid, to double her bets and break the bank."

14 THE AMERICAN WEEKLY August 7, 1955

It's teatime with Mrs. Julio de Diego.

Novak, Marlene Dietrich and the indestructible Mae West. Gypsy and Lili St. Cyr received the nod as "Burlesque's best known attraction."

Strip for Action. In October Gypsy met the creative team of *Strip for Action* to produce an updated version of the original, which was based on a comedy by Howard Lindsay and Russel Crouse. The new show was written by Paul Streger and Eli Basse. Some of the songs from the production, with music by Jimmy McHugh and lyrics by Harold Adamson, were "Gotta Have a Man, Sometime," "Chaps from Annapolis," "Dame Crazy," "Love Me as Though There Were No Tomorrow," "I Just Found Out About Love," "Too Young to Go

Gypsy Rose Napoleona Bonaparte. In another Springmaid ad of 1955 Gypsy appeared as "Napoleona Bonaparte."

Steady," "Rock and Roll Bump," "I Just Want to Be a Song and Dance Man," and "Good Old Days of Burlesque."

Gypsy Shows Off. A small photo of Gypsy appeared in the December 1955 issue of *Show* magazine, accompanying the article "Burlesque — Is It Bouncing Back?" Gypsy was proclaimed one of the "… five top money making exotic dancers of all time," along with Ann Corio, Margie Hart, Lili St. Cyr and Lilly "Cat Girl" Christine.

• 1956 •

New Year's Eve. Gypsy did a New Year's Eve show in a dismal Fort Lauderdale nightclub called The Cavern. According to her son's book, *Gypsy & Me: At Home and on the Road with Gypsy Rose Lee,* she declared that it would be her last performance as a stripper.

Gypsy Is Show Business. Gypsy appeared in the Burlesque section of the 1956 issue of *This Was Show Business,* which presented photographs of her alone and with Bobby Clark. Other burlesque queens featured included Margie Hart and Ann Corio. There was also a photo of Billy Minsky's Burlesque Theatre.

Gypsy Fully Clothed Till 25. "Gypsy Rose Lee Kept Clothes on Until Age of 25" read the headline in newspapers across the country on January 6, 1956.

> Burlesque queens may come and go but Gypsy Rose Lee, a veteran of 16 years on the bump-and-grind circuit, seems to go on forever.
>
> "I'm always amazed that I'm still going strong." Gypsy said today in Atlanta where she is appearing at a night club. "I always think of retiring, but I suppose I never will."
>
> The statuesque, brown-haired stripper, now a sedate 41, made her stage debut at the tender age of three and a half when she and her sister, Actress June Hovac, frolicked at a lodge meeting in Seattle.
>
> "But I didn't start taking off my clothes in public until I was 25," she explained. "I had been playing in the Pantages and Orpheum circuit when I suddenly found myself on the 'starvation route.' It was in Kansas City in 1939 that I decided there would be more money in doing a strip act."
>
> She also changed her name from Rose Louise Hovick to Gypsy Rose Lee because she did not want her grandfather to know of her change of plans.
>
> "Besides," she declared, "the name Gypsy suited me better because I was always traveling and I used to tell my friends' fortunes. I never regretted becoming a stripper for a moment."
>
> She has good reason for not regretting the choice. In the years that followed, her clothes-peeling routine has earned her between five and seven thousand dollars a week.
>
> She has engaged in a busy round of activities which would last most people a lifetime. She is the author of two mystery novels, has traveled extensively over much of the world and appeared in numerous plays, movies and in television and radio programs.
>
> She even found time to wed and shed three husbands and have a baby, Erik, now 11. She divorced her latest husband, Julio de Diego, during an engagement in Reno last August.
>
> "You can't play Reno without getting a divorce," she commented.
>
> When not bumping and grinding out a living, Gypsy putters around in her 26-room New York mansion and indulges her passion for cooking.
>
> "I just love to cook and prefer my own cooking to anything the restaurants have to offer," she said. "I eat anything I like and if I gain three pounds more than my usual 130, I worry so much that they just fall off."
>
> She is also a dabbler in foreign languages and is now attempting to master French. If she gets tired of that, there is always Erik's miniature railroad.
>
> "Erik and I have a great deal of fun with that," she laughed.
>
> But after six months or so of all this domesticity, she "gets to feeling bored," and wheels out her Rolls-Royce to accept a date in Duluth, Los Angeles or Palm Beach.

Piled into the car are her four chorus girls, one or two Siamese cats, and a stack of language books, costumes and Erik who is constantly with her on tour.

"Erik really enjoys my tours," she declared. "As for me, I've lived all my life and I enjoy it so why should I quit?"

Twentieth Century. Ben Hecht's play *Twentieth Century* was produced at the Palm Beach Playhouse in Florida, during the month of February 1956. Gypsy starred with actor Ian Keith.

Gypsy's Tip Off. The April 1956 issue of the tabloid magazine *Tip-Off* queried:

"Marry a Stripper?" Here's the tip-Off:
Is There Too Much Gypsy in Gypsy Rose Lee's Love Life?
by Frederick C. Palmer:
"She's the Best-Undressed Woman in the World.
But When It Comes to Holding a Husband,
the Truth Is: Her Slip Is Showing!"

If the most talented fiction writer, even the best-selling Gypsy Rose Lee herself, were to set down the life of Rose Louise Hovick as a biographical novel, nobody would believe it. There's too much pathos; too much ambition and too much success; too much attempted and too much achieved; too much restless wandering in pursuit of happiness—too much gypsy in her soul.

Nevertheless, Gypsy Rose Lee *is* Rose Louise Hovick, and every word we are about to tell you is true. So if there is too much gypsy in Gypsy's love life, blame the fates and not some hapless writer, because she lived through every minute of it without a script—and is still going strong.

Yes, the gal who has been called everything from an ecdysiast (by H.L. Mencken, no less!) to a diseuse, and whose very name has become synonymous with strip tease; the gal who has played to audiences ranging from Minsky's 14th Street to Ziegfeld's Follies, carnival midways and some of the plushier Broadway houses, is back in circulation and readying something called *Strip for Action* for opening on Broadway at this writing.

And chances are that none of the men in the audience, at least, will go away unsatisfied. Chances are, too, that Gypsy feels the same way about it that she did when she told an interviewer, "Anything I'm in, everybody thinks it has to be burlesque. We hope to give them a show that will take their minds of everything but women."

And Gypsy can do that, onstage or off, with any size audience, down to and including one.

She has used her talents to captivate countless men, including three husbands (one of whom she wed in a water-taxi off the coast of California); wrote two best-selling mystery novels, a successful Broadway show and articles for *The New Yorker, American Mercury, Collier's* and *Variety*. She has also received warm praise for her work in oils, especially a self-portrait exhibited by the exclusive Guggenheim Galleries. Meanwhile, she was appearing on radio and TV, designing and supervising the making of costumes for shows in which she starred, and making a home!

Possessed of Boundless Ambition

What is it then that drives this beautiful whirlwind, whose energy is still as boundless now as it was in 1937, when the students of a toney upstate New York private school voted her "the most prominent woman in the world today" over Amelia Earhart and Mrs. F.D. Roosevelt? It is not material possessions. The fruits of her labors in various vineyards include wealth, a beautiful estate and manor house in the rich Hudson Valley and a 26-room mansion in midtown Manhattan, both elegantly staffed and furnished with such lush items as a 14-foot polar bear rug on which she is wont to frisk of a winter's evening whilst playing backgammon.

But still her restless search for happiness goes on! She has fabulous beauty, wit, charm and vast talent. And she is known to be able to charm the most exciting conversationalist in even a brief and casual meeting. But she hasn't held a husband!

It seems that she is driven by an insatiable urge to achieve merely for the sake of achievement, to succeed for the sake of success. For, having achieved one goal, she moves like a gypsy on to the next, seemingly always just over the horizon.

Some say that her talent and ambition have brought her a long way since she was working for the late Billy Minsky and he characterized her act as "seven minutes of sheer art," but what they don't know is how far she came before that.

It would have been out of character if the girl who was to become Gypsy Rose Lee had been able to choose a more definite birthplace than "somewhere on the West Coast," and if she did, its name has been lost to her biographers. There was a cold, drenching rain falling the night of February 9, 1914, when Gypsy made her bow into the world. Her father, John, a somewhat impecunious newspaperman, had set the family up in a house with a badly leaking roof and the practically minded Mrs. Hovick recalled that at the exact moment of Gyps' birth, she called out to her husband, "Don't mind me; take care of that leak over the piano!"

When the Hovick's separated, Gyps was about four and her sister June (now the famous June Havoc, a last name she acquired through a typographical error in a theater program) was 19 months younger. Mrs. Hovick took the girls to live with their grandfather and pushed them into their theatrical debut before the Knights of Pythias, of which grandpa was a member.

With the alimony she received from three ex-husbands and what the girls could earn by appearing before Grandpa's seven lodges, Mom managed to keep the girls in fancy costumes and gradually built them an act. And that wasn't all she did.

Gypsy recalls, "When we played on the bill with another kiddie act, things always seemed to go wrong — for them. Pieces of their wardrobe would be missing. A toe shoe would get burned. A blonde wig would disappear. The act's music would be lost. Mother was always very sympathetic when these misfortunes happened and would join in the search for the missing articles, and sometimes she was the one to find them, but always too late."

The biggest headache for the Hovick's, though, was the stern-faced policewoman who confronted them at every big town as they rode the circuits. Every female appearing on the stage then, whether six or sixty, had to wear full length opera hose while onstage. Gyps, however, was playing the role of a boy and escaped inspection. But Mama finally had to hire a normal-school grad as a tutor and trick her out in flat-heeled shoes and glasses to impress the authorities and press that the girls were getting a proper education. The little Hovick's were then in their teens and earning as much as $1,250 a week, but with no time for boyfriends or other teen-age nonsense. But they were on their way; the worst was over, yet there was more to come.

June had gone her separate way to fame and fortune in Hollywood by the time Gypsy's shoulder strap slipped one night in the course of a vaudeville act known as Rose Louise and Her Hollywood Blondes and caused a sensation! What started out as an embarrassing episode in an uninspired performance became the inspiration and springboard for a fabulous career.

But not before Gyps had suffered enough disappointment and discouragement to make a soap opera look like light comedy.

Like the time a scout caught her act and got her an audition before the late Earl Carroll, one of the most powerful figures in show business. She was nervous and stiff and knew she hadn't done her best, but she was hardly prepared for what she overheard the maestro telling her mother.

"She's too hefty!" he gruffed. "Put her on a diet! Why do you let a girl with all that beauty put on all that fat? She doesn't even know how to walk — drags her feet! You must have noticed her lisp! Need I tell you more?"

He didn't have to tell Gypsy more. She never forgot. From that day to this, she has watched her figure, along with countless drooling others.

In 1937, another important event in Gyps life took place on (or just off) the West Coast, when she wed Arnold R. Mizzy, a New York dental supply manufacturer, in the aforementioned water-taxi. For three years, then, she continued to grace the runways of Broadway's most luxurious burlesque houses, until 1940, when she opened in the sensational *Streets of Paris* show at the New York's World's Fair, in a $2,500 costume designed by Pavel Tchelichew.

Guested for WW

While doing that stint, she was asked to do a guest column for Walter Winchell, thought it was fun, and decided to write a novel. That was the first of the aforementioned best-sellers. Naturally, there was some speculation as to how much of the book she wrote, and there was a suit filed for collaboration fees by a magazine writer, but everything was settled out of court and Gypsy said it was all a mistake. Meanwhile, she had quietly divorced Mizzy.

Her press agent said she planned to stay single for awhile, "in deference to her fans."

By now the biggest star in burlesque, Gypsy was dealt quite a blow when the late Mayor LaGuardia moved in on the houses that specialized in that art form. She appeared in the big musical revue *Star and Garter* to even greater acclaim, and began consolidating her financial gain.

She had bought beautiful old Witchwood Manor at Highland Hills, N.Y., installed five bathrooms, furnished it in disordered opulence and began to surprise everybody by making wine from her own grapes and doing her own canning. She also began to make life uneasy for assorted "clannish bluebloods" whose ancestral estates lay thereabouts. She gave them their comeuppance, too.

Her first real brush with highbrow neighbors came in 1942, when she heard that the local Red Cross drive might not meet its quota and scheduled a benefit show of her own at the Town Hall. The local ladies were outraged, but somehow the squires swallowed their dignity and turned out to make the affair a spanking success. Now some of the neighboring tycoons are suggesting that she take on directorship of a local bank.

The was also the year she married her second husband, writer-actor-producer Alexander Kirkland, a union which was not to last, but which was to produce her only child, a son, who was born a few weeks after the divorce.

A reporter who dropped by to see how Gyps was taking impending motherhood found that she hadn't knitted anything for the baby, but had finished 12 pairs of argyle socks for nobody in particular.

"All I have for the baby," she confessed, "is a cap and a pacifier. Egad! I was arrested in Boston with more than that!"

She seemed to be concerned that it be a normal delivery.

"Wouldn't I look great with a rhinestone-studded operation?" she asked.

Having garnered more success then anyone else in her field, Gyp's restless eyes began looking around for new pastures, and, in 1949, they lit on a brand new one—the carnival.

She had met and married, the year before, a Spanish painter named Julio de Diego, but her home life was abruptly halted when she accepted an estimated $10,000 weekly minimum, plus a fat percentage of the gross to go on the road with the giant Royal American Shows for a dozen 20-minute performances a day.

With her family packed in an elaborate trailer she took to the road, but not before Julio had arranged for his own girlie show to compete in friendly fashion with Gyps on the midway. The arrangement seemed happy.

But before long the three were back in New York.

No More Trouble

She took to baring her patio for the City Garden Clubs, and the only trouble she got into with the law was over an un-covered garbage can.

Perhaps she gave a hint of the turn things were taking when she told a visitor who had remarked on her ornate Victorian bedroom: "This room is my last stand. It represents the end of my romantic period. I used to have 26 rooms filled with Victoriana and this is all that is left." Julio was not around.

Last August, the marriage that began so gaily in the Bronx license bureau ended in a Reno divorce court.

So now Gyps has a new show and a new challenge coming up. *Strip for Action* is a musical by Jimmy McHugh and Harald (correct) Adamson, based on a play by Howard Lindsey and Russel Crouse, and will feature Jack Whiting, Ben Lessy, Patti Moore, Jessica James and Lois O'Brien.

And, if all goes well, they'll ban or close the show at the Boston tryout, and Gypsy Rose Lee will be made again.

Gypsy Goes to School. On May 25, 1956, Gypsy posed with the students of the Professional Children's School.

Fancy Meeting Gypsy. Gypsy toured for the summer with the play *Fancy Meeting You Again.* The tour began on July 30, 1956, and ended on August 27, 1956. It was written by playwright George S. Kaufman and also starred Ethel Britton and Joseph Warren. The tour included performances at the Somerset Playhouse in Massachusetts, the Lake Whalom Playhouse also in Massachusetts and the Casino Theatre in New Port, Rhode Island.

The United States Steel Hour. Gypsy played the role of Wendy Graves in a teleplay titled *Sauce for the Goose.* This was episode 78 in the show's 4th season; the airdate was October 10, 1956.

Gypsy in Las Vegas. Morey Amsterdam was the emcee when Gypsy appeared at the Hotel Riviera during October 1956. Gypsy usually got $5,000 a week when she worked in Las Vegas.

The Real Gypsy. The November 1956 issue of *REAL: The Exciting Magazine for Men* featured such exciting stories as "Teddy Roosevelt's Rough Riders: They Went for 5 Missionaries," "I Robbed a Bank," and "The Truth About the Negro Soldier." *REAL* also included an article about Gypsy, who they described as "This naked lady — who insists people should pay more attention to her brains — is still the most artistic hip-wiggler of them all."

STRIP-TEASER:
THE UPS AND DOWNS OF GYPSY ROSE LEE
By Roger Kahn

For a woman who has spent a lifetime baring her chest to the world, Gypsy Rose Lee grows surprisingly restless when anyone asks about the flair with which she gets undressed. Swiftly as a Girl Scout troop leader, she steers the conversation away from flesh and toward books, or the theater, or even modern art, before the questioner can blurt out, "Billy Minsky."

"Acting," Gypsy suggests in polished but somewhat urgent tones, "demands technique. How do you talk? How do you walk? How do you move? In writing there are transitions to cope with, and bridges. Painting has to do with form and subtle shading. But stripping? Why, it has no place for technique at all. No matter what a stripper does there's only one question the audience wants answered. You know what it is. How well-developed is she? You've probably asked it yourself."

Despite this coldly practical view, Gypsy Rose Lee has let neither life nor the curious world of burlesque turn her into a cynic.

Somehow, things have always seemed to balance out. The break-ups with three husbands were hard and disappointing, but as consolation Gypsy has been able to ponder her personal fortune and the mansion she owns in New York's stylish East 60s which might well do Bernard Baruch proud. Gypsy is brilliantly aware that she is one of the few women who ever turned stripping into a million dollars. When she dismissed the question on technique, she was merely knocking her own racket even as you and almost everybody else.

But the significant edge which Miss Lee holds is that she can afford to knock her racket whenever it suits her mood. Within burlesque, where the pelvic wiggle seems more profound than all the sonnets of Shakespeare, Gypsy has climbed up on a private pinnacle. She can wiggle with artistry, but with only a bit more effort, she can spell, read and even quote the best sonnets Shakespeare produced. As a result, she has been called an intellectual, and while she frequently protests her innocence, this is one charge she never denies too loudly. Like the very dry martini, Miss Lee is an unrivaled attraction in her field, and her special switch has been this: a naked lady who almost commands that you pay attention to her brains.

All her life there has been a violent conflict between mind and body in Gypsy Rose Lee. In her youth she repeatedly quit stripping jobs that paid as much as $500 a week to join a chorus of $60 and get a chance to appear in legitimate theater. Later, when her success in burlesque was unprecedented, she turned away from it to write books. Even now, when she demands and gets $5,000 a week for stripping in Las Vegas or Miami clubs, she is much more excited about her autobiography.

Harper's, a distinguished and conservative house, will publish the book, probably as *The World on a String*, and Gypsy is extreme proud that when writing the first two parts under instructions to keep them at "about equal length," she finished one part in 215 pages and the other in 216. "I'm working on the third part now," she says, "and hoping. I think my writing is getting better than it was."

To understand just how far removed Gypsy is from traditional strip-teaser, one must first appreciate a few of the professions clichés.

Most important, teasers are supposed to be shy. When Margie Hart had to take a physical examination to qualify for a pilot's license some years back, she balked at getting undressed in the presence of a male physician. "I finally did it," she admitted later, "but only after he told me that he saw so many women without clothes on that to him it was like looking at a ham."

Then, of course, strippers must be homebodies, as any man who ever stumbled into a B-joint has discovered. According to the classic formula, the stripper dresses hurriedly after her act and, while some other girl is grinding away on stage, she walks among the tables out front, looking for a lonely man. As soon as she finds one, she joins him, and chest out, starts to tell the story of her life. Between sustained chatter about the happy times back in good old Hayseed Falls, the stripper whispers orders to a waiter and, when she puts her chest back in and wanders off into the semi-darkness, the waiter hands the customer a $20 tab.

"Scotch for the lady," he explains, although actually the lady was drinking diluted tea or, if the joint is particularly modish, small slugs of cheap, raw rye.

No one looking for Gypsy Rose Lee's queenly frame of 5 foot 9 can think of her as a drink hustler even for a moment. At worst, she might accept a champagne cocktail. Nor can anyone listening to her bright, brittle chatter imagine her holing up in Hayseed Falls for anything but a one-night stand. Coyness is a quality that is never considered with Gypsy around. She admits to 42 and she has lived hard.

Even Gypsy's professional routine is outside the ordinary pattern. On the same stages where hundreds of strippers have labored to lend seductive meaning to the peeling of one long white glove, Gypsy tries to lend seductive meaning to nothing. "It's hard for me to kid," she concedes, "because some people decide I'm kidding highly serious stuff like nudity and the sanctity of American womanhood. But actually, all my act is, frankly, is a spoof on the old strip routines."

Customarily, Gypsy moves on stage wearing a costume that looks fresh out of the 1890's. Then, with exaggerated mannerisms, she tosses a number of ordinary French phrases over the footlights and drifts back and forth in graceful time to the music.

When she begins to take off her costume — in all it costs $3,000 — she adds outrageous winks and looks of almost girlish shock to the monologue in French. Gradually, she works her way free from some of her outer clothing, prances about the stage and, finally, terribly overdressed by stripping standards, she exits.

Inevitably, the audience protests. There is generally a tired businessman down front who finds the energy to shout, "Hey, come back here," or an original thinker in the balcony who bellows, "Take it off."

Suddenly, Gypsy's head pops into view at a corner of the stage. "Darlings," she pleads, "please don't ask me to take off any more. I'll catch cold. Please. I'm embarrassed. I'm almost shivering now."

After the audience rises to her bait, Gypsy works her way down to brassiere and G-string and moves back to the corner of the stage. Carefully, she starts to unhook the brassiere, but just as it is coming off, a woman in the audience shrieks wildly, Gypsy laughs a rich, throaty laugh and the house lights go out with the brassiere somewhere in limbo. Although Miss Lee is certain of the reactions that come from the men, the feminine shrieker is always a paid plant.

It is doubtful that this act can ever rival the poetry of T.S. Eliot as a subtle appeal to human emotion, but judged in context it is undeniably sophisticated. It can hardly be classed with such other standard routines as alternate flexing of the buttocks in waltz time.

"Don't kid yourself about my winking and my French," Gypsy says, "When I come off the stage. It isn't easy to get up a laugh at that same scream five times a day"

Obviously it is not possible to obtain a full picture of Gypsy across the footlights of a burlesque stage. Only a visit to her lair on East 63rd Street will suffice. Fortunately, such a visit was made not long ago. Inevitably, it began with a telephone call to her agent.

"She is still very much in demand," the agent said, eagerly. "Still stripping and still very busy."

"Fine," said the reporter who was trying to locate her. "I'd like to see her."

"She'll call you," the agent promised, and within the hour Gypsy phoned.

"How is Saturday at 6 A.M.?" she asked.

"Perfect," the reporter said.

"After I check my schedule, I'll call you," Gypsy said, "and make it definite."

"No," said the reporter. "Let me call you."

"Ha," Gypsy said in something very close to triumph. "I won't let you have my telephone number. Why, if I let people have the number, I'd never have a moment to myself."

When she called later, Gypsy shifted the date to Monday, but left the hour unchanged. At the appointed time, East 63rd Street was splashed with gentle sunlight and the whole scene was touched with a special beauty. The block on which Gypsy lives is lined with trees and splendid mansions built for another time. At one corner, stands the Barbizon Hotel for Women, a monument to chastity.

Gypsy's mansion, built of white stucco, is four floors high and contains 26 rooms, some of which are rented as apartments. The reporter entered into a spacious foyer and waked quickly into a hall that was painted pale green.

At the end of the hall the reporter found a drawing room, all green and scarlet, in which paintings covered every wall. The most striking was a nude portrait of a youthful girl, larger than life but strangely sexless, which was a gift to Gypsy from Mike Todd, the producer. On another wall hung a much smaller painting which was the only one is the room that could be called so much as provocative. It showed a fleshy lady, undeniably brunette, lying languidly on a bed and clad in one black stocking. The lighting in the drawing room seemed to have been planned as carefully as that in an art museum, and Gypsy's collection of paintings, once widely rumored to be pornographic, might well have been hanging in some fashionable gallery.

An elevator, done in gilt and lined with mirrors, took the reporter to the fourth floor where, erect upon her couch in a spacious, paneled study, Gypsy was sitting. Five cats prowled around indolently.

"Come in," Gypsy said, springing to her feet. "I can offer you Scotch or vodka." The order was vodka and before many minutes Gypsy herself was talking about her writing career.

"Crazy hours," she exclaimed, "but that's the only way for me. Sometimes I'm up at 4 A.M., and often I pound the electric typewriter over there all day. If I finish seven pages I'm doing well."

It was difficult for the reporter to avoid observing that Gypsy's flowery print house dress was not a standard model. It was slit on each side, almost to the waist, and beneath it was a bright pink slip.

"I wonder," the reporter said, "how you ever got started in writing."

"I read all the books my friends write," Gypsy said, "and when I was a child I read *Das Kapital* and the *Decameron*. Now I'm big for science fiction. That's because I liked weird stories when I was a child. Scientific fiction and now, of course, autobiography, to see how other people handled theirs. And theater books. Carson McCullers is a contemporary writer whose works deal principally with decay in the South."

Yet the field of writing was only one small area of the conversational ground covered by Gypsy. She discussed a great range of topics with a great range of skills. Here are a few samples, verbatim from the reporter's notebook.

Hollywood: "I've loved it every time I've been out there. Hollywood is all brittle and over-sexed, but I can't believe it can be bothered by anything but all this genius packed so tightly in one place. Too much genius can be pretty depressing, but the stories that when I was out there I insisted on being different and eating with stagehands are just nonsense. One time I stayed at the home of Fanny Brice, another time at the home of Elsie Mendel, a wonderful friend, and I just loved it. But when I finished my work I came home."

Freudian psychology: "I'm not terribly familiar with Freud, except for a few books, but I'm certain that I have complexes. I wouldn't want to be without them."

Men: "Women should never generalize about men. I think that's too ridiculous. Just the way they look is interesting enough, whether they're big ones, little ones, thin ones, fat ones. I just like nice ones, but most of the nice ones I've met are witty. I suppose wit is the one quality a man must have to attract me."

Polar bear rugs: "Mine was burned up when an ember from the fireplace landed on it, but I can't say I'm sorry. The bear's head was all flattened and teeth kept coming out. Roland Young had sat on it too much during damp weather in Malibu."

Modesty: "I'd never pose in the nude for anybody — and never have, despite all the ridiculous stories that I have."

Work conditions: "If I had a daughter, and she had to be a stripper, I'd prefer that she perform in a TV studio, where they couldn't throw pins, cigarettes, newspaper and other things at her — like they once did with me."

Paintings: "The paintings I have don't really represent my tastes because the painting I want most I could never afford. In Holland, when I looked at Rembrandt originals I saw beauty that I could not believe. I love painting and my third husband was a very fine painter."

Currently, Gypsy is without any husband since No. 3, Julio de Diego, and she have been divorced, and No. 4, if there is to be one, is nowhere in sight. But in addition to the cats, Eric [*sic*], 12, her son by her second marriage, lives in the mansion. "I rent out what used to be the servants' quarters and some other rooms," she says. "That covers taxes and maintenance and leaves me the place clear."

This arrangement lies an entire world away from the roofless house in West Seattle where Gypsy entered the world on a date she gives as January 9, 1914.

Olaf Hovick, her father, was a cub reporter on the Seattle *Post Intelligencer* and was earning the traditionally tiny salary newspapers pay young apprentices. Olaf could afford a house only if he built it himself. He went to work and he finished the floors, walls and basement with such impressive skill that he could not resist moving his wife into the new home before the roof was completed. Under a wide and starry sky, Olaf Hovick's daughter was born. She was named Rose Louise and, of course, she is now Gypsy Rose Lee. Not very long after the roof was finally finished, another daughter arrived. The Hovicks named her June and she, as most theater-goers know, is now actress June Havoc. Not very long after June's birth, the marriage of Olaf and Roanie [sic] disintegrated.

For reasons which have never been explained, Roanie [sic] turned toward the stage when it became a question of work or starve. She had neither a background in show business nor any apparent instinct for it, but fortunately her daughters combined sufficient talent to make eventual success certain.

As the girls grew old enough to appear on stage, Roanie [sic] organized an act called,

"Dainty June, the Hollywood Baby, and her Newsboy Songsters." Although June was feature, Gypsy was prominent as Rose Louise, the Doll Girl.

Since as the Hollywood Baby, June was limited to baby-talk during working hours, she found the role confining and by the time she had reached her 13th birthday the limited dialogue had become unendurable. Without warning, June ran off with one of the Newsboy Songsters, a boy of 21, and later married him. She never went back to the act.

Shunted into a starring role, Gypsy at once began a series of major changes with which her mother, clearly, had to go along. She fired the remaining Newsboy Songsters, hired several chorus girls, ordered them to dye their hair platinum and retitled the presentation, "Rose Louise and her Hollywood Blondes." Rose Louise enjoyed only moderate success until one performance in Kansas City when a should strap broke on stage.

"I noticed," Gypsy says, broadly, "that I'd never gotten such a big hand before. From that minute on, I made sure at least one gave way at every show."

The switch to stripping was considerably more difficult than Gypsy likes to admit. Once Earl Carroll, producer of a famous succession of reviews called *Scandals*, was auditioning for his chorus in Cleveland at the same time the Hollywood Blondes were there. Gypsy tried out, wearing a standard chorus costume, and was hoofing eagerly when Carroll brought her up short.

"Hey," he said. "Stop that dancing and peel down a little. Let's let the customers get a look at what you've got."

In apparently honest shock, Gypsy answered, "Sir!" Then she walked off the stage, and although she still could have worked for Carroll, went back to the Hollywood Blondes. Today Gypsy does not shock quite as easily and no longer treats touchy suggestion in the style of a Victorian school teacher. Whether her basic attitude has really changed is a moot point.

But one year after the Carroll incident, Gypsy became a full-fledged strip-teaser. Her first salary was $75 a week. After a month it rocketed up to $350. Gypsy was a big, dignified nude with an appeal best defined by an old burlesque promoter. "She was the sort of girl," the promoter said, "who'd come on stage and make everyone in the audience want to see her in the raw." For a stripper, this ability is priceless.

The price, however, stayed at $350 for a time, and the work still was far from satisfactory. During early travels around theater circuits, Gypsy had been provided with a tutor and this, plus her frequent reading, plus sheer native intelligence, made it impossible for her to consider strip-teasing as the greatest of all art forms. In 1930, she quit stripping for a job in the chorus of "Hot-Cha," the last musical Florenz Ziegfeld ever produced. Her chorus pay check each week was $60. The problem of art versus stripping is one thread that runs through Gypsy's entire life. Today a good light part, even in summer stock, excites her more than a chance to appear in some huge stripping spectacular. "I don't have a Hamlet complex or anything like that," she says. "I mean I don't feel I must be a great tragic actress. But I do want to be a skillful comedienne. June has studied acting a lot and I haven't, because the way I do things if I ever started I'd never have time for anything else. I think I'm still improving, though."

Still, the truth remains that Gypsy's name will always be more closely allied with that of Minsky than with any great theatrical director. When Billy Minsky first re-named her Gypsy Rose Lee, he was doing more than any acting coach ever could. After "Hot-Cha" folded, and Gypsy had been forced to return to stripping, it was at Minsky's theaters that she was able to raise her salary level to $500 a week. "In the legit," she concedes, sorrowfully, "I made such awful dough I had to hock a few jewels. I lost the house I'd bought in Rego Park (Long Island)."

The compromise which Gypsy eventually made called for her to accept stripping as a means of survival while looking elsewhere for artistic satisfaction. Certainly, she was fearless in her search for art. Among the people she jostled with were H.L. Mencken, the acid Baltimore journalist, and Martin Dies, the Texas congressman who devoted himself to chasing Communists at a time when Nazis and Fascists were working to overthrow the American government.

In the midst of one of his bitter essays, Mencken mentioned Gypsy as an ecdysiast, a word taken from the Greek and which describes "the act of molting."

After checking a dictionary, Gypsy came back strongly, "Mencken," she said "is an intellectual snob. Certainly, I have read his stuff, but only in my youth."

The involvement with Dies stemmed from her support of the Loyalist side in the Spanish Civil War. (At the time, perhaps half of the United States was anti–Franco and pro–Loyalists.) "This man Dies," Gypsy wondered to the press. "Who is going to investigate him?"

On October 13, 1937, Gypsy married a wealthy New Yorker named Robert Mizzy, who made dental supplies. It was a strange wedding, but it conformed with a Norse tradition Gypsy claims for her family. She was married at sea.

Since the cost of chartering an ocean liner was prohibitive, even for Gypsy, the couple settled for a water taxi and then chugged 20 miles from the shore. There the craft's pilot performed the ceremony. "A ship's captain marries people," Gypsy said. "Why not the pilot of a water taxi?" Rather than press this point, she agreed to another ceremony on land.

At best, the marriage was a long-shot. Gypsy was touring the country frequently, dabbling with the idea of trying Hollywood and, from 1939, hard at work learning how to write. On St. Patrick's Day, 1941, she and Mizzy were divorced. It is difficult to imagine how she found time ever to fall in love again.

She had developed swiftly as a writer. Her detective story, *The G-String Murders*, was slick and professional. Her articles were polished enough to meet the exacting standards of *The New Yorker*. When newspapermen asked thickly who she had writing her stuff, she shot back, "Who have you had reading it to you?" She wrote two more novels and a play called *The Naked Genius*, which Mike Todd produced and which lasted 16 weeks. But somehow she managed to sandwich in a wedding, to an actor named William Alexander Kirkland, on August 30, 1942. She had met Kirkland at a dinner party held by Carl Van Doren, a significant literary figure. Van Doren was best man. Gypsy divorced in Reno on October 7, 1944. She gave birth to Eric [*sic*] Kirkland on December 11, just one day before William Kirkland married for a second time. Her final marriage, to Julio de Diego, took place in 1948. Recently came to a quiet end.

Along with husbands, Gypsy has collected houses throughout her career, a pursuit probably related to her earliest days, when first the house was bleak and undersized and then there was no house at all. But unraveling the puzzling personality of Gypsy Rose Lee involves a good deal more than houses. Probably it centers on questions one reporter asked her not long ago.

"Was it difficult for you to become a stripper?" he wondered. "Was it a humiliating thing for you to do?"

Gypsy's reply was fast and glib. "To learn about that," she said, "you'll have to read my autobiography." The answer may be uncovered there, but only if Gypsy still remembers what it is.

Gypsy Behind the Scenes. In November of 1956 Gypsy was in Las Vegas. She sat down with Alice Pardoe West, who wrote a column for the *Ogden Standard-Examiner*. The interview was published in the Sunday Morning issue of November 11, 1956.

As a tragedian wants to be a comic and a comedian, play tragedy — so is world-famous stripteaser Gypsy Rose Lee, modest.

"I scoot like crazy through the lobby," she told me before her show at the Riviera, while in Las Vegas. "Once I comb out the curls on my forehead, no one knows who I am, and that's the way I want it."

"I even wear a bathing suit almost to my knees when I get in the pool, because I can't stand people looking at my figure." We laughed.

She has the reputation of not mingling. "That's also the way I want it," she said. "In my sort of act, I have to create an illusion and it's better not to mingle with people too much."

This led to how she got into a strip-tease act, being so naturally modest herself.

BURLESQUES OR STARVE

She explained it was a case of going into burlesque or face starvation.

She is still beautiful and refined.

It doesn't take long to learn that her act is strictly business.

"I knew it was a terrific step to take," she said as she repaired some loose strands of beads on an exquisite yellow gown which was a mass of dangling beads. "But I thought I could get by with it if I changed my name, so my grandfather wouldn't know. The moment I saw the publicity come out with 'young Seattle beauty' in headlines. I knew he'd catch on — and he did!"

Then there was her sister, movie star, June Havoc.

"I thought she'd die," she said, smiling. "She was dancing in a marathon at the time and she was so upset, she wouldn't let anyone know she was a relative of mine. And Mom — she telling someone about it later and said she cried, and cried, and cried. And I said, "Yes, Mom, but remember you ate and ate and ate."

Gypsy Rose Lee explained she was not frightened as one would think, for her first strip performance.

COMEDY ACT

"It was supposed to be a comedy number," she said, "and I took off each piece of clothing I had to throw it on the musicians. The audience howled and when I got down to the real strip, I knew I was covered with a net and that the trim and flowers were on that net and I felt perfectly all right about it. It was the illusion I was giving and I was so happy about the success of my act that I didn't think a thing about being scared."

She said the applause at the end of her act was so great she couldn't believe it. She had left the stage and slipped into her kimono and the manager came in and asked her to go out there and take a bow. She was about to but her mother said: "Stay where you are!"

Instead her mother went out and demanded a bigger salary for Gypsy Rose.

The last play Gypsy Rose did on Broadway was "The Star and the Garter." She has done many plays since then, but they haven't been on Broadway. She has not made a recent picture but has been playing theatres and vaudeville circuits in Europe and was at the London Palladium. She was over there two years, making a film in Spain.

"I came home on the bias," she said, "taking in the many places I had always wanted to see."

Last year she played six months in Las Vegas, Reno, and at Ciro's in Hollywood and back to Florida to play the remainder of the time. She took her young son, Erik, age 11, with her.

"We zig-zagged around," she said, "and stopped at every historic marker we saw. He knew all about the cities of Europe, but not too much about his own country, so I thought I had better let him get acquainted with America."

ENJOYED SALT LAKE

She was thrilled to see Salt Lake City, as she hadn't seen it since she was a small girl.

She said vaudeville is becoming less and less in demand, but that television is taking much of it over.

"It's so hard to get around," she said. "I can't fly because of my many heavy costumes, and by the time I get them taken care of on and off the train, it really is a job to travel with my show."

She has four girls with her in her act.

"Besides my 26 pieces of luggage," she said, "I have five Siamese cats that have been around the world with me. I hope they aren't tearing things up in the room while I'm out. They know they can't do it at home, but they might do it here."

Before Gypsy Rose Lee changed her name, she was Rose Louise.

"I added 'Gypsy' to the Rose Lee," she said seriously, "to make it more elegant."

UNSUCCESSFUL IN LOVE

Gypsy Rose has been married three times and is not planning on trying it again — at least not at present.

"Each one of my husbands has deeply resented my strip tease work," she said sincerely, "and yet none of them made enough to support me without my taking off my clothes. Men don't feel that it's an art and I can understand it 100 per cent. But I had my own financial problems, and no man wants to be married to a woman who makes more money than he does."

Gypsy Rose has a home of 26 rooms between 3rd and Lexington. It's a four-story house with roof garden and flowers. She recently made it into a duplex, as it seems less lonely, she explained.

Gypsy Rose is genteel, vivacious and gracious. She is a successful writer, having had three books published, "G-String Murders," "Mother Finds a Body," and a play, "Naked Genius" which Joan Blondell did on Broadway. She is writing her own autobiography. "World on a String," which is humorous. Harpers have bought it and she has to December 1 to finish it.

Gypsy Rose gets a real kick out of her work and the only thing about it that amazes her is that she has been doing it for 20 years and she is still in demand.

The Steve Allen Show. Gypsy played a saloon girl in a parody of television adventure shows in a skit titled "The Coward." This was Allen's second season on television, episode 20 and the show aired on December 2, 1956.

Gypsy Hook, Line and Sinker. Avid fisher Gypsy was thrilled to be named Fisherwoman of the Year in 1956. She received the award and title from *Fisherman Magazine*.

CHAPTER SEVEN

Believe It or Not

• 1957 •

Life Is a Cabaret. Gypsy appeared again in the January 1957 issue of *Cabaret Magazine*.

Person to Person. Gypsy and her son Erik were visited by Edward R. Murrow for his popular *Person to Person* television show. The episode was broadcast on February 8, 1957.

Gypsy's Fanny. In their April 1957 issue *Town & Country* magazine featured an article Gypsy wrote about her longtime friend, legendary Fanny Brice: "Fanny Brice and I."

***Harper's* Magazine.** In April of 1957 *Harper's* published the first of two articles written by Gypsy to be featured in back to back issues, to promote Gypsy's new autobiography, *Gypsy*. The first article "Stranded in Kansas City or, A Fate Worse Than Vaudeville," which is described as "A personal account of the turning point in the career of the most famous — and wittiest — practitioner of a unique American art form: The Strip Tease."

In part of the article she discusses the advice she received as a novice from Tessie the Tassle Twirler.

While Mama Rose was happy with the fact that her daughter was doing scenes, Tessie was not. She told Gypsy that it "… detracts from your prestige." She advised the novice thus: "Look at me for instance. I do only two numbers. One in the first half of the show, the other in the second. In Burlesque, you gotta leave 'em hungry for more. You don't bump the whole roast on the platter."

***Harper's* Magazine — May 1957.** The second of Gypsy's *Harper's* articles, "Up the Runway to Minsky's," appeared in the May 1957 issue. Once again, she had pulled off another publicity bonanza. The provocative articles enticed people to buy her autobiography: Gypsy had another bestseller on her hands.

An ad for her memoir appears on page 87 of this issue. The ad reads:

> To the astonishment of no one who has read *Stranded in Kansas City* Miss Gypsy Rose Lee has produced from her electric typewriter a memoir unmatched in its gaiety, refreshing wit and general enchantment. In her candid look backward, her eye takes in the principal cities of America, luminaries of burlesque and other walks of life, gangsters, fashionable society, a number of children and a menagerie of animals. Here, in all it variety and fun, is a life well worth recording.

In an accompanying quote Anita Loos, author of *Gentlemen Prefer Blondes,* says, "I haven't read in years an autobiography that I found so entrancing. You can't get enough of it." John

Steinbeck's quote was succinct. The legendary author proclaimed that *Gypsy* was "Irresistible." The hardcover first issue cost $3.95 and boasted 32 pages of photographs.

Gypsy in Print. Gypsy's memoir, simply titled *Gypsy*, was published by Harper & Brothers, New York.

Author! Author! The author appeared at the Carlisle Book Shop in England to sign copies of her memoir on May 3, 1957.

Gypsy's Life in *Life*. In the May 27, 1957, issue of *Life* readers got a glimpse of Gypsy's life on and off stage.

"Scrapbook Views of a Smart Stripper: After Years of Showing Almost All Gypsy Rose Lee Is Now Telling All."

America's most illustrious strip-teaser, Gypsy Rose Lee, who carried self-revelation to the legal limit on stage, has revealed the story of her early life in a volume of memoirs. Titled *Gypsy* (Harper & Collins) and dedicated to her 12-year-old son ("so he'll stop asking so many questions"), the book begins with the 4-year-old Gypsy trouping with her sister June Havoc and mother Madam Rose, singing in lodges and theaters all over the U.S. Like its author's life, Gypsy's story is gaudy in places, grim at times, rarely dull, and far more entertaining than a burlesque show.

With pictures from her own scrapbooks, Gypsy here re-creates her career. Living in an elegant New York town house, a 26-room establishment on the fashionable East Side, the ex-stripper has now become an accredited member of the city's busy literary set. The captions were written by Gypsy.

The first photo of Gypsy shows her in the bathtub. This photo is similar to the one on the cover of her record album, *That's Me All Over*. She shows plenty of leg, and is squeezing a big sponge: *Today there are seven baths in my house. My favorite has a marble tub with dolphin faucets. I got rid of the mink bathmat: it destroyed the Renaissance quality. Mother stage-managed this shot. "Not too much smile, dear," she said.*

Directly across from this is a photo of a young Mama Rose: *Mother was stagestruck for us. She wouldn't let any of her three husbands interfere with our career. We trouped between marriages. Mother had ambition and she was, in her ladylike way, ruthless — in her own words, a jungle mother.*

Below that is a photo of a young Gypsy in her costume for her song in June's vaudeville act: *When I was 4 I made my debut at Grandpa's lodge hall in Seattle, Wash., singing* I'm a Hard-boiled Rose. *I was still singing it here on the Orpheum circuit stages when I was 10 years old because I couldn't learn a new one.*

Next was a two-page spread with six photographs of Gypsy in vaudeville and burlesque.

Touring with a children's troupe, Gypsy (then Rose Louise Hovick), her sister June and their mother slept three-in-a-bed in theatrical hotels. The truant officers called frequently and the living was not easy.

Vaudeville started to die in the '30s and Gypsy's mother would not believe it. "Nothing," she said, "will ever take the place of flesh." But bookings were scarce. When June, the 13-year-old star, eloped with a chorus boy Gypsy became the headliner. From second-rate nightclubs she moved on to first-rate burlesque, dropping her costumes, raising her fees. Other strippers took off more, but Gypsy disrobed with queenly style, tossed out a few French phrases, and seemed to be kidding the customers. "You don't have to be naked to look naked," she said. "You just have to think naked."

There are four photos from the vaudeville years. The first shows the original vaudeville act in which June and Gypsy (Louise) performed: *The name of the act was "Dainty June and Her Newsboy Songsters." My sister June was the star. I was one of the newsboys and mouthed the words while they did the singing. None of the boys were paid. Mother told them the experience was worth more than money.*

Below that is a picture of the new act that was created for Louise after June left: *The act after June eloped was "Madam Rose's Dancing Daughters." These were my dancing partners in* The Doll Dance. *The theatre manager in Saugerties, N.Y. billed us as the "most beautiful act that ever appeared in this town," but after we opened he tried to cancel us.*

A fantastic photo runs across the top of both pages. Gypsy's caption says it all: *In Yuma, Ariz. 1929 I bleached the girls' hair and changed the name of the act from "Madam Rose's Dancing Daughters" to "Rose Louise and Her Hollywood Blondes." I was the only brunette. I made all the costumes, and scenery and sang* I'm a Hard-boiled Rose. *But even with all this we still couldn't get work. We were stranded in Kansas City when Mother booked us by mistake into a burlesque theater. The star of the show was "Tessie, the Tassel Twirler." We got bottom billing, and from the way the act went over that's all we deserved.*

Below this is a charming photo of the reunited Hovick sisters, Louise and June. The caption that accompanies this photo reads: *Most times I had been wearing boys' clothes, a knicker suit and brogues, so I liked wearing a dress as I am above, even if just to have a picture taken. June (right), who came back briefly to the act, had always hated our hair bows and ruffled dresses. "I'm not a baby anymore," she would say. School, for us, was a problem. We trouped for a while but she left before we got past our foursies in multiplication. One day just before June got married, a woman stopped us in a dime store to ask the time. June looked at her watch. "Big hand is on the six," she said, "and the little hands on four."*

Across from this photo are two photos from Gypsy's early days in burlesque. She appears in an ad for Billy Minsky's Brooklyn Burlesque: *When I was 16 my picture was on the front page of the* Police Gazette, *the* Evening Graphic *and I was advertised in Chinese. The show's name changed every week, "Ada Onion from Bermuda," "Iva Schnozzle from Red Rock," but my name was always on the top.*

Below the Chinese ad is a stunning photo of the young stripper posing perched on the top of what looks like a big round pillow standing upright. She is nude, except for the white fox fur draped over her shoulders, and covering her breasts and another fur on her lap: *Billy Minsky told me to wear my hair back. "It's more ladylike," he said. The white fox came in handy on my last encore, I used to drop it in the tuba. I was called the Gene Tierney of burlesque, and Jean Cocteau, after watching my show blurted, "How vital."*

On the next page there are four pictures of Gypsy headlined with "On to Broadway, books and baby." The photos begin with a shot from *Star and Garter*: *From burlesque I went to the Ziegfeld Follies. Then Hollywood, the World's Fair and Mike Todd's* Star and Garter *(above). Bobby Clark wore painted on spectacles. Under spangles I wore three pasted-on gardenias.*

A doting mother changing her baby's diaper: *Along the way I married three times. My son Erik was born in 1944. He trouped with me with his bathinette [sic], then, as he grew older, with his kiddie car, tricycle and schoolbooks, a guinea pig in his pocket.*

Gypsy the author at work: *During the World's Fair, I rented a typewriter to do a guest column for Walter Winchell. I had three and a half weeks left on the minimum rental so to get my money's worth I started my first book, the* G-String Murders.

Gypsy on tour: *In 1949 I spent 23 weeks touring the country with a carnival sometimes playing 18 shows a day, never without sailors in the audience. Variety said I parlayed a G-string into 100 Gs, actually it was closer to 125 Gs counting my take from the hot dogs and soda pop.*

The final photograph shows a resplendent Gypsy sitting in front of a fountain in the courtyard, with one of her Afghans by her side: *Now, after almost 40 years in show business, I can relax in my patio, pat my dog, and contemplate my future. But not for long. First I have to take the kimono off the Corona and get back to work on a Broadway musical of my book. Then I must pack the scenery, beaded dresses, music, cats, dogs, guppies, frying pans, fishing tackle and Erik's schoolbooks for 10 days in a nightclub. Royalties are nice and all that but shaking the beads brings the money in quicker.*

Gypsy Gets Bought. On May 27, 1957, *The New York Times* announced, "David Merrick apparently was successful in outbidding a couple of formidable competitors, Leland Hayward and Herman Levin, for the privilege of escorting a musical version of "Gypsy, a Memoir" to the stage...."

Gypsy & June Handle Men. In Earl Wilson's "It Happened Last Night" column of June 11, 1957, he included a piece, excerpted below, about the famous sisters, Gypsy and June.

"How to Handle Men"

I've been a one-woman guy for years, so I was amazed when June Havoc told me how she and Gypsy Rose Lee handle their various husbands.

"Julio," she said, "kept us up till 6 A.M. the other day laughing."

"Who's Julio?" asked a guy with us.

"Julio De Diego, the painter, one of our removed husbands," June explained. "He's very talented. We couldn't handle him. He was a bit too much for us."

He was Gypsy's husband — so I asked her about her mate, Bill Spier, the TV writer and producer.

"Bill's remarkable!" laughed June. "I was on the verge of running away and hiding from everybody. Gypsy said, 'Don't run off and hide without Bill. We'll never find another like him.'"

"Do you often run away and hide?" I asked.

"Oh, Gypsy and I often sign our letters, 'Goodbye forever, darling, I'm going to take the gaspipe,'" June admitted gaily.

"It took me four months to get Gypsy back to America after her marriage to Julio broke up. I brought her home via Africa...."

"Then Gypsy wrote her book, titled 'Gypsy.'"

"She was putting it off," June said. "I told her, as a last resort, that I was writing one, and she finished hers in three months. I am writing one, too."

Sunday with a Stripper. Gypsy wrote "My Life and Good Times" for the *Chicago Sunday Tribune Magazine*, which ran in the July 28, 1957, issue, and included four black and white photos of Gypsy, and one of Mama Rose. Ever the savvy promoter, Gypsy got additional publicity for her autobiography by writing condensed versions of the stories in *Gypsy*. This was a two-part series, the next installment appeared the following Sunday.

Fanny Butcher, the *Chicago Tribune*'s literary editor, wrote the following:

Gypsy Rose Lee may have won initial fame in lesser pursuits, but there are some of us who want to claim her as a litterateur. Her greatest natural blessing may be her talent for putting into print the world around her. Her mystery book, *Mother Finds a Body*, proved that Gypsy has a sense of humor and can write. Now comes *Gypsy*, a story of her own life in "show biz" a tale full of "yaks" and hearttwangings, written with wit, frankness, and a keen eye for phonies.

Watch out, Jason Lucas! There's a new angling
authority on the scene. This gal puts into her fishing
the same skill and determination that made her the Queen of
the burlesque runways. Here she tells you

HOW TO
CATCH A MUSKY

by GYPSY ROSE LEE

Gypsy's Gone Fishin'. The July 1957 issue of *Sports Afield* magazine proudly featured an article written by Gypsy about one of her favorite pastimes. Here is her story about the one that didn't get away.

"How to Catch a Musky"

You don't have to be born in Seattle, Washington, to like fishing—but it helps. Everyone in Seattle goes fishing. And why not, with Puget Sound as a back yard? I didn't have the chance to fish when I was a child; we left to go into show business when I was four years old. My sister June could dance on her toes, like a real ballerina, when she was 2½ years old, and Mother was ambitious.

The next time we visited Seattle I was nine, and we were on the Orpheum Circuit. We played a matinee every day so there was no time for fishing then, either. But in 1946 I went back home—not exactly as a local girl who had made good—Seattle wasn't sure if being Gypsy Rose Lee was what they could call making good, but they rolled out the carpet for me anyway. The red carpet being in the Northwest a rowboat with an outboard motor. That first day I caught a nine-pound salmon and joined the fishing fraternity.

Since then I've fished whenever and wherever I could: between shows, after performances at night, at dawn before catching a train, and sometimes during my dinner hour instead of eating. I've fished the Campbell and McKenzie rivers, trout streams in Wyoming, rapids in Canada, the Gulf Stream, and the Great Lakes. I've caught bonito off Montauk Point, striped bass in the Chesapeake, halibut in the Pacific and gar in the Mississippi. With my son Erik, aged two, tied to the pontoons of a plane, I've fished for walleyes in Ely, Minnesota. But next to that salmon I caught in Puget Sound my favorite fish is musky.

I like muskies for many reasons, but most important I like where they live. I like the cool green-blue lakes and the crisp air and the deep, deep silence. I like fishing from a rowboat, too. I like being close to my fish. When he's on the end of my line I want to be able to look him straight in the eye. Then, if I lose him, I've at least had a chance to meet him face to face.

Meeting a musky face to face is an experience. The first time it happened to me I was playing one-night stands in Wisconsin and fishing between shows, with Bill Waggoner and Red Leekely. The musky struck my plug on my first cast of the morning. The rod bent almost double and the reel sang as the line went out, and then suddenly slack—the musky has whirled and was making straight for the boat. He was two feet away when his head broke through the water. I took one look at those crazed yellow eyes, those double rows of teeth, and dropped my rod in terror. That was no *fish*, it was a monster!

I saved my gear but the fish was gone. Bill told me to forget it, he'd been through the same thing with other fishermen. "We'll go after bass," he added. "Musky is a man's fish anyway."

My hand was trembling. I could feel cool rivulets of sweat rolling down each side of my arm. "To hell with bass," I said. "I'm going to catch that musky if it takes all day.

All day? The sun traveled its course, and I tried every lure in my tackle box. I tied on plugs, spoons, wigglers and wobblers. I didn't have a strike. I knew the fish were there. I could see them nosing at my lures, smelling around the boat, surfacing for flying bugs and whipping themselves into a fury through the weeds, but they didn't want anything I had to offer. At 6:30 A.M. Bill kicked over the outboard motor and we went back to the lodge. It was the first time I'd been fishing without catching *something*, and I felt cheated.

The other boats were coming in when we got to the pier. The fishermen were unloading their gear and tying up for the night. They were all so pleased with themselves, slapping one another playfully and shouting back and forth about what a great day it had been. "We had a lot of action around four o'clock," one of them said. Then they all started talking at once: "They bit hell outta that new plug of mine."

"I thought he'd turn over the boat—"

"One of the best days I've ever had!"

I looked for their fish. The boats were empty. No one had a fish slung over his shoulder, not even a little one. I nudged Bill and asked, "Why are they so happy?"

He didn't answer me. He was too busy telling them what a great day *we'd* had!

That night, after dinner, I met fishermen and their wives who had come along for the air and knitting. We sat around the fire and talked about muskies. That is, the men talked and I listened. These weren't men who were just fishing, they were muskie fishing, and there's a big difference. They wouldn't take a pike or a walleye. If a bass got on their line they let it go. Their tackle boxes were filled with plugs that rattled and clanged, and bucktails as big as the whole buck. I'd never, in all my life, seen such hardware. And I'd never heard so many diverse opinions about one kind of fish.

"I've been hunting musky for 40 years," one man said. "I must have had 100 strikes or more and I know what I'm talking about. Muskies will strike at anything! Why I once hooked one on a hunk of bread–"

"Bucktails," another man said. "Only sure musky lure there is." He was polishing a spoon while he talked, but it wasn't an ordinary spoon. There was a pork rind dangling from it, and a shaggy bit of hair made more or less attractive with a red feather. He held up the lure and gazed at it appreciatively. "If they don't like that," he said, "they don't like home cooking!"

"Muskies want a noisy lure," a third man said. "They strike out of anger, not hunger. The noisier the lure, the madder they get and the harder they hit. They KNOW a plug when they see one, of course, but their character won't let them admit that a chunk of wood is more formidable than they are." He leaned back in his chair and his smile warmed his face. "Yep," he said, "I'd rather lose a musky than catch any other kind of fish there is."

His wife looked up from her knitting. "You won't lose them all again this year, dear," she said.

There was a strained silence, then someone got into another favorite argument about muskies: how they got their name. I heard four versions that night, but the one that made the most sense to me was how the Indians named them *Maskinonge* because of their long, ugly mask. I'd had a look at that mask and it was very *nonge* indeed.

Stories about the record musky taken on a light tackle were conflicting, too: almost six feet long, one man said, and another added that the net marks were found on the body, and besides, it was 5½ feet. They told how cheats had added weight to muskies by shoving bits of iron and rocks down their gullets and how when one fish was cut open it was found to be filled with roe—PIKE ROE—added no doubt by an eager record-seeker.

Muskies they told me, weren't friendly like trout or salmon. There were treacherous, tricky and temperamental. They would tear a hole in a wading boot, and had bitten off a woman's finger. They were sly and dangerous and above all a man's fish.

I felt eight pairs of eyes rest on me when this last remark was made. I wanted to tell them of other fish I'd caught, that I'd never dropped my rod before, but I couldn't. I'm not an angler. I just like to fish. I've caught my fish with more luck than skill. Oh, I can drop a plug on a lily pad with a fair sense of accuracy and I have the patience and endurance to outwait a fish, but I can't roll cast or skimmer a fly or do any of those fancy things. I don't even have any theories on fishing. I just keep my hand steady, my head clear and my bait in the water.

"I'm sure muskies are smarter than I am," I said. "But maybe I'll find a nice stupid one who doesn't know I'm a woman."

My tackle box must have weighed 35 pounds when I stowed it away in the rowboat the next morning. It was filled with every kind of lure I could beg, borrow or buy. Not that I didn't trust my luck, but I wanted the equipment to go with it. My casting rod, everyone agreed, would do. It wasn't too supple or too stiff. My line, an 18-pound test nylon, was okay. There were a few arguments about my cable leader, which was wire, of course, so the musky couldn't bite through it. Some said it should be 12 inches long with a double swivel, others said eight. So I tied a ten-incher to keep everyone happy. The boat sank a bit deeper into the water as I dropped my gear aboard.

Bill did the rowing and Red and I fished from opposite ends of the boat. Bill had told me consistency was important in musky fishing, to keep a rhythm in the cast and the retrieve, so I found myself counting under my breath: one, two, three cast; one, two, three, retrieve. After an hour I stopped and checked the sharpness of my hooks. I'd seen that bony mouth and knew how hard it would be to set a hook in it, let alone a dull hook. I examined the line near the swivels and cable; I didn't want to lose my fish through carelessness.

Red was casting bucktail, so I tied on one equipped with a weedless hook and a bright new red feather. I tried a swifter retrieve for the next hour, giving my rod a flip to activate the lure. It didn't help. I tried a slow, wobbly retrieve — maybe the musky would think it was an injured something or other. Red switched to a jointed plug with spinners fore and aft like a Calder mobile, so I switched to the same lure and the noise we made echoed over the lake. I could see the muskies following the lure, but they wouldn't strike. Once or twice I felt them flip their tails against the side of the boat; a fish's way of thumbing his nose.

Red reeled in and unhooked the hardware. "I don't know about you," he said, "but I'm ready to try a sucker."

"Sucker?" I replied, "I'm ready to try a club!"

The suckers cost a dollar each. The bait man told us they had to be transported in aerated tank trucks and the mortality rate was high. Red and I settled for four weighing about a pound

Musky bait...suckers at a buck each

a piece. Carrying our precious bucket filled with bait I would have settled for on the end of a fly line, we got back in the boat.

We had switched rods, too. I borrowed one of Bill's, a deep-sea rod with a foot cut off at the tip to give it stiffness. The heavy-duty reel with a foot cut off at the tip gave it stiffness. The heavy-duty reel was set with 200 yards of 18-pound-test nylon line and ten-inch cable leader.

Bill rowed us to a spot near a half-submerged log, where a weed bed made the deep water blue. I reached into the bucket for a sucker. All women should bait their own hooks, but hitching up a live sucker is something else again. I love the feel of a trout in my hands, but a sucker is slippery and unpleasant to touch. Gritting my teeth, I got a firm grip on one of then and held it between my knees the way Red was doing, the head and "shoulders" are free. While it was wriggling and squirming. I strapped it into a harness of heavy nylon line with hook secured in such a way that it was under the body. I crossed the line over the hook, then under the pectoral fins and back again and tied it off. Bill and Red complimented me on my cleverness. I didn't remind them that I was an old hand with strings of various sorts. Besides, I had recently seen a slow-motion movie dealing with this very subject. The film showed other ways of harnessing a sucker; gang hooks for instance, and another where the hook came through the mouth of the sucker, which seemed unnecessarily cruel.

Watching Red I discovered that one doesn't cast sucker bait, you heave it. Standing up in the boat you use both hands to get your bait out. On the retrieve you jerk your rod leftward, with a gentle, rhythmic stroke. After a few casts this retrieve action is very important, because the sucker has given up and you must make it lifelike. When the bait became too battered I changed to a fresh one. Red said muskies like to think they've killed their own food.

An hour later I ached in every muscle, but I didn't dare stop. My bait had attracted interest. I had no proof of this, but I knew, that a pair of yellow eyes had fastened on the sucker. I knew a musky was down there, perhaps an inch away from my bait, trying to make its mind when and how to strike. That swig of coffee I wanted and the puff on a cigarette had to wait.

Then, when I least expected it, the musky hit. I felt the pull on my line and my first instinct was to set the hook. "Easy, Gyp," Bill whispered. "He's nowhere near your hook. You jerk that line now and you've lost a fish."

The tug was almost gentle, not at all like the frenzy of a strike on a plug. "Quiet," Bill said. "Don't stomp around in the boat, don't scuff your feet — anything can distract him now."

I heard Red reeling in — two lines over the side of a boat could be dangerous — then suddenly the musky's tail flashed and my line went out, straight down! I could feel the pressure of the weeds as the musky went deeper and deeper with the sucker in its mouth. Then there was no movement at all, and I could almost see what was happening at the bottom of the lake. I could see my fish holding his prize and taking bows as the other fish gathered around to watch and applaud.

"How still he is," I whispered.

"He's scaling the sucker," Bill said, sitting back in the boat and lighting a cigarette. "He'll play with it awhile, and then flip it around in his mouth so he can swallow it headfirst."

The smell of his cigarette reminded me how much I wanted a puff, but I was afraid to move, even to breathe.

"How long will it take him?"

"Ten minutes, maybe half an hour — depends on how much fun he's having. When he flips that fish be ready. You've still got a split second to set the hook."

There was absolutely no movement on the end of my line. Bill finished his cigarette, then he and Red settled down for a wait. All at once I had the feeling my musky was gone! I leaned over the side of the boat and tried to see down through the weeds. Then I felt it, the tug on my line. He was flipping it and I wasn't ready!

"Set your hook!" Bill yelled. "Up with that rod, hard!"

Using both hands and every bit of strength I had left, I pulled up on the rod and felt the hook set in. Or was it the weeds? I jerked up again, and again, to make sure. The water churned and roiled, and a second later the musky surfaced. The sucker was gone but the hook was set. The line went out and I felt a fingernail snap as the musky made for shore. I didn't need Bill and Rod to tell me I'd lose him if he ever got under the submerged log. I thumbed down on the line and prayed the nylon would hold. The fish stopped suddenly and threw himself into the air, and the water sprayed off his body like rhinestones glittering in the spotlight. How lovely, I thought. Then he came at me, his yellow eyes gleaming with fury. Halfway to the boat he whirled and headed for the shore. Bill was yelling at me to take up slack, and I reeled in as fast as I could. Then the musky stopped and pulled on my line. "I can't hold him," I cried. Red shouted at me to give him his head, as though I could do anything else.

He surfaced again, shaking to get rid of the hook. I thumbed my line, hoping he'd take a rest, the way a pike does, but there was no rest for that fish, or for me either. He came at the boat churning the water and leaving a path in it that widened at the end and tapered to a thin streak at his head. Then, when he was close enough, he threw himself out of the water and our eyes met. I laughed right in his face. "Not this time," I shouted down at him. "You scared me once, but never again!"

The action and my whooping and hollering brought other boats around us, close enough for the men to yell out advice.

"Tighten your line!" someone shouted.

"Give him room — don't horse him!"

"Lift your rod!"

I was too busy to tell them to shut up. Bill and Red were standing beside me now, and when they knew the fight was over Red leaned down and thrust his hands into the water. Coming up in back of the musky, he sunk his fingers into the gills. Holding him firmly, he stood there for a second so everyone could get a look, then he reached back for a club and tapped the fish sharply on the back of its head. "Here's your musky," he said, handing me the fish.

I remember Flo Ziegfeld handing me my contract; my editor handing me my first book when it was published. Big moments in our lives are few, and so well remembered.

Holding the fish in my arms, I ran a finger down his long slim body. How ugly he is, I thought, and yet how beautiful. For an instant I was sorry I had caught him. Then I heard the bell clanging at the lodge telling everyone a "keeper" was coming in. The boats began nosing toward the pier, and Bill started up our outboard motor and we followed. The bell also meant the bar was open and the drinks were ready — to be paid for, of course, by the one who brought in the fish.

Over a beer, I gazed proudly at my musky lying in state on a bed of ferns at the end of the bar. He was 35 inches long and weighed 18 pounds. Truly the guest of honor!

"You ought to have him stuffed," Red said.

"I intend to," I said, and took him into the kitchen and stuffed him then and there with chopped fresh tomatoes, onions and a pinch of oregano, and baked him ten minutes to the pound in a medium-hot oven. Any fish that's good to catch is good to eat, and that musky was no exception.

The head was sent to a taxidermist. It sits now, mounted on polished wood, open mouth, teeth flashing, as a door stop. People don't

A northern I caught in Wisconsin

believe it, but to this very day that musky is fighting me. Every time I pass I give him plenty of room, or that devil reaches out and bites me.

Gypsy and the Literati. Gypsy, the best-selling author, attended the July 1957 Pacific Northwest International Writers' Conference in Seattle, Washington.

Minsky vs. Mama Rose. The August 4, 1957, issue of the *Chicago Sunday Tribune Magazine* ran a piece by Gypsy entitled "How Mother Fixed Minsky: Wherein the Author Learns Something of the Might of a Mother's Wrath and Meets a Sentimental Snake Charmer Called Nudina." The magazine included six photos of Gypsy, including a rare photo of her as a baby, along with Billy Minsky and Abbott and Costello, who Gypsy had worked with at the World's Fair.

Gypsy Goes Stag. The August 1957 issue of *Stag* magazine ran a "Where Are They Now?" article with a 1942 photo of Gypsy just beginning to roll down her stockings, captioned: *Her bawdy act took her half-round the world in various stages of undress.*

Gypsy Rose Lee:

WHERE IS SHE NOW? Gypsy now lives in Manhattan, raises Siamese cats, and has been an officer in the Greenwich Village Humane League. She still struts a mean wiggle occasionally in night clubs, but she's more interested in the legitimate stage, recently appeared in a TV play[s] as a fully-clothed lady novelist.

Now 41, she is a publicity girl for a bedsheet company famous for it's *double-entendre* advertisements, has staged fashion shows, and finally, she's gotten around to the thing every red-blooded American male has been waiting for — her memoirs.

Steel Gypsy. On September 29, 1957, it was reported in *The New York Times* that Gypsy was returning to television's *U.S. Steel Hour*. This would be her second dramatic role for the TV show, which broadcast plays written for television.

Gypsy the Rogue. Gypsy appeared in the September 1957 issue of *Rogue* magazine.

Gypsy Wanted by the Police. Gypsy was once again the subject of a tell-all article, which ran in *The National Police Gazette* of September 1957. Gypsy was on the cover between Billy Graham and Sugar Ray Robinson, each captioned with tantalizing headlines: "Exclusive Interview — A Candid Talk with Billy Graham on Sex — Sports — Crime," "Inside Dope on Robinson Basilio Fight — Will Sugar Ray be 'Ready?'" and "Famous Stripper Gypsy Rose Lee's Intimate Confession."

"Gypsy Rose Lee's True Story"
by George McGrath

The theatre lights dimmed and the spotlight splashed on the solitary, shapely figure of Gypsy Rose Lee — the girl who has become the world's most famous stripper.

"Do you believe that I am thinking of sex?" she asked, softly dropping her petticoat.

"I am wondering how much I should contribute to charity," she said, and she unbuttoned her blouse. The audience sat tensely, silently watching as her white, rounded figure was slowly disrobed.

"Art is my favorite subject," Gypsy murmured, discarding a garter belt.

"I like Shakespeare, too," she said, and she slid off her stockings.

She stood quite naked except for three tiny bows.

"Do you still believe that I'm thinking of sex?" she asked with a seductive pout of her lips. "WELL — I CERTAINLY AM!"

With that spectacular finale she ducked behind the velvet curtains amid a crash of applause and delirious cries from the audience.

That's how Gypsy Rose Lee made her fame and fortune.

What She's Really Like

At home she's quite a different kind of girl. Sort of demure. And she *really* does like art.

Gypsy, well clothed from knee to neck-line and surrounded by antiques and oil painting, achieves an air of gracious culture.

You'd hardly believe she's had a rough, tough up bringing. But when she first went on the stage Gypsy used to sing a song called, "I'm a Hard-Boiled Rose."

A notorious New York gangster helped her to become famous by getting her a part in a Flo Ziegfeld show on Broadway.

Today Gypsy lives, in a certain amount of splendor, on Manhattan's East side. Her house has 26 rooms, a marble floor in the drawing room, a fountain in the patio, an elevator and seven baths.

The walls are lined with paintings, the furniture is antique and the collection of curios includes a number of nude statuettes.

"They have no connection with strip tease," smiled Gypsy. "Actually I know nothing about art. I have more pictures than I can hang at one time — but they're not valuable. I just buy things I like."

She sat down and crossed her legs — the legs that have been gazed at by thousands of eyes all over the world. They're rather good legs too.

I visited Gypsy because she's just writing her third book — this one's an autobiography called "Gypsy — a Memoir." She confided to me some of her ambitions, some of the things that have made her what she is.

Gypsy is still stripping because she loves the limelight. But she'd like to do some serious acting. Her reputation stops that.

"When people know you are a stripper they seem to have pre-conceived ideas..." she said, petulantly.

"I know what you mean," I murmured.

"How could I be an actress — the moment I walk on stage people forget the play, forget the part I'm acting and start wondering when I'm going to take my clothes off."

Gypsy was 4 years old when she first went on the vaudeville stage. Her sister, June, was 2 and their father and mother were divorced. Taking the two girls, her mother plunged into showbusiness.

"Mother was very ambitious — and a bit ruthless," smiled Gypsy. "She use to say 'God will protect us — but just to make sure we'll carry a heavy club.'"

Besides her real father, Gypsy had two other fathers during her mother's other two marriages.

"But I never got to know them very well," she told me. "They weren't around long enough." One was a chiropodist. One day a friend called him a corn doctor. Mother was very sensitive about things like that. 'Corn doctor?' she repeated.

"A month later she left him and we were back on the road in showbusiness again."

Another Husband — Another Divorce

Gypsy's third father was a wholesale grocery salesman whom they called Bubs. Her mother divorced him because she said he was cruel and inhuman — he wanted to send the girls to Sunday school.

One of Gypsy's favorite pastimes as a child was a visit to a dime store with her sister June.

"June engaged the salesgirl in conversation and I clipped," she recalled. "Then it was my turn to talk to the salesgirl while June clipped.

"We didn't take things we needed, or anything we wanted. Our aim was to take as much as possible."

One time June took a tin spectacle case, a jar of pomade, two compasses, a can opener and a tea strainer. Gypsy's haul was similarly assorted. They were trading articles among themselves when they were caught by Miss Tompkins, their tutor. She was shocked and made the girls take the stolen articles back to the store and apologize for taking them.

Later, just before they were due to go on stage for their act, Gypsy and June threw a bout of crying hysteria and told their mother how Miss Tompkins had humiliated them.

Their mother promptly fired Miss Tompkins for subjecting her daughters to such nervous strain.

Gypsy lived mostly in hotels as a child, sleeping in the same bed with her mother, her sister and her mother's two pet dogs.

Her mother would frequently dispute hotel bills if she thought she could get them reduced by a dollar or two.

"It's not the principle of the thing," she would shout. "It's the money."

How She Started Stripping

Money has always been a big thing to Gypsy. She knows what it's like to be without it. She always saved as much as she could.

"But I didn't invest my money, so my savings are not worth as much as they should be," she told me. She waved a shapely arm towards her house. "It costs me $1,500 a year just to heat this place — so you can see I'd have to keep on working, even if I wanted to retire."

Gypsy became a stripper after her sister June eloped at the age of 15. That left Gypsy and her mother alone. They arrive one day in Toledo, Ohio, and went to the Gaiety Theatre, a burlesque house. The manager said he wanted a stripper.

"Well, that's just what Rose Louise is," said Gypsy's mother. "Haven't you heard of her success in St. Louis and Milwaukee?"

The manager hadn't heard, but he nodded politely and signed Gypsy to star on the bill.

Actually Gypsy had never stripped in her life before.

"It was typical of mother to do that," Gypsy told me. "She'd bluff her way into anything."

"Now she's bluffed me into a starring role in the show — and I was terrified. Mother spent the rest of the afternoon rehearsing me and we changed my name from Rose Louise to Gypsy Rose Lee. It sounded better.

"I was too tired and nervous when I went on stage. I dropped my shoulder strap, unhooked the side of my dress and went into the routine."

The applause at the end of her act was terrific — and that was the beginning of Gypsy's career as a stripper.

Her next big break was when she met Waxey Gordon, the underworld kingpin, who put in a good word for her with Ziegfeld.

"I was playing at Minsky's Republic, on Broadway," said Gypsy. "One night after the show Mother and I were invited to a stage party. While we were there a short, squat man walked in. He was surrounded by four big bruisers with their hats pulled over their eyes and their right hands in their coat pockets.

"There was no mistaking what they were — gangsters.

"Somebody told me the short man was Waxey Gordon and introduced us. Waxey stared at my teeth.

"'Be nice if you got your teeth straightened out,' he remarked.

"Mother said I was going to when we could get enough money saved. Waxey said nothing more. But a few days later one of Waxey's henchmen called on us and told us to go to a Dr. Kraus, a Broadway dentist.

"'The boss took care of everything — you go,' he insisted."

So Gypsy got her teeth straightened out. Shortly after she got another message from Gordon. This time he wanted a favor from Gypsy — he wanted her to appear at a benefit show at Comstock prison.

"It struck me as funny," Gypsy laughed. "Here was one of the country's top racketeers putting on a show for the inmates in prison. He had big names, too — including Al Jolson, Jimmy Durante and Florence Ziegfeld.

"I was rather nervous. It was all right for the others but I wasn't at all certain how the hard-boiled, sex-starved prisoners would react to my strip tease. Seemed hardly fair..."

But Gypsy went just the same. She hoped to meet Ziegfeld.

"On the train going down," she told me, "I told Waxey that my big dream was to be in the Ziegfeld Follies. He thumbed to a group of men and one of them came over.

"'This is Gypsy,' he said, pointing to me. 'She's a real good-looker and I think she'd be good in your show. I'd like to have her put in.'"

The man told Gypsy to report to the Ziegfeld Theatre the next day for the show Hot Cha. It was as simple as that.

After that Gypsy soon reached the big time and stayed there. She knows the value of publicity, and usually manages to cause a sensation wherever she goes. In London she bought a Rolls Royce. It was made to order in maroon and gray with her initials on the door. When Gypsy travels it usually carries a vast assortment of baggage.

Santa's Beard Came Loose

She posed for photographers in Paris, lifting her skirt to show her legs. Behind her were 27 pieces of luggage, five Siamese cats in plastic carriers, a guinea pig in a box, a typewriter, a portable television set and a net shopping basket filled with oranges, jelly beans, cat food, and dried bugs for the turtles.

"I've always been fond of animals," said Gypsy. In her New York home she keeps the cats, the turtles and the guinea pig plus an Afghan hound and 140 guppies. The guppies are small fish and they live in a large tank in her son, Erik's bedroom.

Erik is 12-years-old and as well as collecting fish he collects stamps. He loves to listen to his mother's stories of her experiences in showbusiness, and usually travels with her wherever she goes. As a result he is wise for his age.

He lost his belief in Santa Claus when he was five years old. It was Christmas time and Gypsy was playing in Dayton, Ohio.

Between shows comedian Tiny Pierson was doubling as Santa Claus at the local orphanages. Tiny's pink face and plump stomach were very convincing, but when he took Erik on his lap Erik noticed that his beard was coming loose. Leaning closer he smelled the glue that held it on.

"That's spirit gum," said Erik. "That's what Mommy glues her brassiere on with."

Gypsy was once invited to join in a plot to assassinate a king.

"It was in 1931 when I was playing at Minsky's," she told me. "My mother came to my dressing room backstage with a strange man who had a foreign accent. She introduced him and he told me he was a lieutenant in the personal guard of King Carol of Roumania.

"He said he had been watching me for days and he wanted me to go to Roumania with him to meet the king.

"I thought for sure it was an invitation for me to become the king's mistress. But it wasn't.

"The man explained later that after he had introduced me into the court circles he wanted me to act as a decoy to lure the king into a secluded part of the palace grounds. An assassin would be waiting there to shoot the king.

"I politely declined the invitation."

Gypsy doesn't intend to retire for a long time yet. But she does plan to write more books.

"People think that just because you're a stripper you don't have much else except a body. They don't credit you for your intelligence. Maybe that's why I write. I've had two mystery novels and dozens or short stories and articles published," Gypsy told me.

So next time I see Gypsy strip I really am going to wonder if she's thinking about sex. Maybe she isn't. Maybe she's really thinking about art ... or Shakespeare ... or something...

Gypsy Abroad. Gypsy boarded the S.S. *Flandre* in October of 1957, destination: Europe. She ate at the captain's table and entertained with the ship's band.

Gypsy's Artistic Inclinations. The October 1957 issue of *Pageant Magazine* ran an article on Gypsy that discussed her art collection and her work as a painter. There is a full page photo of Gypsy sitting at her desk at home. On a nearby wall there is an incredible female nude painted by French artist Adolphe William Bouguereau.

The painting was given to Gypsy by Mike Todd during the run of his show *Star and Garter*. Todd left the price tag on the painting, which cost $3,999.

Gypsy's enormous and ever expanding art collection included works by well-known artists such as Jean Charlot, Max Ernest, Georgia O'Keeffe, Marc Chagall, Dorothia Tanning, Marcel Vertes and her own former husband, Julio de Diego.

Although Gypsy rarely tried to paint in the abstract, she did have a penchant for creating her own collages, created from things she had collected, aiming for a surreal effect. Gypsy said she acquired her taste in art from her friend, Fanny Brice. She joked that it was Brice and husband Billy Rose who taught her "... the difference between Rubens the painter and Rubens the delicatessen." Fanny Brice also painted a Degas-like study of Gypsy and gave it to her. Gypsy it seems didn't like to get into analytical discussions about painting. Her advice was, "Don't talk a about painting — just look at it and let it talk to you."

For *Pageant* Gypsy created a special collage entitled "Sarah Bernhardt," after the famous stage actress. She would not talk about her artwork's meaning saying, "I'd rather each person make up his own interpretation."

Her art collection also included several rare posters on tattooing, as well as sketches of various tattoos. The article states that her theatrical appearances are all but a thing of the past. When asked about her striptease career she said, "All that has changed, darling. You may refer to me as an authoress who sometimes strips."

Gypsy the Scamp. In the November 1957 issue of *Scamp Magazine* Gypsy was quoted at the start of an article titled "Notes on a ... G-String."

"Nowadays," she said, "I sit back and wait for the royalties to roll in." She was referring of course, to her successful career as a writer of fiction, articles, and books. "But if the royalties ever stop," she added, "I can always go back to shaking the beads."

No one can deny that there will always be a place in burlesque for the incomparable Gypsy Rose Lee. What bothers some devotees of the art — Art (there's a question about its being capitalized and we'll come to that in a minute) — is whether or not that great American contribution to entertainment, burlesque, will stay around long enough for Gypsy to return to it if she wants to.

Gypsy's Tipsy. On December 8, 1957, Gypsy participated in the 4th annual American Society of Bar Masters Mixed Drink Competition. The competition took place at the Park Lane Hotel in New York and her competition included Frank Farrell and Joan Harvey.

Comden and Green Abandon Gypsy. *The New York Times* announced on December 21, 1957, that the celebrated team of Betty Comden and Adolph Green would not be adapting Gypsy's autobiography for the Broadway stage. One can only wonder what *Gypsy* would have been like if Comden and Green had written the book and lyrics. Comden and Green had a long string of successful Broadway shows, including *On the Town, Bells Are Ringing, Two on the Aisle, Say Darling,* and *Wonderful Town* (which starred the future Mama Rose, Rosalind Russell). Many of these Broadway shows went on to become Hollywood musicals. The team also created the MGM movie musical *It's Always Fair Weather.*

Gypsy Takes the Plunge. At the end of 1957 a new ad for Springmaid Sheets appeared in women's magazines. Gypsy relaxed in a hot tub located in the natatorium of her old friend, Col. Elliot White Springs. The elderly gentleman is also in the photograph, standing nearby while his famous friend enjoys a therapeutic soak.

• 1958 •

Gypsy Rose Lee. Gypsy had a television talk show during 1958, details and airdates are unknown. The show was broadcast from New York.

The United States Steel Hour. *The Charmer* was episode 110 of the show's 5th season. Gypsy appeared as Lorraine Anderson. Her co-star was Martin E. Brooks. The airdate was January 1, 1958. *The New York Times* reviewed the show on January 2, 1958. In part, the review read: "Despite her manifold attainments, Gypsy Rose Lee hardly can be expected to be convincing in the part of a sentimental, guileless theatrical agent...."

Gypsy & June: Friends, Pals, Chums. "Sisters Gypsy Rose Lee, June Havoc Going to Russia" was the headline of an article by Olga Curtis that appeared in national newspapers on January 24, 1958.

Sisters Gypsy Rose Lee and June Havoc are friends, pals, chums to the end. But only personally. "Professionally," the sisters insist firmly, "we have no connection at all."

"I'm just an actress," says June.

"I'm always the world's oldest stripteaser," says Gypsy.

So keep in mind that Gypsy is Gypsy, June is June, and never their acts shall meet.

Older sister Gypsy, tall, dark and still rightly-dimensioned, told her plans for the future while presiding over a teapot.

"It's a switch for me," said the former G-string player as she poured Lapsang Souchong into China cups. "I used to have 98 percent male audiences — now they're 98 percent female.

"I'm a real paid lecturer — I show a home movie of my backstage life and then I talk for half an hour. The only thing is I take off is my gloves."

Younger sister June, who's small, blonde and bouncy, outlined her next project — a serious stage role — while munching garlic spaghetti and garlic bread.

"It really isn't much of a departure because I haven't done a musical since 1944; I've been doing serious films and TV dramas," said June.

"But I'm really excited about this new play. I'm the wife-mother in this French version Oedipus Rex, and I hang myself for six. With a red scarf."

And so Gypsy will be pounding the podium in Albuquerque, Dallas and Colorado Springs while June opens Feb. 9 in New York in Jean Cocteau's "The Internal Machine."

"Are you lecturing for art's sake?" Gypsy was asked.

"For money," she replied. "I can still make a good $5,000 in a night doing the same old strip — but I'm sure I won't be able to do that act ten years from now. So I'm getting set for the future. I only get $500 a lecture now, but I'm getting to know lots of people — and there's lots of money to be made in it when all I can do is talk!"

"Are you acting for money?" June was asked.

"For art," she said. "I'm financially independent now and can do what I like. Years ago I had no choice, I had to play anything and everything and save every penny I earned. So now I can enjoy doing what I want to — like this version of Sophocles."

Is there anything the sisters agree on?

"Real estate is a girl's best investment," said June. "I have this little Brownstone on East 95th which I cut into apartments. I rent three of them and keep one big room for myself."

"Tenets? Not for me," said Gypsy. "I've got these 26 room town house on East 63rd Street and I keep all 26 for myself. I mean, for myself and my son, two maids, the carpenter, three cats, the dog and the guppies."

So how can anybody see this personal sister act without shuttling 32 blocks or buying lecture and show tickets?

"Come to Russia," was the answer. "We go touring together. Did Europe and Africa last year. This summer we're going to Russia."

Screaming Mimi. *Screaming Mimi*, written by Fredric Brown, was first published 1949. The dark theme made it a cult classic. In 1958 German-born director Gerd Oswald turned it into a movie.

The amply bosomed Anita Ekberg starred as the title character. The film's opening scene shows Ekberg coming ashore after a swim in the ocean. She enters an outdoor shower. A stalker with a huge knife comes upon her while she is helpless and unable to escape.

Unsettled by the sudden attack, Mimi seeks the counsel of a psychiatrist, Dr. Greenwood, played by Harry Townes. On his advice she takes a job in a questionable nightclub, where she becomes the star with her interpretive (and awful) dance.

Gypsy is the nightclub's owner Joann. Her routine to "Put the Blame on Mame," the song that catapulted Rita Hayworth to great fame in the film noir classic *Gilda*, is the film's one bright moment. Gypsy is in her element, she certainly understood the nightclub world and had interacted with club owners. She is relaxed and obviously having fun. This is the movie in which she came the closest to playing herself.

Leonard Maltin has this to say: "Lurid ... melodrama ... woman who cracks up after being assaulted, takes a job as an exotic dancer in Lee's nightclub ... remains under the

The original caption for this still read: "Newspaperman Phil Carey, left, is introduced to the El Madhouse's latest attraction, Anita Ekberg, right, by the club's owner, Gypsy Rose Lee, in this scene from Columbia's 'Screaming Mimi.'"

influence of a possessive psychiatrist. Strange, kinky … sounds more interesting than it really is." He gives the film two stars out of four.

Gypsy the Viking. Gypsy and her Royal American Beauties appear at the Casino Theatre in Oslo, Norway, during June of 1958.

Life **Magazine — June 16, 1958.** A photo of Gypsy dressed in a leopard-spotted dress and wearing a necklace made of bone decorated the article *Hawaii Hoopla in N.Y.* This party for more than two hundred guests was given by Richard Burton for his wife Sybil. Other photos show guests Lena Horne, Jules Munshin, Tony Perkins, Judy Holliday, Henry Fonda and Peter Ustinov having a wild time.

glance at Gypsy. *glance*, with a small "g," was a 25 cent mini-magazine. The June 1958 *Special* BURLESQUE *Issue!* included *"over 70 photos!"* The cover displayed a photo of Lilli "The Cat Girl" Christine.

    "With [Ann] Corio setting the pace, and such immortal ecdysiasts as Gypsy Rose Lee and Sally Rand to speed it up, burlesque was a bonanza right up to World War II": *That's Gypsy Rose Lee bedecked in a black lace teaser.*

The one bright spot in the noir world of *Screaming Mimi* is Gypsy's musical number — her singular version of the Rita Hayworth classic "Put the Blame on Mame."

Hunting Down Gypsy. Gypsy played summer stock, also known as the tent circuit, beginning in June of 1958. She appeared in a new musical *Happy Hunting* in a role that had been written for Ethel Merman, who was most definitely not happy while starring in it on Broadway. Merman, who was well known for a long string of successful Broadway musicals, called *Happy Hunting,* "A jeep among limousines."

With Gypsy at the helm, the ill-fated show performed in Pennsylvania at the Valley Forge Music Fair, the Camden Music Fair (New Jersey), Westbury (Long Island) and in

Atlanta, Georgia. It was rough going for the cast, and especially for Gypsy, who was not a trained singer and had frequent problems with her voice.

The summer heat, especially under the canvas tent at the Valley Forge Musical Fair, was unrelenting. Valley Forge was also a theatre-in-the-round, which meant that whenever Gypsy had to enter and exit (the stage) she had to run up and down long aisles. The aisles were at an incline, with the stage at the bottom. During matinee and evening performances she made the steep journey to and from the stage more than thirty times.

One afternoon she fainted after a matinee and was revived with smelling salts. The woman handling Gypsy's wardrobe suggested salt tablets, but there wasn't enough time between the matinee and the evening performance for them to take effect.

That night, with only seven or eight minutes to go till the final curtain, Gypsy collapsed on-stage. The cast took her to her dressing room.

The stage manager was ready to send Gypsy's understudy on-stage to finish the show. Ever the trouper, Gypsy told him, "When I'm dead you can send in my understudy." Within ten minutes she was back in front of the audience, finishing the performance before an amazed audience. She was front page news the following morning.

And She Cooks Too! In July of 1958 the story of Gypsy's fabulous kitchen, excerpted below was seen in newspapers from Paris, Texas (July 10), to Ada, Oklahoma (July 16), to Fresno, California (July 25).

"Gypsy Loves Kitchen of Town House."

By Vivian Brown

IT MAY UPSET a man's preconceived notion of glamorous woman to learn that some of the world's most fascinating women are mad for kitchens. Gypsy Rose Lee, for instance.

The vivacious, versatile star of stage and screen has two kitchens in her household, for the very good reason that she wants one for herself.

"I love to cook," says Gypsy, who lives with 13-year-old Erik and a housekeeper in a pair of New York townhouses that comprise 26 rooms. "My little kitchen is stocked with just about every utensil a woman could want for kitchen fun."

Her culinary equipment runs the gamut from the traditional melon-shaped pudding mold down to a paella pan, the latter for holding the mouth watering paella dish, a gastronomic achievement that includes chicken, shrimp, rice, lobster and what have you. Utensils hang from the kitchen ceiling, and decorate walls and shelves. "My stove is the 1913 Rolls Royce of stoves," says Gypsy, pointing proudly to the old-fashioned black stove that is her personal love.

Gypsy's Gone Fishin'. The August 25, 1958, evening issue of the *Wausau Daily Record-Herald* (Wisconsin), featured a photo of Gypsy laying in the shade, fishing pole in hand and wearing high-heeled shoes! "It's the Gypsy in Her." *Former strip-tease queen Gypsy Rose Lee found the 96-degree weather in Atlanta, Ga., just too hot for activity. So someone (a press agent, maybe?) gave her a fishing rod and she stretched out on a grassy bank under a shade tree to present this charming picture of curvesome angling. Now a "legitimate" actress, Gypsy is starring in "Happy Hunting."*

Gypsy in the Everglades. The September 22, 1958, issue of *Life* ran black and white photos showing Gypsy, and the rest of the cast, on location for *Wind Across the Everglades.*

Here, on a marshy island in the Florida bogs, a flock of famous faces from widely different worlds gathered to act in Wind Across the Everglades, *a movie about feather-hunting "swamp angels" who years ago all but wiped out many species of fine birds. LIFE photographer Yale Joel persuaded Bud*

The original caption to this publicity still reads, "Ex-stripper Gypsy Rose Lee stars in a straight dramatic role with Christopher Plummer in the new Warner Bros. motion picture release, 'Winds Across the Everglades,' written by Budd Schulberg and filmed in WarnerColor in Florida. Burl Ives also stars in the Schulberg Production in which Gypsy portrays the proprietor of a turn-of-the-century Miami salon. Warner Bros. 1958."

Above and opposite: Rocky Weinstein and Gypsy Rose Lee try their hand at some fishing in between scenes for *Across the Everglades.*

and Stuart Schulberg, who produced the movie for Warner Bros., to dress the actors as the public knows them best and pose them around the Everglades set. In the movie MacKinlay Kantor, author of Andersonville *and other best-sellers, plays a judge. The roles of swamp angels are taken by Emmett Kelly, the renowned clown, Tony Galento, the famous boxer, Burl Ives, once a ballad singer, and Sammy Renick, a former jockey. Gypsy Rose Lee, the strip-teaser, plays the owner of a Miami fancy house. Christopher Plummer, famous Shakespearean actor, is the hero—a brave Audubon Society agent who puts an end to the nefarious traffic in feathers.*

Gypsy on the Lecture Circuit. During 1958 Gypsy appeared, as she frequently did, on the lecture circuit. A photo of the event shows Gypsy at the podium. The photo shows three older women listening to the burlesque queen. Radio station WPAT in New York was involved in Gypsy's appearance as sponsor or host. The photograph was seen in newspaper ads for WPAT.

Gypsy and the Beast. Gypsy's costume was created for the "Beauty and the Beasts" tableaux at the Imperial Ball, which took place on December 4, 1958. Other notable guests included opera singer Patrice Munsel and ballerina Vera Zorina.

American Legion Christmas Party. Gypsy attended the American Legion Christmas Party on December 15, 1958.

CHAPTER EIGHT

Broadway, Broadway, How Great You Are!

• 1959 •

Casa Gypsy. Gypsy was asked to appear at a Manhattan nightclub called Casa Cugat in February of 1959, but she declined.

Gypsy Asks for It. Gypsy appeared on the hit television show *You Asked for It*. This episode was seen on March 1, 1959. On March 3, 1959, she was on a television program called *Galaxy*.

Gypsy Once a Week. Gypsy was given the opportunity to host her own weekly television show. Her show premiered on April 7, 1959. Unfortunately, for Gypsy and her loyal fans the show was cancelled after the first broadcast.

    The New York Times journalist Jack Gould reviewed the show in the newspaper's April 9, 1959 issue.

> GYPSY ROSE LEE, author, art collector and doyenne of the runway, joined the lobster shift of raconteurs on Channel 13 Tuesday evening. In her program, running from 11 A.M. to 12:20 A.M., the stately subject of a forthcoming musical quickly proved one of the medium's most attractive test patterns.

The musical was, of course, the upcoming *Gypsy*. Gypsy's friend, and one-time costar, Paulette Goddard was one of her guests. Evidently, there were some risqué remarks made by the two stars. Mr. Gould referred to them as "priceless observations," observations he was not willing, or able, to repeat in his column. He did however, point out Gypsy's "formidable good humor" and her "very considerable charm."

Gypsy & Jack. The witty talk show host, Jack Parr, welcomed an equally witty guest, Gypsy Rose Lee, on the *Jack Parr Show* on April 29, 1959.

Gypsy's Echo. In 1959 an enterprising publisher named Barrie L. Beere and his editor John Wilcock introduced a new magazine entitled *Echo — A Magazine of Sight and Sound*. *Echo* had a unique format. It had standard magazine articles with the issue of a record, which was included in the magazine. Each article was followed by a recording directly impressed into the magazine's extra thick pages. The premiere issue of *Echo* included "Gypsy:

A Backstage Preview," supplemented by music "On the Record: Gypsy Rose Lee and Jule Styne."

The article was also accompanied by two photos of Gypsy. In the first she is at a microphone, singing and holding a piece of sheet music (probably a song from *Gypsy*). In the second photo she is seated and reading from her autobiography.

Gypsy's Triumph! *Gypsy* opened on Broadway May 21, 1959. *Gypsy* is inarguably in the pantheon of great Broadway musicals, and some consider it the perfect Broadway musical. It certainly has stood the test of time. *Gypsy* has been revived on Broadway numerous times, starring an array of talented actresses in the demanding role of Mama Rose. The quintessential stage mother has been played by Angela Lansbury, Tyne Daly, Bernadette Peters, and Patti LuPone. Other television and theatre stars such as Yvonne DeCarlo, Kaye Ballard, and Betty Buckley have also played Rose. In the 1993 television film of *Gypsy*, Bette Midler tackled the role.

It has been said that Gypsy walked into the Broadway opening of the musical based on her life as a star, she walked out a legend. The new musical had to bear the title *Gypsy: A Musical Fable*. The word "fable" was added to appease an unhappy June Havoc.

Havoc was not pleased with how she was portrayed in the show. Some changes were made to make her character more sympathetic. Luckily, June was persuaded not to pursue legal action to block the show from opening. For the sake of her sister and the time-honored tradition of the theatre, she let the show go on.

***The New York Times*— Review of *Gypsy*.** The May 22, 1959, issue of *The New York Times* ran theatre critic Brooks Atkinson's enthusiastic review of *Gypsy*, which applauded the show as a whole and in particular gave high accolades to Ethel Merman's performance as Mama Rose.

June Follows Gypsy. Like her older sister before her, June Havoc wrote her biography and published it in 1959. The book, *Early Havoc*, was mentioned in *The New York Times* on May 24, 1959: "Like the Brontës — well, perhaps not entirely like the Brontës — The Hovick sisters are writers, pretty fine ones."

***Theatre Arts Magazine*.** In May 1959 the venerable theatre magazine presented an article titled "A Memoir with Music (for G-String)," which included a three-page photo spread of the dancers appearing in *Gypsy* on Broadway. There is one photo of Gypsy backstage with the some of the dancers who were auditioning for the show.

> The fine art of the strip tease is only one of the components of Gypsy, the new musical arriving on Broadway this month, but it is obviously a rather integral one in any show based on the early career of the celebrated Miss Lee. During auditions for the short scene in which the strip-teasers appear, more than two hundred obligingly followed the instructions of director Jerome Robbins: "All we want to see is your best feature." Most of the aspirants were experienced performers from burlesque, and when the two-day period of gyration was over, three successful contestants remained. "One of the best shows I've ever seen in my life" was the verdict of photographer Slim Aarons on the audition period, which he recorded in elaborate detail. The show scheduled to come to the Broadway Theatre in mid–May derives From *Gypsy*, the autobiography of Gypsy Rose Lee, and it stars Ethel Merman. Arthur Laurents adapted the memoir into a musical-comedy book, Jule Styne composed the music,

and Stephen Sondheim contributed the lyrics. Mr. Robbins is the director and choreographer.

Gypsy's Parr for the Course. On June 2, 1959, Gypsy was once again one of the welcome guests on the popular *Jack Parr Show*.

Life Magazine. In the June 29, 1959, issue of *Life*, Gypsy divulged her secrets for success in one of her favorite pastimes, shopping for antiques.

Tips by an Improbable Pro
by Gypsy Rose Lee

Brought up as I was in hotels and dressing rooms, with the Pantages circuit for a backdrop, my heirlooms are few: a crotched afghan Mother made between shows and a faded Santa Claus I swiped from a backstage Christmas tree in Bradford, Pa. when I was 10 years old. I treasure them, but they aren't exactly heirlooms. Heirlooms, to me, mean permanence, continuity and family roots. Maybe that's why I began collecting antiques. Having no roots of my own, I guess I tried to latch on to other people's.

I began collecting Victorian when I was working for Minsky, not just because I liked it but because it was cheap and there was a lot of it. Suddenly Victorian became fashionable and the beaded footstools, tufted Turkish chairs and papier-mâché tables I had bought in junk shops were being sold on Madison Avenue. My $10 chairs were worth $500, so I had an auction, sold my surplus Victoriana and used the profits to buy what I called French Provincial but was actually Queen Anne, Directoire, Italian and even Early American. To me, the rake of a leg meant nothing if the woods matched and the price was right. I was ahead of that market, too, so I saved out the best for myself again and had another auction. I used the money to buy English Regency. My house is filled with a combination of all three periods, making it sort of Early Halloween.

I've learned from my mistakes, from dealers and from books. Although I don't pretend to know antiques, I sure know how to go antiquing: flat shoes, no girdle and two shopping bags. I never wind up empty handed. Empty pursed, maybe, because I always find something I can't live without. Most of my bargains — a few of my treasures — I've found among the broken unsalable things hidden away in the back rooms of antique shops, in cupboards or in boxes under counters. A Lowesoft teacup with a chip in the lip and broken handle will sell for a fraction of its value, and I'm handy with a glue pot.

For my fancy restoration job I use powdered plastic made for replacing broken fingernails. Adding liquid and dropping layer upon layer upon layer, I shape the filler as I go along. Then when it has dried, I file it smooth with an emery board and paint it with dope and gloss used for painting model airplanes. If a large piece is missing, I carve a replacement from balsa wood, secure it into position and cover it with the nail repair goop. For repairing busted corners on Barbizon and ornate frames, I use modeling clay with several layers of glue to make it solid. Wet newspaper soaked in thinned-out glue is messy to work with but perfect for repairing mache pieces. I upholster all my own furniture. Stripping it (if you'll forgive the expression) down to the frame, I retie the springs, replace the webbing, add new stuffing and do all the things a man does on the TV commercial. It took me a full week to reupholster a 10-foot free-foam sofa. It was a week of broken fingernails and bleeding knuckles, but I saved $300 and gave myself something to talk about on the Jack Paar show. I made all the draperies and curtains in my 26-room New York house. I rewired most of the lamps and made all of the lampshades. Now I'm making patchwork crazyquilts. I usually quilt in my bedroom which is sort of patchwork, too. To mention some of its charms, I have a bell filled with waxed flower and stuffed birds, a hat stand holding a collection of old parasols, a Franklin stove — it really works, I never paint anything white and fill it with flowers — a clock that plays music and rings gongs every 15 minutes and also has a waterfall, a collection of pincushions and some tiny shoes. Cluttered but cosy.

Six months of every year I'm on the road, shaking the beads for a living, so working around my house is a holiday for me and antiquing is my relaxation. I antique on the road, too. I accepted my first engagement in Atlanta for short money because I heard antiquing there was good. It was, too. I've been lucky in Boston, Philadelphia and Los Angeles. But most of the dealers know me in those cities now, so I'm looking for new territory. It doesn't seem to matter if I'm known to dealers in New York or not, but too often when I'm recognized out of town, the prices shoot up.

I bought a pair of bronze herons when I was playing New Orleans. Because of their size the birds had to be dismantled, wrapped in paper-covered excelsior, then crated and sent home by freight. It took seven weeks to deliver, cost $62, and when I was unpacking the birds I turned one of them upside down and saw the label on his bottom, "Made in Japan." I sold them two years later for a profit, but that's beside the point. A New York dealer who knew me would have told me they were fakes. I learned a lesson, though. Now I examine everything from all angles, especially the bottoms, before I buy.

I don't know why I feel as though I should pack an overnight bag and fill a Thermos with hot coffee every time I go to Brooklyn, but when I get there I find the antiquing good. One wonderful junk shop off Flatbush Avenue is owned by a woman who lives, not in the back room, but right smack in the middle of her store. She has a hot plate set up on a Biedermeier table with a price tag on both, heats a can of soup in the 18th Century pewter bowl marked $37.50 and sleeps, so help me, rolled up in an Aubusson rug. When I asked her the price of a Charles Dana Gibson plate, she talked it over with Ginger, her tomcat, whose sandbox is a Flora Danica fruit bowl. "The lady wants to buy our Doulton dish," she said to the cat. "What shall we charge her for it?" I finally bought the plate because I collect them, but that tomcat drives the hardest bargain of any dealer in the business.

Bon Voyage! Gypsy and her son, Erik, boarded the S.S. *Flandre* in June of 1959. Their destination: Paris. *Life* photographer Walter Sanders accompanied Gypsy and Erik when they visited a nightclub in the City of Lights, but *Life* never used the photos.

Gypsy's Got the *TAB*. The August 1959 issue of the racy *TAB* magazine took readers on a trip "Down Memory Lane": by running photos of three of the greatest stars of burlesque: "Remember When?" *In burlesque's salad day, when Boston's famed Old Harvard theater packed in the stolid citizens, this trio of torso tossers, (l. to r.) Margie Hart, Lili St. Cyr, Gypsy Rose Lee, lit up the stage. The Howard's closed now, but the memories remain.*

Gypsy's Bed of Nails. In a popular ad for Springmaid sheets Gypsy dressed in a harem girl outfit, lifting a Springmaid sheet up to reveal a bed of nails beneath.

Gypsy meets the Modern Man. Gypsy was profiled in the September 1959 issue of *Modern Man Magazine*. The cover of this Playboy-type publication promised an "Intimate Profile of Gypsy Rose Lee," written by Morton Cooper.

For most practical purposes, the school of culture known as strip teasing is as alive and kicking today as the three-tailed toad. Burlesque shows, complete with sleepy drummers, baggy pants comics and candy butchers who sell chocolate bars and intimate French photographs of Gen. Charles DeGaulle, are still being operated here and there, of course, if you're will to do a bit of excavating. And in them you are bound to see a stripper or two who will be worth at least a quarter of the admission price. Also, the naked eye can view semi-naked girls strutting their conventionally exotic stuff on the stages of nearly any side street quenchery. Sipping your beer — which at said quencheries costs little more than the National Budget — you can watch a strawhaired, pot-bellied Venus make like an organ grinder, and you can forget for a moment that the art of stripping, like the Essex and Terraplane, has fallen on hard times.

"I'm going to spike a rumor,"

says Gypsy Rose Lee, famous author, actress and landlady, "that Springmaid
sheets won't fit a fakir. I know better because after the Communists took Viet Nam,
the Socialists took France, the Hindus took India, the Battenbergs took England,
the PX took Germany and the Russians took exception, I took nothing home
from my world tour but my costumes and you know that's only token pay.

"So I have had to take roomers but since the rumor spread that I was using
Springmaid easy-to-fit sheets, I have had a waiting list that would reach from
Moriarity's to Morocco and my roomers, if laid end to end would reach from
Burke's Pier to Burke's Peerage. And that's no rumor."

During the '30s, though the stripteaser had a prestige second to none. Taking up the bra mantle of Hinda Wassau, any girl could make a fortune if she was over 12, had most of her teeth, a prominent bosom, a prominent behind, and a talent for shaking most of her apparatus concurrently.

The '30s was the age of the bump and grind, and men, worried about the Depression, discovered that half a buck exchanged at Minsky's window could give them a few hours of rest from job-hunting, a few hours to realize again that life was still worth living.

As in every big business, competition quickly appeared. Suddenly it was not enough to simply disrobe, in a hurry, bump two or three times, and jiggle off. You had to have "A Gimmick." The girls who did not realize this perished in the business and today are successful counter girls. The ones who did realize it strove to find a way to sell the old merchandise in a new package.

The scramble was on. One exotic hired birds to remove her clothes while she panted sensuously. Another played suggestively with a snake. Still another performed the entire sex act with every available equipment except a man. One more endearingly set fire to her G-string.

Then, as if from nowhere, appeared a not-too-beautiful, not-too-fantastically built, slightly buck-toothed girl who single-bumpedly made the weary world of Stripsville a decent place in which to live again. Her name was Gypsy Rose Lee. Her gimmick? She showed a great deal less skin than her professional fore-barers. She flounced on-stage, smiled sweetly, kidded the men out front unmercifully but cordially, and said good night. Not much more than that happened. In doing so, she got away with burlesque murder. And the crowds ate it up.

Who, her co-workers asked, was this odd ball? Who was this Rose Louise Hovick who had tabbed herself Gypsy Rose Lee and decided to enter a career not otherwise open to Jennie Come Latelies who thought they were too good to show all?

Soon the shocking facts came out. She was beyond moral contempt. When she went to bed, it was reported, she was both sober *and alone*— reason enough to drum her out of the society. Vulgarly, she used good English. In her free time, instead of shacking up with the trombonist or smoking tea or scratching the eyes out of one of the troupe with gossip — as any normal stripper was expected to do — she spent her time *reading!* And deep stuff at that!

Although Gypsy (she was given the nickname as a kid, when she gave most of her afternoons over to having her palm read by gypsy fortune tellers) could not have cared less what a bad reputation she seemed to be giving her profession, the other girls came to like her for her salty frankness and honestly. Before long her name became a household word through-out the world. Her sophisticatedly roughhouse act was called "Seven minutes of sheer art." Between turns at removing underclothes and singing songs about virgin sturgeons, the 130-pound Amazon with a passion for everything intellectual busied herself in reading Thomas Mann and Marcel Proust, gardening, selling millions of dollars worth of war bonds by auctioning off her garters, hobnobbing with some of the great thinkers of her time, divorcing a husband because he ate gefulte fish in bed, writing novels and plays, getting herself involved in fights with labor leaders (the Harry Bridges forces considered her a political menace) and lecturing United Mine Workers on their right to strike for better working conditions. As the uninitiated outsiders looked on agog (who'd ever heard of a stripper who read anything more complicated then the menu or knew anyone beyond the stage door?), the active Miss Lee intelligently expressed herself on every subject from fine arts to photography to precious stones and trade unions.

Unlike many of her sorority sisters who called themselves serious *artistes* and insisted they had entered burlesque only because they had heard an aesthetic Call, Gypsy often spoke French but never double talk. To all the highbrows who were positive she had attained her huge body of knowledge at fashionable finishing schools and had become a stripper as a lark, she immediately put them straight. She was born in 1914, in Seattle, in what unfashionably amounted to poverty, to a German mother who had a towering ambition and a Norwegian father who made $8 a week as a newspaperman.

Never one to do anything in undramatic halfway measures, she arranged to come on the scene during one of Washington's heaviest rainstorms while her parents were trying to put a roof over their house, literally. A midwife was hurriedly summoned and placed a canvas sheet over Mrs. Hovick to keep her partially protected from the hammering rain. Mrs. Hovick, who was known as something of a character herself, noticed through her contractions that her beloved piano was getting wet from the torrent. "Hurry up and cover the piano," she yelled. "Don't mind us. You can always get more babies!"

Mother separated from the reporter two years late, shortly after Rose's sister June (now movie star June Havoc) was born, having discovered the $8 every seven days would not buy mansions or minks for her daughters, even with a dollar or two set aside every now and then. She took the girls to Hollywood when Rose was four and June was two, determined to have them escape the poorhouse jungle. That she succeeded was shown less than 25 years later, when her daughter Rose commanded $1,000 weekly as the most inspiring thing to hit burlesque since the runway and who, among numberless other monumental achievements, posed for the cover of *The Plumbing and Heating Journal.*

It was agreed from the beginning that June was the singer, dancer, comedienne, and all around romper talent, that Rose would, like her mother, supply the brains and natural shrewdness. A rickety act called, coyly enough, "Dainty June, the Hollywood Baby, and Her Newsboys," was devised for vaudeville, and within three years was earning as much as $6,000 a month. The original idea had been for June to star and for Rose, the gawky one, to play the supporting role in men's clothes ("Gyp wore suits in the act for so long," friends remember, "that we called her Baby June's big brother"). But before long, without planning it that way, Rose had the reins handed to her; her saucy personality connected with the audiences so instinctively that, by merely walking on stage and singing in the voice that sounded like a cow being milked with cold hands, she became the Bernhardt of the toddler set. Soon the act's name was changed to "Madam Rose's Dancing Daughters."

Because no one has yet figured out a way to adequately educate children who must move from town to town, as did the Hovick's, Rose did her reading on the run. At one point her mother hired a tutor only because, after successfully keeping her kids working by lying about their ages, the law discovered that the birth certificates she had provided were fakes and ordered her to get those youngsters educated, or else. While June avoided studies as much as possible, concerned more with romance (at 13 she ran off with a chorus boy) and hard work ("I wanted to die," she has said, "just for a vacation."), Rose took to the books, an addiction she has never been able — nor ever really wanted — to break.

Despite her mother's protests, Rose eventually switched from vaudeville and clubs to burlesque, for the simple reason that the paychecks were fatter in the skin shows. Still no raving beauty and not endowed with the kinds of assets that have immortalized Evelyn West, she became Gypsy Rose Lee and most of the serious students of the science of Ann Corio, Georgia Sothern and Margie Hart still have not fully recovered from the shock.

She stripped, to be sure, but in doing so she created the most fiendish optical illusion in the delusive annals of peeldom: By taking off her gloves, hat, hair bows, petticoat and other strategic articles of underwear, the boys out front were hypnotized into not noticing that her skirt and shirtwaist was kept intact. This art was achieved by continuously conversing with such teasers as, "Darling, please don't ask me to take off any more. I'll catch cold. No, please, I'm embarrassed. No, honestly, I can't. I'm almost shivering now," or by talking vaguely smutty songs less depraved than Little Bo Peep.

By 1931, hardly weeks after she had joined the burly wheel, Gypsy Rose Lee was yanking down $1,000 a week. Old-time strip fans, used to the poetry of the low female growl, the seductive grind, the meaningful bump, and the all-purpose G-string flash were, without quite knowing why, beating paths to the front row of New York's Republic Theatre to view this upstart. A now dead breed called Café Society, in bored search of thrills, heard about her and went slumming on Times Square just to sit with the bald, T-shirted guys and applaud her. The word got around that she was a wit and an intellectual, and the cream of the society crop invited her to tea.

Gypsy broke a record at The Republic before she walked out on burlesque, 12 weeks after she had walked in, to play a small part at $60 a week in a Ziegfeld show. But having decided — as her mother had decided years before — that wealth beats poverty, she soon returned to the runway. Billy Minsky, irked that she had left him, took her back but at a figure considerably lower than $1,000. The big money returned quickly, though, when he rediscovered that no attraction kept the cash registers humming at his store as vigorously as did the toothy girl who sold brains as well as breast.

As aware as her detractors that her skills were limited (the late Mike Todd once hired her and her dog, a Chihuahua who could get mass applause just by darting across a stage, for his Broadway show *Star and Garter*, billing them as "the two greatest no-talent queens in show business"), Gypsy nevertheless did not diffidently refuse when she was offered $2,000 a week to go to Hollywood. She accepted. But even before she arrived in California, many church groups and organized den mothers got to work protesting that if "That Lee Person" ever reached the silver screen, American morality was doomed. Their screams of fear and rage were so piercing that one would have thought Shirley Temple was about to be replaced in the movies by Adolph Hitler.

The Hays Office ordered Gypsy to bill herself, as long as she was on the coast, as Louise Hovick. This tactical maneuver, brilliant in that it automatically undoomed impressionable mankind, calmed the religious folk somewhat it did nothing to help Gypsy's career. One critic, in reviewing her first picture, wrote, "Hollywood has given Gypsy the two things she needs least: another name and several complete changes of clothing."

Although the $2,000 checks were sent to her every Friday to two years, few of her employers at 20th Century–Fox were pleased with her. They did not enjoy her boasting, for any available ear, that she owned more that 160,000 feet of stag movies and did not hesitate at showing them to her guests. An even more unforgivable sin was that she just did not behave in the way a movie star was expected to. At her home she chose to entertain not other stars, producers and directors, but the grips and electricians from the studio.

"They wanted me to play down my background and act sedate," she said of her bosses. "And you can just imagine me doing that."

The ensuing years have heard the death rattle of burlesque and, with it the last feeble gasps of most of the once-honored strippers. But Gypsy Rose Lee, the absent minded institution who once strode from the stage to the runway and fell into the orchestra pit because she had forgotten that the runway had been removed that morning, goes on forever. Her memoirs of a few years ago made the best seller lists and provided the basis for Broadway's current musicomedy hit, *Gypsy* (MM August, 1959). Her sophisticated girlie shows in cross-country carnivals have brought her new fortune. She drinks perfumed tea, lives in a 26-room mansion on New York's East 63rd Street, still chatters enthusiastically on subjects that may range from her three husbands to Picasso, and is constantly planning new projects.

One of the reasons for The Gyp's unflagging popularity is that she has never stopped being outspoken and thoroughly truthful. Not long ago an admirer gushed, "You look marvelous, Gypsy. Your figure is marvelous. In fact, you look as well as you did 25 years ago." "Yes, it's all the same," Gypsy said with characteristic — though in this case inaccurate — honesty, "but everything's just a bit lower." Her reply was inaccurate because she looks sexier today than she ever did.

Gypsy Rose Lee was one of the few characters (in a profession that makes a *requirement* that its members be characters) who never needed a press agent to invite brains and wit for her. One of the best recalled of these happened during the war when she was invited, along with Clifton Fadiman, to address a Victory Book Committee rally. At the microphone she nervously picked up Fadiman's speech instead of her own and read, for the assembled throng to hear, "All my life has been spent in the world of books."

Later, still ruffled, she blinked as a fan asked her, "What's the matter, Gypsy? Scared of crowds?"

As she has done all her life, Gypsy instantly rose to the occasion. "How would you like to stand up here before such a mob," she asked, "with all of your clothes on?"

Gypsy joined fellow partygoers Jack Carter, right, and Jule Styne (who wrote the music for *Gypsy*). Pearl Bailey, Ruth Gilbert, Dorothy Loudon, and Les Charlivels also performed.

Winter Antiques Show. Gypsy and her sister June were seen at the Winter Antiques Show in October of 1959.

Gypsy and Paris — A Perfect Match! Princess Grace (Grace Kelly) of Monaco adorned the cover of the October 17, 1959, issue of *Paris Match* magazine. The article "L'honorable Gypsy reine de Broadway" featured five black and white photos of Gypsy.

Gypsy Throws a Big Party. The November 5, 1959, episode of CBS's show *The Big Party* was hosted by silver screen legend Irene Dunne.

Gypsy's Brain and Brawn. In December of 1959 Gypsy appeared on a television show called *Brains and Brawn*. This game show was hosted by Jack Lescoulie (The Brawn) and Fred Davis (The Brains). The exact airdate of the show is unknown.

• 1960 •

Sunday News — January 3, 1960. Gypsy was on hand to celebrate the release of Broadway producer Leonard Sillman's book *Here Lies Leonard Sillman: Straightened Out at Last*. The celebration took place at a New York club called The Living Room. Other stars in attendance included Jeanette MacDonald, Margaret Leighton and Celeste Holm.

Gypsy Is a Lady. The January 17, 1960, issue of *The American Weekly*, which invited readers to "Meet the ex-strip-teaser who has become a best-selling writer, art collector, a woman of fashion and for the current Broadway hit musical."

"The LADY Behind the GYPSY"
by Louis McLain

RUNNING THE GAUNTLET of fancy antique shops and art galleries, the maroon Rolls Royce bowls along Madison Avenue, turns into 63rd Street and comes to a stop before a charming three story house.

Madame has returned from a weekend in the country.

Esther, the maid, helps the chauffeur with the luggage, tenderly divests her mistress of her mink coat. Erica, the secretary, runs around, giving instructions. A magnificent Afghan hound celebrates the occasion with frenzied barking and leaping, while three Persian cats — Gaudi, Tina and Sub-Gum — drift across the floor like shadows.

Madame trips down the hall, plastered with paintings and etchings, passes the dining room, with its frescoes by Vertes, steps into the patio and draws a satisfied breath.

With a house like this (26 rooms, seven baths and an elevator), smack in the center of sky-scraper-studded New York, she has every reason to feel satisfied. The whole show suggests not only money but old money, a long established family fortune. However, despite the enthusiasm of a Chicago critic who wrote: "General Robert E. Lee would have been proud to count such a woman among his relatives," Gypsy Rose Lee, the svelte chatelaine of this mansion, definitely does not count the General, or anybody else for much distinction, among hers.

Gypsy amassed her fortune by herself, in a profession (or art, if you will) of a highly special-ized kind. She has been called a burlesque queen, sometimes, in scientific circles, "a kimonophode." More commonly, she is referred to as a strip-teaser, the greatest of them all. Connoisseurs still consider her act a classic. That it proved profitable is not strange. But how, at the same time, it prepared her for a literary career and a life of fashion is rather puzzling.

To date, she has written three books. One of them, an autobiography, not only made the best-seller lists but provided the inspiration for *Gypsy*, one of the biggest hits now playing on Broadway. Its muse, the real-life Gypsy, nowadays is sought after by the best society. She talks stylish English, sprinkled with French. Her son, Erik, is being given a gentleman's education, plays the piano, takes fencing lessons and attends an exclusive school.

Under furs and a Vassar accent, it is hard to recognize the little girl who in the 1920s hacked back and forth across the land with a moth-eaten troupe of child actors.

At that time, she slept on the back seat of a beat-up car, while her mother, the driver and Porky (a pet pig that strutted around on its hind legs and wore a hat) took up the front. She and her younger sister June, who later became the actress June Havoc, never went to school. Their childhood was passed on the road, at one-night stands and in shabby hotel rooms. Always they were exposed to the overpowering company of their mother, Rose.

That astonishing woman, a mixture of hen, pioneer and monster, is the real heroine of the play, *Gypsy*, in which Ethel Merman plays her to the hilt.

Rose was determined to make a success of the child act she had put together. The troupe was composed of June, whom Mama considered the infant prodigy of the family; Gypsy, then called Louise; and a number of other girls and boys. There was no question of paying any of them. Rose had persuaded their parents that theatrical experience was more valuable than money.

It was a rough kind of education and, to make it worse, vaudeville was dying. Rose refused to accept this fact, despite the increasing rarity of jobs. With frightening energy, she bumped her way across the country, arguing with theater managers, out-shouting them, cajoling them into signing contracts they later regretted.

One day she and her troupe found themselves stranded in a burlesque house in Toledo, Ohio. Opening night, a catastrophe: the star, a stripper who appeared in five scenes, was missing. Rose had a brilliant idea.

"Louise can fill in," she announced.

The frantic stage manager broke off his lamentations.

"Can she strip?"

After a moment's hesitation, Rose produced a stout "Yes."

Panic gripped Louise, but her mother reassured her.

"Nobody's going to ask you for a real strip-tease. Just go out there and loosen a few things."

Half-paralyzed, Louise obeyed to the letter; she just let down the straps of her evening gown. At the end she had a happy idea: pretending to shed her dress entirely, she wrapped herself in the curtain.

During the following years, this curtain-wrapping gambit became her specialty. Its effect was amazing. Audiences knocked themselves out applauding and shouting for encores.

Cincinnati, Chicago — the jobs began pouring in. Mama stood guard everywhere to see that her daughter's name headed the notices, that her daughter, in person, was given the star's dressing room. At the end of a show, Gypsy would receive a magnificent bouquet, with a card reading, "From an admirer."

Whenever she had to share top billing with some other actress, the latter always would get anonymous letters, full of abuse. Gypsy soon discovered that her unknown admirer and the author of the scurrilous notes were one and the same person — Rose, naturally.

Stripping, Rose kept insisting, was just an interlude; presently vaudeville would pick up again and they'd be back at their lasts. But Gypsy was getting ahead in her new profession. She became dedicated to it when Billy Minsky, king of Burlesque, engaged her for a New York appearance. Under his aegis, she really came into her own.

She bought a house in the country, an automobile, jewelry, furs — and fame finally cut her loose from Mama's apron strings. Rose fought the inevitable as long as she could but in the end complainingly gave in. Loaded with loot, she let herself be packed off to the country house, after which she saw her daughter only once a week in town.

Gypsy's success lasted for years without much change in her act. On stage, she always managed to reveal a lot less than the ads promised. To put it simply, she gave the customers more tease than strip. Nevertheless, they seemed to love it.

Today, all that is behind her. Rose, cranky and courageous to the last, died in 1954. Following in her mother's footsteps, Gypsy went through three husbands; then she wrote her three books and developed a taste for painting, reading and traveling abroad.

She is not ashamed of her memories, pictured forth in scrapbooks, which she is always leafing through. For her son, Erik, her childhood represents a world, vanished but endlessly enchanting. Although by now he knows many of her stories by heart, he still dies laughing over the antics of Porky, the pig, and is full of questions about the celebrated gangster, Waxey Gordon, who paid a dentist to straighten Gypsy's teeth because he found her sympathetic.

After immersing himself this way in the past, Erik reluctantly returns to the present. And what a present! Climbing into the maroon Rolls-Royce, he is whisked off to his fencing lesson....

Gypsy in Disguise. Gypsy appeared on the popular television show *Masquerade Party* on February 5, 1960.

Gypsy Lights Up the Sky. In March of 1960 Gypsy and Harvey Korman appeared in Moss Hart's play *Light Up the Sky*. The production was presented at Chicago's Drury Lane Theatre. The world-renowned author Studs Terkel was also in the cast, along with the actress Mary McCormick Best.

Gypsy's Curious Evening. After she quit stripping, Gypsy was always searching for another way to make a living. Of course she was receiving royalties from *Gypsy*, the two murder mysteries she wrote, and her autobiography. One of her most creative, and frustrating, projects was a documentary titled "A Curious Evening with Gypsy Rose Lee." This monumental task involved taking the hours and hours of film she had taken over the course of her life, and editing them down to a ninety minute film. Gypsy, the perfectionist, tinkered with this project for many years.

In *Gypsy & Me,* Erik Lee Preminger described his mother's work ethic, determination, and eventual resignation when she realized that the film was not going to generate any income.

On May 10, 1961, the film premiered at the Mayfair in New York City. The show was a flop — during its short run of two and a half weeks it lost seven thousand dollars.

Erik had better luck with the footage documenting Gypsy's life when he created *Gypsy Rose Lee's Home Movies* in 1998. The following excerpt is from a favorable review written by Heather Clisby for *Movie Magazine International*.

> With Preminger doing a live narration, "Gypsy Rose Lee's Home Movies" is a highly personal look at an extraordinary human being that lived and breathed show business.
>
> This patchwork of film — which includes both personal and public footage — is likely to make a Gypsy fan out of anyone ... she was a pioneer at bringing sexuality and laughs together and dared fans to hoot at their own hang-ups.

Gypsy Meets Mame. During the summer months of 1960 Gypsy Rose Lee, America's favorite stripper, met Mame Dennis Burnside, America's favorite aunt. When Patrick Dennis wrote his classic book *Auntie Mame* he unwittingly created a role that perfectly suited actresses who were of "a certain age," as they say. Gypsy and Mame was a match made in heaven. Coincidentally, the part of Mame was first played on Broadway by Rosalind Russell, the future Mama Rose.

Dennis' book was adapted for the stage by the successful team of Jerome Lawrence and Robert E. Lee. Rosalind Russell played the title character in the original Broadway production. The wonderful character actress Peggy Cass played the supporting role of Agnes Gooch.

Rosalind Russell and Peggy Cass received Tony Award nominations; only Cass won. Russell lost the well-deserved Tony to Margaret Leighton, who won for her performance in *Separate Tables.*

Gypsy was a smash hit in the role of Mame. She had a lot in common with Patrick Dennis' wildly eccentric, hilarious and lovable aunt. It was a case of an actress and a role melding together seamlessly. Gypsy toured in *Auntie Mame* to rave reviews.

Playing Mame Dennis requires a great amount of energy. The character is never off stage. The play spans approximately 15 to 20 years, the passage of time is shown with changes to Mame's New York town house, her wardrobe and her hair. This requires numerous quick-changes. Gypsy had a trained pro as her dresser, her son, Erik.

Mame changed her hair color at least once every 5 years. The play calls for eighteen costumes changes, and at least seven different wigs. In *Gypsy & Me: At Home and on the Road with Gypsy Rose Lee* Erik recalled how, by the end of the performance, Gypsy was a sweating, exhausted mess. Then, by chance, she hit upon something that endeared her to the audiences, a bit that garnered both hysterical laughter and applause.

During her curtain speech one evening Gypsy decided to show the audience just how bedraggled she was at the end of a performance. She did so by removing her wig. At first the audience was shocked to see Gypsy's own matted and frayed hair, but then they joined in as she laughed at herself. The old pro quickly realized that this endeared her to the audience. The removal of the wig after the final curtain became a regular routine. Gypsy would keep the bits that got a big laugh, and drop those that didn't.

Erik also makes an interesting observation. He felt that Gypsy was unaware of the reason why her curtain speech was so successful. She assumed the audience was responding to her jokes. Erik goes on to explain that it had nothing to do with what Gypsy said, the audience responded to the fact the Gypsy was being herself. Even after all of her years in show business Gypsy was unaware that audiences loved her all the more when she was relaxed and natural.

Gypsy on the Silver Screen. On September 21 of 1960, *The New York Times* reported that Warner Brothers bought the screen rights to *Gypsy.*

Visiting with Gypsy. Gypsy appeared on the front cover of the October 22, 1960, issue of *Star Weekly Magazine*, wearing a costume from her 1958 film, *Wind Across the Everglades.* In another photo inside the magazine she's dressed to the hilt for an evening at the theatre, her escort is Billy Rose. She towers over the diminutive theatre impresario. The following article was a highlight of the issue.

A Visit with Gypsy — Meet the best undressed woman of our time
By Richard Gehman
Whenever the name Gypsy Rose Lee is mentioned, nearly everybody I know — including prim old ladies and clergymen — thinks immediately and affectionately of the word "strip-tease." Although it has been several years since Gypsy has stripped, or seemed to strip (for it was always more promise than peeling) in public, she is still the acknowledged queen of them all. A musical made from her book, *Gypsy*, starring Ethel Merman (who plays not Gypsy but her mother, Madam Rose), opened in 1959 and is still running to capacity audiences on Broadway. Gypsy herself makes irregular appearances on the stage in the United States and Canada, traveling in a maroon Rolls-Royce which often has a trailer hitched behind it. She says that it is the only Rolls in the whole world with a trailer hitch, and that may be true. It is hard to tell when Gypsy is serious and when she is joking.

Whenever the name Gypsy Rose Lee is mentioned, nearly all her friends — including stock-brokers and beatniks, other old strippers, the cream of café society, fine artists and lord knows who all else — smile immediately, not with affection alone but with pure delight, for Gypsy is a character invented by Gypsy. She has sketched this character, cut her out and stitched her together out of scraps of satin and velvet, much like the patchwork quilts she makes while lying in grand repose in the Victorian bedroom of her magnificent 26-room house — with seven gold-fixtured baths and an elevator — in Manhattan's smart East Sixties. This house, which resounds continually with the calls of beasts and the chatter of guests, is a living part of the Lee legend. I paid a visit to it not long ago, and left with a scrambled impression of lights and colors and animals and showbiz talk and prepschool talk, like one of those quilts Gypsy is continually working on, which is the reason, dear reader, I want you to think of this not as a piece but a patchwork....

"Mother's allowed her dates to overlap, as usual," Erik said, opening the front door. Erik is 15, well-built, tall, and blond; later when we had a minute to talk, he confided he planned to be a mathematician. He was born just after Gypsy divorced her second husband, Alexander Kirkland, the actor-writer. Her first husband was a man named Arnold R. Mizzy, about whom not much is known except that he had the stamina to live with the legend for four years. Kirkland had less staying power: he was with her for two. The title goes to her third husband, a small, muscular painter with a marvelous gnarled and seamed face, Julio de Diego. They were together for seven years. Julio was a great cook.

Between husbands there was a long relationship with the late Mike Todd, who once gave her a fantastically expensive diamond bracelet, casually, as they were having supper at Sardi's, a restaurant populated mainly by theatrical people. Just as casually, she left it by her plate. Vincent Sardi retrieved it and gave it back to Todd. He sent it back to the shop the next day and used the money to buy her a huge painting, four feet wide by eight feet tall. "You ain't going to leave *that* in no restaurant," he said.

As Erik led the way over the Italian marble floors. I noted that the walls were jammed tight with pictures overhanging tufted velvet chairs and chaises, in rich deep reds and yellows; tassels and gewgaws were everywhere, with hunks of ironwork throwing shadows. Gypsy's mother had a deep acquisitive instinct. So has Gypsy. People who have been to both houses say that only that of Billy Rose, the showman and art collector, is more elegant, but it was done for him by a decorator, and Gypsy's was done for her by Gypsy. Billy Rose is her most frequent escort these days. There is nothing between them but old friendship, they both protest, and we might as well take their word for it. On a table by her bed is a silver-framed photograph of him. It is nearly life-size, since Rose is a tiny man. Mike Todd was small. So was Julio de Diego. Gypsy appears to love tiny things.

She greeted me from a low, backless sofa, where she sat like a gentlewoman of exquisite breeding receiving in her drawing-room. We had reached this room by crossing an open court, tiled underfoot, lush with ferns and new flowers, with a small solarium tucked off in a corner. From an open window above, two huge Afghan hounds peered down at us and barked angrily. From another window three Siamese cats nosed timidly around the drapes.

Gypsy extended a long, slender arm, slightly freckled. She was wearing a dark blue dress, cut low as though in deference to her public image, with a long full skirt; her sandals were made of tiny thongs, with high heels. A pair of glasses on a ribbon lay against her bosom. My first thought was one I'd had when I'd seen her before: Her protruding teeth get in the way of her speech. Her voice is out of the far country, somehow, comfortable, folksy, and almost school-marmy.

She introduced me to the two men who made up the other half of what Erik had called her overlapping appointments. They were from RCA-Victor Records, and this was business. Nearly everything Gypsy does is business. Just as her mother was able to transport her, her sister June and assorted other child performers and animals from city to city, when they were in vaudeville, by spending practically nothing, so Gypsy turns nearly everything she does to a profit. I have heard that she often sells paintings and antiques to people who admire them in her home.

I know, from talking to bookers of talent, that when she bargains for her services, she is as cold-blooded as a Las Vegas blackjack dealer.

The business at hand was listening to a tape unwinding on a portable recorder at Gypsy's feet. The tape sounded as though it had been made at a bull-fight. The men from the record company were listening hard, their faces shrewd with appraising.

"It's a recording of a party I had here the other night," Gypsy explained to me. "At my parties, everybody performs. We had Red Buttons that night and Ethel Smith — the organist, you know — and Jane Kean, the comedienne, and Fay Emerson ... oh, and my son's English teacher with his banjo. I thought it would make a marvelous record, and I called my agent, and he invited these gentlemen over and now we're going to make another record, just a record of one of the parties...."

"We'll need four microphones," one of the men said.

"Oh, dear," Gypsy said, "will we need that many? Won't it make the people self-conscious?"

"They're performers, Miss Lee," pointed out the other man.

"But that's the whole idea," Gypsy said, patiently. "We don't want them performing. We want them having fun at a party."

They rattled on and on, the three of them. I had a word or two with Erik who was acting as bartender, plate-passer and amused, detached observer. He looked at his mother with pleasant tolerance as she spoke. His is a most sophisticated teenager. Like his mother, Erik was all but raised backstage; as Gypsy's mother, who was known as Madame Rose, had done with her and her sister, June Havoc. Gypsy had taken Erik everywhere as she stripped across and up and down the country. The story goes that when she was working at the Carnival, a New York night club, a stooge in the audience was, on cue, to yell, "Take it off!" One night the stooge did not show up. Gypsy made her usual move, but the cry did not come forth. She made it again. Erik was watching from the wings, and he came to her rescue. "Take it off — mommy!" he cried, and brought down the house. I asked Erik if that story was true. "I can't remember doing that," he said, "but maybe I did. I never know, with mother what's fact and what's fiction." He grinned across at her.

"Erik darling, go out and get us some more of these cheese puffs, darling," said Gypsy, handing him a plate on which one cheese puff remained. "That's an angel, sweetheart." Erik trudged off, bearing the plate.

The discussion of the record-to-be went on. And on. I remembered that this desire to make a record of her ordinary daily life was no new idea of Gypsy's. Some years ago she organized a quilting bee and sewing circle that meets regularly at her house. Some of the communicants are Celeste Holm, Faye Emerson, Mrs. Nicky Blair (wife of the proprietor of Blair House, a restaurant), Hermione Gingold and, on occasion, Paulette Goddard. June Havoc attends when she has old clothes to sell to the members; Miss Hovac's sense of business is as highly developed as that of her sister. Once Gypsy decided to record the quilting bee and put it out as a record. She abandoned the idea, she later said, because all that came out on the tape was "Lend me your thimble, please" or "Pass the thread."

While I was recalling this, the discussion of the record finally came to an end. The men stood up and we all shook hands, they a good deal more enthusiastically than I, for it was my jaundiced view that they had gypped me out of my Gypsy interview, although not intentionally. Gypsy then quickly made up the lost time. She said that in the spring she had been in Chicago, playing *Light Up the Sky* at the Drury Lane theatre, and she had invited Paulette Goddard and June Havoc out there for company, and some burglars had got in and stolen all her jewels (which fortunately were insured) and all Paulette's furs and, I gathered, all the clothes June was preparing to sell, and wasn't that terrible, but there had been one funny thing connected with it, and did I want to hear it, and I got to hear whether I wanted to or not, for by now the words were coming torrentially, and she told the funny thing. Paulette had been concerned over what her husband, Erich Maria Remarque, the novelist, would think when he learned that she had been careless enough to let her furs get stolen. And when she told him he had not been very angry at all, but had said that in a way it was fine, because he never knew what to give Paulette for Christmas. "Oh, wasn't that a scream?" Gypsy asked, and I said: "Oh, yes, indeed, it was." Erik, who had returned, looked bored.

Gypsy asked me if I thought the party record would go over. I said I was no good at predictions.

"Oh," she said, "we probably won't make enough out of it to buy a clean tape." I thought otherwise: When Gypsy decides to promote something, it gets promoted as nothing in the world does. She is her own best press agent; the man she employs is superfluous. Somehow, a few months ago, she became associated with the distributor of a British film called *Jack the Ripper*. She wrote the liner note for the record of its sound track, and she was hostess at screenings of it. To the public, she gravely announced that it was a good film for children. Coming from anyone else, that would have aroused indignation. Coming from Gypsy, it was funny.

I asked her what else was new. Her hands fluttered every which way. She said "they" were after her to go on the road in *Show Boat.*

"The Capt. Henry part?" I asked, with unseemly facetiousness.

"Oh, you" she said, giving me a push. "Also," she said, "I might do *Auntie Mame* in summer stock, here and there. I love to travel. Oh, I so love the country. When mother was living and had her place in Nyack, we were up there every weekend, Erik and I, weren't we, darling?"

"Not *every* weekend," Erik corrected, with the teenager's characteristic passion for accuracy.

"Nearly every one," Gypsy said, reprovingly, but placidly.

A dog came waddling in. It was easily the most repulsive dog I ever have seen in my life: It was hairless, like a Chihuahua, of a nondescript brown-gray or grayish-brown color, with a gray tuft atop its foxy little skull. It looked as though it had been shaved all over, except for the tuft. "What in the name of heaven is that?" I asked my hostess.

"It is a Hairless Chinese Crested," she said solemnly.

"Come on," I said.

"It *is*," she said, drawing herself up, cuddling the dog against the spectacles on her breast. She kissed it. "He's an orphan. Very rare."

"There is no such dog," I said. "You're pulling my leg Gypsy."

"There is, too," she said, firmly. "He's in The Beast Book."

"*What* Beast Book?"

"*The Beast Book. The standard one. You know, The Beast Book.*"

That was that. She began to tell me about the rest of her animals, the two Afghan hounds and the three Siamese cats, and I remembered from Gypsy that her mother had been in the habit of traveling with various odd pets — monkeys, chickens, etc. The Hairless Chinese Crested was actually June's dog, she said; and the dog was just living there waiting for her to come home. "He's an orphan," Gypsy said, pityingly, "and has no place else to go."

I found it hard to find any sympathy in my heart for the orphan dog, and changed the subject to her work. *Gypsy* has been a best-seller, as had her two previous mystery novels, *Mother Finds a Body* and *The G-String Murders*. Her only disaster was a play, *The Naked Genius*, which was produced in 1943 by Mike Todd. After that she had written to *Variety*, the showbiz newspaper. "For the sake of the legitimate theatre, I have just tossed my typewriter out of the window." (She evidently had sent Erik to get it back; it is difficult to think of her throwing *anything* away, except possibly some out garments, and those only temporarily.)

"I'm haphazardly working on a couple of projects," she told me. "I'm doing a cookbook. And, maybe, a continuation of *Gypsy*. The book only takes me up to the burlesque period, you know — that was the mid–30s, and a lot has happened since then." The story of how Gypsy, born Louise Hovick, became a stripper, is told in the book. She became one because the indomitable Madam Rose told a manager she already was one. The fact that she seemed to regard it all as a joke was what set her apart. She was a legend even before she began consciously creating it, I reflected. I asked her if writing was all her own.

"Oh, my, yes," she said. "I'm not very good at punctuation, you know, but the words and the arrangement of them are all mine. Why, I wouldn't have it otherwise."

David Merrick, the producer of the musical *Gypsy*, had told me that he had conceived the idea after reading one fragment in a magazine two years before it was published as a book. I never know whether or not to believe anything Merrick says: in his own small way, he is the Barnum of our day. I asked Gypsy if this were true. She replied with a straight face, that it was. It may be. Then I asked her how it felt to be impersonated. She assured me that she loved Sandra Church, the young actress who plays her in the musical. "She's delightful," she said. "Of course, she isn't really me. June says she's what I would have liked to have been."

"What does that mean?" I asked.

"I don't know," Gypsy said. "I suppose she means she's sexier. I can't say I really ever *tried* to be sexy. June says she should have more vitality, too. Maybe she should. I *did* have vitality."

I said that I had read June's book and had liked it. She said she liked it, too. June's book, published a little after Gypsy's is called *Early Havoc*. Both books are a little frightening, if only because of the extreme energy of their characters. This energy was now beginning to tire me. Gypsy is a marathon talker, and she talked all the way to the door. I forget what about. We stood outside, looking at the houses of her neighbors — Jock Whitney, U.S. ambassador to the Court of St. James, lives nearby, and so do Mrs. Roosevelt and Tallulah Bankhead. We admire the flowers that the people have set out in boxes. I thought of the patchwork of this lady's life: Born in 1914, forced into show business by the domineering mother, dragged all over the country, a gangly girl who eventually became a kind of sex symbol, let alone a legend, and I marveled. Some distance this one has come, I thought as we said good-by. Some distance; some lady.

• 1961 •

Mame Visits San Juan. Gypsy returned to the role of Mame in January of 1961. She trouped to San Juan, Puerto Rico, to perform at the Tapia Theatre.

Gypsy ran into some unexpected trouble in Puerto Rico. The San Juan Drama Festivals were picketed. At one point the picketers entered the theatre, interrupting the show. Gypsy took it in stride, saying, "... no more bother than the usual opening night mishaps." Gypsy also observed, "If they had been actors they wouldn't have tried to spoil opening night for another actress." Actually, some of the crowd were actors. The fifty-some picketers were from the Puerto Rican Association of Actors and Technicians.

Mrs. Julio de Diego Travels. "Gypsy Rose Lee, who couldn't get a reservation at Claridge's in London, got in by using her old marriage name, Rose del [sic] Diego." This story ran in *The Salt Lake Tribune* on February 4, 1961.

Two days later, February 6, 1961, in *The Salt Lake Tribune* she was expressing her concern for her sister who was playing the part of the rejected girl in *Glass Menagerie*, Laura. Gypsy didn't think it was the right part for her younger sister. "No sister of mine would ever be rejected by those stage bums," she declared.

The Royal York Magazine. This 1961 publication was a monthly theater magazine from Canada. A stunning photo of Gypsy graces the cover. She looks regal in an elegant black dress, with a slit on one side that lets her show off her legs. There are feathers in her hair and white satin opera gloves, which goes up past her elbows.

Gypsy was making her premiere performance as Jenny Diver in Kurt Weill and Berthold Brecht's legendary show *The Threepenny Opera*. She appeared in a three week run of the show at the Royal Alexander Theatre in Toronto.

When this engagement ended the company went on the road, seeing fifteen cities in thirty weeks. At age forty-seven Gypsy was still the trouper, with wanderlust in her soul. However, the show was a flop. It closed in Toronto, and the tour was canceled.

This article is titled "Gypsy Premieres in *The Threepenny Opera*."

The combination of Gypsy Rose Lee and "Mack the Knife" is the big news of the fall touring season. Word that the famed ecdysiast would be playing the role of Jenny Diver in Kurt Weill and Berthold Brecht's "The Threepenny Opera"—the longest running musical in world theatrical history—has been called the most imaginative casting in years.

Toronto will be the first city to see Miss Lee play the role in a three-week engagement at the Royal Alexandra Theatre beginning September 19.

Gypsy Rose Lee is putting on her black lace dainties again for musical comedy instead of burlesque.

"I thought I'd packed 'em away forever," said the demure former queen of genteel strip-tease. "I'm getting some back from museums."

Producer Carmen Capalbo, who also directs, regards discovery of Gypsy's melodic ability as "absolutely fascinating."

"I'm supposed to sing like a tart and that's what I do," blandly replies the 47-year-old star who since 1942 has concentrated on such off-stage careers as writing, art and real estate.

"The nice thing about such a show is that you can use costumes like this," she continues, holding up sundry gossamers of glamour dishabille.

"I don't mind in the least," the star said. "I'll sing in whatever key you want. I'm like a drum—it doesn't have a key either."

Although Miss Lee has not been in a musical production since 1942 when she was the star of Mike Todd's "Star and Garter," she has not been idle. There have been national tours of her own variety show and most recently a national trek in a one-woman delight called "A Curious Evening with Gypsy Rose Lee." There have also been TV shows, movies, lecture tours, personal appearances in book stores to autograph copies of her best sellers.

When the producers approached her with the suggestion that she'd make a wonderful Jenny, Gypsy was still working out her one-woman show tour schedule. They didn't think that the fantastically energetic star would be daunted by the prospect of hitting the road again—and they were right.

"It's time I got into a real stage role again," she admitted. "Jenny is as *real* a role as has been offered me." With predictable practicality, she noted: "Besides, I was really dreading the idea of unpacking."

...

Until now, Gypsy hasn't been tempted by the musical stage. She is making the move now because the role of Jenny Diver is irresistible. "The Threepenny Opera" has its comic aspects, and it's also tough, bawdy, bitter and sardonic.

"Threepenny" is based on underworld characters—Jenny, a madam, and the notorious MacHeath, known to his pals—and now to every pop music fan in the world—as "Mack the Knife." Their adventures in London's Soho at the time of Queen Victoria's coronation create exciting theatre. "The Threepenny Opera" celebrates its seventh year at the Theatre de Lys in New York City this fall.

Ultimately the show did not go on the road. It closed after a handful of performances. As part of her pay Gypsy was given a golden harp.

Painting Gypsy. Gypsy had always dabbled in painting. So it was no surprise to read the headline "Art: Notable Collectors; Gypsy Rose Lee, Inge and Others in the Theatre Display Their Works Here" in the April 10, 1961, issue of *The New York Times*. "Inge" refers to William Inge, the playwright who wrote *Bus Stop, Dark at the Top of the Stairs, Come Back, Little Sheba* and *Picnic*. He won the Pulitzer Prize for *Picnic* and an Academy Award for *Splendor in the Grass*.

Mistress Gypsy. "International Ball Set for Washington Friday" was an article in the November 8, 1961, issue of *The New York Times*. The ball had been held on the previous night, November 7, 1961. The article began: "Gypsy Rose Lee, entertainer and author, will be mistress of ceremonies at the International Ball here Friday night." The ball was held to celebrate the tenth running of the "International at Laurel, MD."

CHAPTER NINE

Hooray for Hollywood

• 1962 •

Gypsy sees *Gypsy*. In 1962 Warner Brothers released the film version of the beloved Broadway musical, *Gypsy*. The film starred legendary movie star Rosalind Russell. Gypsy was portrayed by the stunning Natalie Wood, who brought a tender innocence to the adolescent Louise and titillating sensuality to the adult and newly christened Gypsy Rose Lee at the beginning of her burlesque career.

Ethel Merman wanted to re-create her role as the indomitable Mama Rose. However, Rosalind Russell's husband, Frederick Brisson, was a major power in Hollywood and a producer at Warner Brothers. Therefore, the coveted role of Rose went to Russell. While a brilliant comedian who had honed her skills in the screwball comedies of the 1930s and on Broadway as Auntie Mame, Rosalind Russell was not a singer. Mama Rose dominated the musical with a staggering seven numbers, including the challenging musical monologue that closes the show, "Rose's Turn."

Russell had brilliantly bamboozled her way through her performance in the Broadway musical *Wonderful Town*, winning her audiences over with charm and verve. However, wiser heads prevailed at Warner Brothers.

Rosalind Russell's singing was dubbed by Lisa Kirk, who filled in the spots where Russell floundered. A recent CD re-issue of the original motion picture soundtrack includes five outtakes of Russell's vocal attempts at "Some People," "Small World," "You'll Never Get Away from Me," "Everything's Coming Up Roses," and "Together Wherever We Go." The recordings are nearly impossible to listen to for those blessed with a pure sense of pitch.

Contrary to popular Hollywood lore, Natalie Wood's vocals are not dubbed (as they were in *Westside Story*). She turns in a rousing "If Mama Were Married" with future television star Ann Jillian. Her "Little Lamb" is wistful, fragile and full of shattered dreams. Wood's "Let Me Entertain You" does exactly what it is meant to do — showing the young Gypsy's confidence grow as she gains experience in her career as a professional stripper. She starts in a near whisper, then slowly increases her volume as she reaches one triumph after another as a star.

Bosley Crowther of *The New York Times* wrote a review when the film premiered at the Radio City Music Hall. The review "'Gypsy' Arrives: Role of Mother Played by Rosalind Russell" was published on November 2, 1962, and begins by mentioning Ethel Merman as that "tornado of a stage mother." He then goes on to say Rosalind Russell's Mama Rose amounts to "little more than a big wind...." He refers to her vocal chords as "rusty," and

says that Russell does not display the magnificence, or the magic, that Merman brought to the role. Evidently, like many fans of the Broadway musical and its star, Crowther hoped that Merman would recreate her stage role. He feels that the casting of Russell was the "misfortune" of the film.

He does, however, praise Russell for the light-hearted way she handles the scenes depicting the early days when Mama Rose, June, Louise and company were trouping in vaudeville. The critic also felt that Russell brought a warm tenderness to the song "Some People."

Her rendition of the powerful, do-or-die "Everything's Coming Up Roses" does not meet with Crowther's favor. He states that "Russell simply doesn't have it." Again he compares her to Merman, who interpreted the song in a confident and courageous manner.

The review goes on to praise the performances of Natalie Wood and Karl Malden, Natalie for her portrayal of a child who has been upstaged for all of her life by her favored sister. Wood is also congratulated on the "solidity and sparkle" she brings to the role of the grown-up Gypsy. Similarly, Crowther clearly sees Malden as the kind of actor he always was, "solid and agreeable...."

As usual, the critic singles out the strippers who teach the neophyte Gypsy the burlesque traditions and tricks of the trade with their riotous the show-stopping "You Gotta Get a Gimmick" number.

Leonard Maltin gave the film three stars and had this to say: "Entertaining ... bittersweet Broadway Musical about the ultimate stage mother, Mama Rose ... her daughters Baby June (Havoc) ... Gypsy Rose Lee. Can't lose with ... Stephen Sondheim–Jule Styne score."

Gypsy Wept. "Gypsy Rose Weeps" was the headline to the following article, which appeared in the *Winnipeg Free Press* on August 22, 1962.

> It doesn't shed its petals to music, but the new Gypsy Rose brought tears to the eyes of the former strip-tease queen.
>
> Gypsy Rose Lee wept demurely when the new 30-petal rose, named in her honor, was unveiled at a reception here.
>
> "I can't help it," she said, wiping away the tears. "After all only two or three others have roses named after them. And they were opera singers.
>
> "It's the first time for somebody in my business."
>
> Miss Lee's business once was confined to undressing artistically in public. Now she is a serious actress and author.
>
> She flew here from her California home for the debut of the new rose, a product of a Brampton, Ont., and nursery.
>
> The rose is said to retain its "deep velvety, romantic red" even in the winter. Fittingly, the stems are long and sturdy.
>
> Miss Lee was presented with a package of cellophane-wrapped roots to take to her home.
>
> "The bare roots," she exclaimed. "Play a little music and I'll take the cellophane off."

Gypsy on a Saturday Evening. An article in the September 15, 1962, *The Saturday Evening Post*, "Star Without an Image," about Joanne Woodward, describes how she perceived Gypsy.

Opposite: **Gypsy meets Gypsy. Natalie Wood and Gypsy meet on the set of the 1962 Warner Brothers production of *Gypsy*. The stunning Natalie Wood was perfectly cast in the part of Gypsy. She played the teenage tomboy Louise, nicknamed "Plug," and then emerged as the sensuous woman who was the "Queen of Burlesque"— Miss Gypsy Rose Lee.**

In 1963's *The Stripper* Gypsy played a mature burlesque star to Joanne Woodward's younger stripper.

Occasionally her [Woodward's] efforts to fit into other people's shoes have put her in a tight squeeze. One day, practicing the bumps and grinds for *A Woman in July* in front of her dressing room mirror, Joanne glanced up to see Gypsy Rose Lee, who has a small part in the film, looking on. "I stopped dead," Joanne recalls, "as if somebody had shot me. It was like strumming a guitar and finding Segovia looking over your shoulder."

A Woman in July was released as *The Stripper*.

United Gypsy. Gypsy was seen at the United Funds Campaign on October 11, 1962.

Natalie in Gypsy's Life. The November 2, 1962, issue of *Life* featured an article about Natalie Wood in the film *Gypsy*.

• 1963 •

Gypsy 90210. Earl Wilson mentioned Gypsy's new home in his "It Happened Last Night" column … "Gypsy Rose Lee now has a beautiful home in Beverly Hills — thanks to selling her New York town house for $175,000 (she paid $12,000 about 20 years ago)…." This bit of gossip appeared in newspapers nationwide on January 10, 1963.

Natalie Is Gypsy. The cover of the February 1963 issue of *Screen Stars* magazine had a full color portrait of Natalie Wood as Gypsy Rose Lee. The magazine included a short synopsis of the movie *Gypsy* and a small photo of Miss Wood tossing her corset aside during her strip.

Gypsy Eats Her Veggies. The recipe for Gypsy Vegetable Casserole appears in *Cooking as You Like It* by Jane Weeks Martin (Macmillan 1963). Gypsy is given the following brief biography:

> Star of stage, screen, radio and television, Gypsy Rose Lee literally grew up on the stage. She made her debut with her sister, actress June Hovac, in Seattle. This was the beginning of a new way of life for "Madame Rose's Dancing Daughters" and a lucrative spell in vaudeville. Then came burlesque, Minsky's Theatre and its Queen, Gypsy Rose Lee. As Miss Lee has often said, "Royalties are nice and all that, but shaking the beads brings the money quicker."

Gypsy Vegetable Casserole

½ cup olive oil	2 teaspoons salt
4 cups thinly sliced onions	½ teaspoon white pepper
4 large tomatoes, thinly sliced	2 cloves garlic, minced
4 cups thinly sliced potatoes	⅓ cup minced parsley

Pour ⅓ cup oil into a casserole. Spread half the onions on the bottom, then half the tomatoes and half the potatoes, sprinkling each layer with salt, pepper, garlic, and parsley. Repeat layers and pour the remaining oil on top. Cover and bake in a 325 degree oven 1 hour. Serve as an accompaniment to broiled or roast meat. Serves 6–8.

Fractured Gypsy. On September 29, 1963, Gypsy was interviewed on popular TV show *Fractured Flickers* by host Hans Conried.

Gypsy Spots a Baldy. Gypsy always had a thing for bald men. During her burlesque days at Minsky's, and other burlesque theatres, she used to go down into the audience whenever she saw a bald gentleman. It is probably one of the reasons she chose Otto Preminger to father her only child. Things hadn't changed by 1963. On December 8, 1963, *The Press-Courier* ran this humorous tidbit: "So what happened when Gypsy Rose Lee appeared the other night on the Les Crane show over at ABC? She spotted a baldy in the front row. 'It's like old times at Minsky's,' she crackled. 'I never forget a bald head.'"

• 1964 •

The Steve Allen Show. Gypsy begins 1964 with an appearance on *The Steve Allen Show*. The show was broadcast on January 12, 1964.

Darling, You Look Marvelous! Journalist Hal Humphrey wrote a column called "TV Viewing." His January 5, 1963, entry featured an interview with Gene Reynolds, who had been a child star. He played Jimmy Stewart as a boy in the 1938 picture *Of Human Hearts*. Reynolds, currently enjoying success as the director of the television hit *My Three Sons*, reflected on things he had heard from other child stars, such as, "I believe it was either June Havoc or her sister, Gypsy Rose Lee, who tells of the time their mother rushed to her daughter after a performance and cried, 'Oh, darling you were marvelous and you looked fine — nobody would suspect you had a hundred-and-five temperature.'"

Back to Burlesque? On February 22, 1964, columnist Earl Wilson wrote that a "Broadway producer is trying to coax Gypsy Rose Lee to star in a burlesque show to nab the World's Fair trade...."

Gypsy and the New Flying Wallendas. Hedda Hopper reported on the rough gang Gypsy was palling around with in her column on February 25, 1964:

> Gypsy Rose Lee, Bette Davis, Imogene Coca and Leonard Sillman have been seeing so much of each other somebody tagged them the mouse pack.
>
> "We're more like leftover vaudevillians," said Gyp. "We got to calling ourselves the New Flying Wallendas and decided we'd go to our next party as acrobats."
>
> They all showed up at Western Costumes, Inc., for fittings, reported to Bette's house to rehearse their entrance, and went together to Teddy Lynch Gaston's party.
>
> "We rented the suits for a week, just in case we're invited out again," Gypsy said.

Gypsy, Ethel and Ernest. In her autobiography Ethel Merman has a chapter about her marriage to Ernest Borgnine. That chapter consists of one blank page. The union was very short-lived, and one of the most infamous showbiz marriages. Gypsy, along with Barbara Nichols and George Jessel, was in attendance when the couple celebrated their newly wed bliss. Columnist Earl Wilson wrote this on July 2, 1964:

> "Doesn't Ethel look happy?" said Barbara Nichols ... then over sailed Gypsy Rose Lee, slim and beautifully coiffed, announcing she'd just have a soft drink. She's a new confirmed Californian who rises at 5 A.M. to enjoy the morning, and write. She goes to bed at 9 P.M.
>
> "We gave Ethel a shower," she said, "The big question was who had glasses so we could read the cards," she laughed.
>
> SUDDENLY GYPSY hopped on Ernie Borgnine's lap for a picture.
>
> "It's all right, Ethel, because he's sort of my father, you know," Gypsy said, referring to Ethel having played her mother in "Gypsy."

Gypsy Debates Woody. Gypsy was a frequent guest on Steve Allen's show. On the episode airing on July 13, 1964, Gypsy and comedian Woody Greene took sides in "a humorous debate on Las Vegas 'nudie' shows."

Television Rolls On. Gypsy was mentioned many, many times by Earl Wilson. Her name was dropped again in his July 14, 1964, "It Happened Last Night" column.

> Bill Harrah, the Reno and Lake Tahoe multimillionaire, was sending the B.W. [Earl Wilson always referred to his wife as the B.W., short for Beautiful Wife] and me to his private plane in a chauffeured Rolls.
>
> "Is there an ashtray around anywhere?" the B.W. said.
>
> "I don't see any," I said. "Wait. What is this little knob here?"
>
> I pulled the little knob. Out came a Sony TV set. We watched TV through the desert. Desert! I saw a sign that said: "Cocktail Party Ice Cubes."
>
> I was telling Gypsy Rose Lee about the Rolls Royce TV set in Los Angeles, forgetting that she had a Rolls.
>
> "Doesn't everybody have a TV set in their Rolls?" she asked. "I have ... and also a stereo."

Gypsy's Game. Gypsy was much in demand for television game shows. On August 2, 1964, she joined a rather unusual lot for a show called *The Celebrity Game*. Aside from Gypsy, the celebrities on this telecast included Gary Crosby, Dennis Day, Hedda Hopper, George Jessell, Paul Lynde, Della Reese, Ann Sothern and Mickey Rooney. The game consisted of contestants querying the celebrity panel for their opinions on everything from the benefits of old-fashioned spanking, to whether the wife or the husband changes more after marriage, to whether a "computing machine" could mate people successfully. This type of gabfest was perfect for quick-with-a-quip Gypsy.

Smile! You're on Gypsy's Camera. This tidbit appeared in Hedda Hopper's column on August 11, 1964: "June Havoc is here visiting sister Gypsy Rose Lee. The girls are mad about home movies and spent last Sunday shooting Lucille Ball and her family. Next day they discovered they had no film in their cameras, so they'll have to drag out their cables and lights and do it all over again."

TV Rolls on Again. On August 14, 1964, Gypsy visited *The Steve Allen Show* again. This time she brought along a small surprise for Steve ... her Rolls Royce!

Gypsy was in Hedda's column again on September 11, 1964. This time she was photographing other stars. Hedda wrote:

> Gypsy Rose Lee is still photographing stars for footage she'll use on Mike Douglas' show in October.
>
> She got Polly Bergen in a bath towel; Hank Fonda in a parking lot ("I had him blocked with my car"); and Walter Slezak.
>
> She's out to get her neighbor, Rock Hudson.
>
> "When I show people his house they fall down in my driveway. I want a shot of him standing on his terrace looking at my place through binoculars. His career needs a slight stimulant, and this should do it."
>
> She invited me over to see her new Cinerama-type portrait: "It's like wallpaper. There I am with all my dogs, birds and cats.

Gypsy's School for Strippers. The September 12, 1964, issue of *TV Guide* included a review of the television show *Burke's Law* in a brief article bearing the title "Gypsy's Rose Lee's School for Strippers. Short course: How to Undress Gracefully in Front of Millions. The instructor: Gypsy Rose Lee."

> Whatever *Burke's Law* may lack in realistic, penetrating drama, it makes up for in its fun — including famous personalities who stroll through so-called "cameo" parts. It was thus inevitable that Gypsy Rose Lee would turn up — she will be seen in an episode, scheduled for September 23, titled "Who Killed Vaudeville?" In it Gypsy portrays a Miss Cathcart, who operates a school for young ladies who intend to become strippers. When the scene was filmed, the girls drew so many onlookers — including producer Aaron Spelling and star Gene Barry — that Gypsy looked around and wondered aloud: "Who's watching the front gate?"

Prior to the broadcast of *Burke's Law* ABC sent out a press release dated September 15, 1964, which read:

> *DON'T MEAN A THING IF SHE AIN'T GOT THAT ZING*
>
> She observes that the modern strippers are more beautiful that those she worked with in her "heyday." However, she feels that they are missing an important element. That element was "zing." In other words, they were lacking "style."
>
> She also feels that the strippers in the 1960's didn't work as hard as those in what she refers to as burlesque's "glorious age." This is due in part to the fact that the gowns worn by the current exotic dancers were easier to take off (they were what designers referred to as breakaway costumes). Next, Gypsy pointed out that the new acts lacked a theme. Strippers no longer dressed as a character, such as a French maid, a young bride or an exotic animal.

She ends this press release saying that she enjoyed working with Gene Barry, the star of *Burke's Law*. She sums up working in television as follows: "'It seems like such a — excuse the expression — grind. And, besides,'" she added with a wink, "'I'm afraid of overexposure.'"

Gypsy Obeys the Law. *Burke's Law* (Episode 34 Season 2). Gypsy plays Miss Bumpsy Cathcart in the poplar show starring Gene Barry. Gypsy's scene is described as follows:

> A maid escorts Burke to a classroom at a posh estate where Miss Cathcart is training aspiring ecdysiasts to the tune of the Minuet in G. She tells Burke, as she escorts him away, that burlesque is a true art form and the girls have a lot of work to do as graduation is near, G-strings to sequin and zippers to oil. When he tells her he's a policeman, she assures him that all her licenses are in order. He tells her of Rags' murder and the terms of the will (which makes her laugh — the best laugh she ever got from Rags). Miss Cathcart says Rags' death couldn't have happened to a nicer fella. She was the first girl Rags ever used in his act. She says she made him a star. He was ambitious and really stingy. She tells Burke Rags' probably "took it with him." He saw her the day he died; he didn't like the girl she had sent him for the act — probably because the girl wanted to get paid. Miss Cathcart says everyone wanted Rags dead. She then propositions Burke. When he declines, she tells him to see Gus Watt, bartender at the Golden Garter, because Rags had been blackmailing him for years. Miss Cathcart escorts Burke to the door, telling him she used to be called "Bumpsy." Just then a shoulder strap slips provocatively.

Gypsy the Grande Dame. On July 4, 1964, Gene Barry filled in for vacationing journalist Joseph Finnigan, writing Finnigan's Hollywood column. Barry wrote of the success in having prominent co-stars cast in minor roles on *Burke's Law*. The actor remembered his work with Gypsy as follows:

> … with Gypsy Rose Lee as the operator of a school for strippers. You might say Gypsy was type-cast. True. But we laced her part with an implausible embellishment. In "Grande Dame" manner, she routinely had the girls shedding clothing to the "Minuet in G!"

Gypsy's a Celebrity Again. On July 11, 1964, Gypsy returned to (Carl Reiner's) *The Celebrity Game*. The other stars surrounding her included Paul Lynde, Gisele MacKenzie, Julie Newmar, Barry Sullivan, and one-time husband and wife Howard Duff and Ida Lupino.

Gisele in *Gypsy*. "'Gypsy's' Staging Will Draw Notable Guest" was the headline that ran in *The Valley News* on September 13, 1964. The Valley Music Theatre was producing *Gypsy* with Gisele MacKenzie as the "fearless" Mama Rose.

The notable guest was none other than Gypsy. She would be seeing the show for the first time since opening night on Broadway. The article quotes a young Erik Lee Preminger as saying, "I wish I could have been in the act with you, but I guess your mother couldn't have found a place for me. I can't sing or dance or do anything." To which Gypsy responded by saying that she too had no singing or dancing abilities.

After this exchange, Gypsy thought to herself, "Mother had been many things, but never 'nice.' Not exactly. Charming, perhaps, and courageous, resourceful and ambitious, but nice…." Mama Rose called herself a "… jungle mother." Gypsy went on to observe that vaudeville was Rose's jungle. She also remembered her mother saying, "God will protect us," but just to be sure she warned her daughters to, "… carry a heavy club."

Gypsy and the Golden Harp. The queen of Hollywood gossip, Hedda Hopper, had a regular column in *Chicago Tribune's Sunday Magazine*. Her article "The Girl with the Big Golden Harp," which follows, ran in the September 27, 1964, issue, and was accompanied by a nice black and white photo of Gypsy standing in the living room of her Beverly Hills home, next to her is the golden harp.

> Gypsy Rose Lee, world's most famous ecdysiast, raised the strip tease to such an art, but she never really took 'em off. She's now absorbed in an era of domesticity oddly alien to her glam-

our years. Gypsy keeps all her clothes on, while our movie actresses are taking them off. "What will happen now that civilians have taken over?" I asked Gypsy.

"You know the old saying," she laughed, "nobody can sell it when amateurs are giving it away. It will never become a fad; too few women are equipped. Most of the girls stripping in films are actresses, and there's a reason for it. They don't just get up in front of the camera and take their clothes off pointlessly. It'll be a terrible day when men get tired of naked woman, but probably the wives and sweethearts will get sick of it on the screen and won't take their men to movies. Men rarely go alone to the theatre. Tickets are sold to people who go together, and most of the time it's the woman who wants to see the show."

"Men used to go see Mae West, and then write her obscene letters," I protested.

Gypsy shrugged: "A detective on the Brooklyn vice squad once told me that after a Shirley Temple picture, the crimes against children went up 82 per cent. I don't think Mae West, or Natalie Wood in 'Gypsy,' incited depraved minds. I think burlesque served a good purpose. It was a refuge for kids who wanted to disobey their parents and went where they could scream and yell and feel they were being very naughty. Economically you can't bring burlesque back. They can't even afford a chorus line except in a place like Las Vegas."

Gypsy always had a domestic streak. In her heyday, it was a 27-room townhouse in Manhattan, complete with Rolls Royce and chauffeur. Today she lives in a multi-curved hilltop mansion of highly imaginative architecture. The house has a 180 degree view of Beverly Hills on one side, and Hollywood and Los Angeles on the other. When you ring at the wrought iron gates, Gypsy comes down the garden path to let you in. There's a pool on the terrace, and the fruiting lemon and orange trees which flank it were planted by Gypsy herself. You follow the curving pool past a solarium glimpsing tropical plants thru the glass.

Gypsy had her dressmaker working when I arrived. The 14-foot round dining room table, which could seat King Arthur and his knights, was piled high with materials.

"She'll be here a week," Gypsy said, "and I've laid out enough to keep her busy."

She had that table in her New York house. It was taken down to be moved out here, and an expert accompanied it to put it back together again.

The house is filled with furniture and objets d'art from all over the world. Gypsy has them assembled without any regard to period, and everywhere there are mementoes of her professional years. Her New York bedroom has been faithfully recreated even to the curtains and draperies. The bath has ornate green and gold designs done by an artist she imported from New York. There's a suite, too, for sister June.

"June has five Malibu houses," Gypsy said. "But she stays with me when she comes out."

There is a large circular chamber lined with books on the third story. It has a view to the sea, and will eventually become her work room, as she's still writing. A separate suite downstairs with its own entrance from the garden is for her son, Erik, who is now away.

Gourmet cooking is one of Gypsy's hobbies. Her kitchen is specially designed to incorporate all modern conveniences. She has one room in which to store her large movie film collection. Next to it is a room devoted to the burlesque days — posters, pictures, programs, photos of old friends, including Mike Todd.

She maintains the house with a live-in couple. "Ed does the gardening, and Nellie takes care of my laundry. They have their own suite with a view," Gypsy told me.

She found this home when a friend casually mentioned there was an old house on a hill above Beverly for sale, adding, "It looks like you, Gypsy."

"I called the real estate agent," Gypsy said, "and he said, 'Sorry, we only show it until 4, it's past that now.' So, I asked the name of the bank and went up to look it over. Next morning I showed up at the bank and learned they were closing out two bids that afternoon. They wouldn't tell me what others had bid so I had to go on intuition. It turned out my bid was $2,000 higher than anyone else. The house had had only one owner and it was built in the early 30s."

I was curious about the big gold harp in Gypsy's living room. When I asked her if she played it, she laughed, "No. I took it once in lieu of salary when I was with a show on the road."

Gypsy's home is filled with antiques she collected over the years while haunting Third Avenue shops. "I learned to be cagey while searching for antiques," she said. "When haggling became too intense over something I really wanted, I'd feign an ulcer attack. They'd feel sorry for me and let me have it. That ulcer came in mighty handy, and helped to furnish a lot of beauty for my home."

Gypsy Unveiled. In addition to the Hedda's September 27, 1964, *Tribune* article, Gypsy was also in reporter Mike Connolly's column on the same day. Connelly wrote, "Gypsy Rose Lee tossed a party at her place in Malibu to unveil a new oil painting of her fully clothed self."

• 1965 •

Gypsy the Trader. On April 6, 1965, Gypsy was spotted in the famous San Francisco eatery Trader Joe's.

The Windy City Loves Gypsy. A joyous Gypsy Rose Lee is on the cover of *Chicago Tribune TV Week* (August 14 — 20, 1965). The color photograph shows a laughing Gypsy, swinging her beads. The headline reads "Stripper Turns Yakker: Gypsy Rose Lee Has Daily TV Show," and the inside article, "Meet the 'New' Gypsy Rose Lee — She's a TV Yakker Now," follows.

On our cover this week, we present the "new" Gypsy Rose Lee — the head-and-shoulders version.

This attractive lady, who started her climb to stardom on the burlesque runways of New York City, is now featured in a 30-minute week-day talkfest at 12:30 on ABC-TV (channel 7) called "Gypsy." The chatter as uninhibited as the star herself, and that's considerable.

At Tribune Tower, where the cover photograph was taken by Earl Gustie, Miss Lee talked of many things, all of them interesting and most of them funny.

One subject was her show — "We yak about this and that, and people seem to like it. Phyllis Diller was with me on several programs, and she is totally wonderful. One minute she'd be talking, with love in her voice, about her daughter, and the next she was complaining about her contact lenses — she's forever dropping them into the plumbing."

Gypsy's show is produced by the ABC-owned television station in San Francisco. Which means that she commutes by air several times a week from her Beverly Hills home, lugging costumes, make-up, et cetera, in a two-wheeled folding shopping cart.

"I got it with trading stamps," she said. "It has it all over suitcases. I even carry a coffee-maker and cups."

Gypsy Stars and Strips. The September 19, 1965, issue of *Stars and Stripes* featured the article "GI Son Greets Gypsy Rose Lee," excerpts below, by Ralph Bennington.

MUNICH (S&S) — Gypsy Rose Lee is just as affable, bouncy, flamboyant, and, in her own laughing words, big-mouthed as ever.

The still-youthful, 51-year-old burlesque queen, author and TV and movie star hit Munich with a splash, promptly starred in a Hollywood-style plane "departure," then offered spicy quotes on a wide variety of subjects.

Her only son, Pfc. Erik Kirkland, stationed with the 24th Inf. Div. in Augsburg, Germany, met her at planeside along with Army and official observers and the press. With cameras grinding and clicking, she made a number of trips up the plane ramp and had plenty of affection for the 20-year-old son she hasn't seen in a year.

"Prop" Luggage

Miss Lee's famous furs and costumes came separately, but this didn't stop the show. She climbed aboard a nearby luggage tractor, with assistance from her son, and hoisted her skirt several inches to display a still curvy leg. Her apparel was a Technicolor delight — bright lavender for shoes to wraparound turban. Her rings and bracelets bore amethysts.

While scrambling to keep up with cameramen — she wanted movie shots of her own for publicity purposes — Miss Lee ignored the cart of personal belongings. "I don't have any money and worry only about my knitting," she said.

After admonishing a photographer for a long series of pictures by stating "Don't take more pictures ... It's hard work holding my stomach in and my chin up," Miss Lee explained that she made her unofficial stage debut at the age of three, "in my grandpa's cabin by singing 'Hard-Boiled Rose.'"

The seasoned star still created an endearing and hectic scene just by showing up. Gypsy had the crowd in Munich right in the palm of her hand. She was the star, and the focus of her arrival. She played it for all she was worth.

Gypsy in the Mirror. In October 1965 Gypsy appeared in the popular *TV Radio Mirror* magazine.

Gypsy and Leonard. Gypsy attended a party hosted by producer Leonard Sillman on November 7, 1965. "Leonard Sillman produced the legendary Broadway revues *New Faces,* which introduced talents like Eartha Kitt, Carol Burnett and Imogene Coca."

CHAPTER TEN

Visiting with Gypsy

• 1966 •

Heads Up! On January 5, 1966, reporter Mike Connolly included this tidbit in his "Notes from Hollywood" column: "Gypsy Rose Lee sat for one of photographer John Engstead's glamour sessions in stretch pants so tight you can tell if the dime in her side pocket is heads or tails...."

Gypsy's Chit-Chat. On January 23, 1966, *The New York Times* announced, "GYPSY ROSE LEE, an author, art collector and erstwhile ecdysiast, picked up another television station last week for her syndicated chit-chat show."

Gypsy in *Time*. The January 24, 1966, issue of *Time* featured Truman Capote on the cover. Capote was then at the peak of his career, having just released his masterpiece, *In Cold Blood*. Inside the issue a photo of Gypsy accompanied an article about one of her favorite topics, television censorship, entitled "Time of the Bloop":

> On Gypsy Rose Lee's syndicated talk show, Gypsy mentioned the LeRoi Jones play "The Toilet." Or, rather, tried to mention it. As it came out, "Jones has written "*The Bloop*." "Darling," said Miss Lee, "it was ridiculous."

Look at Gypsy. In the February 1966 issue of *Look* featured an article about the success of Gypsy's talk show, which was filmed in San Francisco at ABC Channel 7, and eventually broadcast as far away as Australia. The following excerpts highlight her hard-won business savvy.

> [L]ast April, the peace of America's dowager stripper was interrupted again, when she was hauled back to work as hostess of a TV gabfest called simply, Gypsy Rose Lee, a runaway that can now be seen, heard and not quite believed, nationwide.
> Suddenly, on your early morning TV, there's that boisterous good-humored Gypsy, looking great, even though she's been up since 4:30. She's winking and mugging and leering at you in conversation that makes her seem very confidential, and then she's chattering away with discoveries like: a beauty expert who does facials with tomatoes, a widow who got rich dreaming up a sponge-plastic dress form, Sally Rand on needlepoint, a girl who makes her own shoes, and even Mrs. Edward G. Robinson, who invented a rubber band that stretches four ways. Gypsy, the homebody, thinks her show, syndicated by Seven Arts, is a hit because viewers are made to feel they, too, can go out and invent a gadget or cook with flowers ("but of course they can't, darling").
> The show's launching pad is her slightly disreputable past, and Gypsy does what's expected

of her, like an occasional, "I have a kaffeeklatch show that strips away the bare facts," accompanied by that bad leer. ... But she's annoyed by being "blipped" so often by the show's censor when she says "anything anatomical.... Is there *another* word for pelvis?" ... Her chief peeve, though, is that the men producers of her show don't always understand that women are interested in other women's cooking, clothes and kids. "My only disastrous shows have been with men guests," she says. "Like show business types who moan about their budgets."

The guests she likes most are those who excite her gadget-gimmick-gourmet passions. She thinks that most men in charge of TV programming today have never really known the reactions of a live audience.... Behind the scenes, she is tough, loud and nervous in her demands for perfection. "There's no time for hurt feelings. After all, we're not going out dancing."

Gypsy doesn't always win in the selection of her guests, but she fights a good fight. She surprised her producers by refusing to invite a onetime madam, now an acceptable matron, along with a nightclub owner employing topless waitresses. "I spent a lifetime kidding nudity," she says, "but there's no humor there for me. I'd rather invite one of the whores, or one of the waitresses, instead. I can't relate to people who profit from human misery. I deplore a man who exploits nude waitresses, even though he is usually considered a respectable citizen. The waitress, with her minimum wage and limited tips, is the one who's always criticized. I would like to advise her, that she's misguided, if this is her idea of breaking into show business.

Gypsy's Celebrity Guests. The guest list for Gypsy's show reads like a veritable Who's Who of famous film and stage actors, artists, authors, chefs, comedians, costume designers and anyone else who could match wits with the quick witted hostess, including Jack Albertson, Steven Allen, Hermione Baddeley, Kaye Ballard, Ernest Borgnine, Victor Buono, Sid Caesar, Pat Carroll, Imogene Coca, Dick Clark, Bob Crane, Richard Deacon, Jimmy Dean, Gloria De Haven, Phyllis Diller, Nanette Fabray, Eddie Fisher, Annette Funicello, Beverly Garland, Judy Garland, Tammy Grimes, June Havoc (Gypsy's sister), Edith Head, Celeste Holm, Robert Horton, Tab Hunter, Van Johnson, Carolyn Jones, Laine Kazan, Stubby Kaye, Eartha Kitt, Sybil Leek, Liberace, Robert Q. Lewis, Jane Meadows, Ethel Merman, Haley Mills, Agnes Moorehead, Charlotte Rae, Don Rickles, Colonel Harland Sanders of Kentucky Fried Chicken fame, The Smothers Brothers, Jacqueline Susann, Mel Torme, Andy Warhol, Jane Wyman and Cornel Wilde.

A Russian Gypsy. Gypsy arrived in Moscow in May of 1966.

Gypsy Meets Phyllis. Gypsy appeared three times during the first season of *The Pruitts of Southampton*, a sitcom starring Phyllis Diller. The title was changed to *The Phyllis Diller Show* for the second and final season.

Gypsy played the role of Regina Wentworth in "Phyllis, the Milkmaid," episode 2, which aired on September 13, 1966. She was on hand again in "Phyllis Goes Commercial," episode 8, aired on October 25, 1966.

To promote *The Pruitts of Southampton*, and Gypsy's appearance on the show, ABC's press release hailed Gypsy as a "legend in the creative arts...." As usual, her success in numerous areas of the performing arts world were cataloged, she was painter and art collector, lecturer and panelist, a writer of novels and plays.

The write up of her film career put emphasis on some of her well-known co-stars like Fred Allen, Alice Faye, and Tony Martin. *Stage Door Canteen* and *Belle of the Yukon* were listed as two films in which she starred using the name Gypsy Rose Lee. Next came the obligatory rundown of her literary triumphs: the best-selling mystery *The G-String Murders*, and its follow-up *Mother Finds a Body*. Her play *(The) Naked Genius* was on the list, the fact that it was a flop was not mentioned. The path of *Gypsy* from best-seller to "smash hit musical comedy" to film was there too.

Gypsy's numerous guest appearances on a wide variety of shows, such as Jack Paar's talk show, were highlighted, and her own talk show, which was on the air at the time, was plugged as an "internationally syndicated ... femme forum...."

Current info on items such as Erik being in the U.S. Army (and stationed in Germany) and Gypsy's interest in knitting, her animals and residence, the "17-room Beverly Hills estate, Naked Acres," brought her fans up-to-date.

Phyllis Remembers Gypsy. In a telephone interview conducted by the author on August 20, 2008, a very lovable and gracious Phyllis Diller shared these memories of her friend, Gypsy:

> Gypsy was booked as a guest star on my show *The Pruitts of Southampton*. She played the role of my neighbor, Regina Wentworth. It was a running part, in other words she made several appearances. She was very rich, and I was broke pretending to be rich. Every time she showed up she was wearing jodhpurs, which indicated that her character had horses. Gypsy was volatile and very bright. She loved people, and they loved her.
>
> Her mother chose her over her sister, June, to be the breadwinner of the family. Her mother, Rose, would have liked to have been the star. She invented Gypsy. It was definitely a case of a woman living through her daughter.
>
> Gypsy and I became close friends because we had a lot in common. She really *lived* her life. She made sure every moment of it was *interesting*. For example, when I visited her home she had 85 birds flying around her kitchen. They were *loose*, baby! ... and you can quote me on that.
>
> She grew up in hotel rooms. Her mother made all of their clothes, including those coats that were made from the hotel blankets. Gypsy made all of her costumes as well; even the gloves that she stripped off. She liked to make homemade gifts. In fact, she made me a pair of those gloves and a matching scarf in very bright colors. They're in my archives.
>
> Of course you know she had that affair with who was it? Alfred Hitchcock? No, no ... Otto Preminger. They had a son.
>
> She had her own TV show broadcast out of San Francisco. I was on the show. She had this wonderful director and producer, Marty Pasetta. She could be difficult, and for a man to tell her what to do, forget it. One day he'd had it and he quit. He quit on the air! It was a big scene. He went on to Hollywood and eventually won eight Oscars.
>
> Of course she always had that Rolls Royce, you know. She would put some things in a shopping bag and off she went!
>
> One funny moment that comes to mind is when she was sitting, waiting to get her hair and make-up done. The hair-dresser approached her, and she let out a huge scream! He asked her, "What's wrong? I haven't hurt you." She replied, "No, but you're going too!"

Gypsy and 007. In November of 1966 Gypsy travels to Tokyo. She interviewed Mr. Connery, Sean Connery, who was promoting the new Bond movie *You Only Live Twice*.

Gypsy's Last Visit to Southampton. Gypsy played Regina one last time in "Phyllis, the Dressmaker." This was episode 12, which was aired on November 29, 1966.

The Trouble with Angels. Rosalind Russell appeared as Mother Superior in this Haley Mills movie. Mills was the quintessential teenager in early 1960s movies, including the wildly popular *The Parent Trap*. The film had a great cast of character actresses including Binnie Barnes, Mary Wickes, Camilla Sparv and the one-and-only Gypsy Rose Lee.

In the 1966 film *The Trouble with Angels* Gypsy portrayed the free-thinking dance instructor, Mrs. Mabel Dowling Phipps.

Film critic Leonard Maltin gives this romp two and a half stars. He sums it up as follows: "Cutesy study of ... convent school, with students Mills and Harding driving mother superior Russell to distraction. Episodic ... touching comedy."

Taking It Off on TV. An article about Gypsy's new talk show appeared in the December 11, 1966, issue of *TV Guide*.

Here are a few excerpts from "The story of *GYPSY ROSE LEE*, from 'TAKE IT OFF' to 'KEEP THEM TALKING'" by Charles E. Alverson:

> … [O]ne day last April, an agent called. Would Miss Lee be interested in summer stock? No, she wouldn't, Miss Lee replied. Then how about doing a morning conversation TV show from San Francisco? Why not? said Miss Lee, and the next thing she knew she was winging north to talk to David Sacks, ABC vice president and general manager of KGO-TV.
>
> And how has Miss Lee made the transition from "Take It Off!" to "Keep Them Talking"? Not without certain problems.
>
> "We had an awful time with Gypsy at first," says Marty Pasetta, director and executive producer of the show.
>
> "She was so used to being a guest that she'd rattle away for the whole show instead of drawing her guests into the into the conversation. But lately she's become fantastic at getting the best out of the celebrities who visit her."

Still glamorous at fifty-six, this is how Gypsy appeared on her popular television talk show *Gypsy Rose Lee*. The postcard was used to promote the show. This collector's item bears Gypsy's signature. 1967.

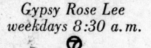

Gypsy Rose Lee
weekdays 8:30 a.m.

Dear Valerie,
Thank you for your letter and the clippings.
I have sent your letter on to Nanette - thought she might enjoy it also.
Hope you'll continue to enjoy the show.

Valerie Cox
58 E. Barrymore
Stockton, Calif.
95204

"Fantastic" is a bit of an exaggeration. There are few signs that Miss Lee has given up running her guests off the conversational road. On a recent show she was nattering away with a flock of male stars doing the heavy listening, when one of them, Jimmy Stewart, suddenly fell out of his chair sideways onto the floor. Miss Lee stopped talking long enough to ask: "What happened?" "Sorry," Stewart said, "I was just trying to get a word in edgewise."

… But so far Miss Lee may rest easy. Her fans range from John Wayne (who says, "Like eavesdropping on a ladies' powder room") to the secretary of a chapter of the Hell's Angels motorcycle club, a band of California bike riders often in the headlines. Says he, "You kind of hate her at first because she talks so much, but after a few times you really get hooked."

Gypsy in Europe. Gypsy traveled throughout Russia and Europe in August of 1967.

• 1968 •

Gypsy Squared I. During 1968 Gypsy made a total of fifteen guest appearances on the popular game show *The Hollywood Squares*. The show was hosted by Peter Marshall. It had several regulars among its cast, including Wally Cox, Cliff Marquette (as Charlie Weaver), Rose Marie and everybody's favorite center square Paul Lynde. Aside from Gypsy other frequent guest stars were Gypsy's friends Kaye Ballard, and Nanette Fabray. Other stars like Charo, George Gobel, Charles Nelson Reilly, and Vincent Price made frequent guest appearances.

Gypsy was on *The Hollywood Squares* on the following dates in 1968: April 15 and 22, June 17 and 24, July 1, 15 and 29, August 12, September 2 and 9, October 14 and 28, November 18, December 16 and 30.

Gypsy and Johnny. In August of 1968 Gypsy is Jonathan Winters' guest of *The Jonathan Winters Show*.

Voila, It's Gypsy. Pet lover Gypsy became a spokesperson for Voila Pet Foods as announced in *The New York Times* on September 6, 1968: "The Curtain Rises on Gypsy Rose Lee in New Job — Making Pitch for Pet Lovers": "Gypsy Rose Lee, who unzipped her way to immortality as the first lady of burlesque, is now out to tempt America's four-footed friends…." A great photo of Gypsy accompanies the article: *Gypsy Rose Lee, new vice president of Voila gourmet pet food company, cuddling a Chinese hairless puppy at a party for people and dogs in Washington.*

Gypsy and Mike. Gypsy had a "strip" of co-hosting *The Mike Douglas Show*. She gave Mike a helping hand from September 23 through September 27 of 1968.

CHAPTER ELEVEN

Gypsy the Trouper

Gypsy Invades Okinawa. In November of 1968 Gypsy, the ultimate trouper, entertained U.S. troops in Okinawa. She was presented with a lacquer-covered photo album as a thank you from troops stationed there.

Around the World of Mike Todd. Gypsy appeared as herself in this documentary about her former director, producer, and lover Mike Todd. The film, written in part by Mike Todd, Jr., was released in August of 1968.

• 1969 •

Gypsy on Ice. On January 2, 1969, Gypsy boarded a bus with celebrity friends Paul Lynde, Jo Ann Worley and Steve Allen. Their destination was the Forum Theatre, where they saw the show *Holiday on Ice.*

Gypsy Squared II. During 1969 Gypsy made eight appearances on *The Hollywood Squares.* The shows aired on January 13, March 10 and 31, April 28, May 19, June 16 and 30. Her final appearance was on July 14, 1969.

Gypsy also appeared on the *Steven Allen Show* in March and July of 1969.

Gypsy Goes to the Front Lines. In 1968 Gypsy was given the USO Woman of the Year Award for the work she did in Southeast Asia. In early 1969 Gypsy made her first tour of Vietnam with the USO. Gypsy made two tours during the Vietnam War. Unlike the big USO shows, starring celebrities such as Bob Hope, Gypsy traveled on her own. This allowed her to visit remote places, and visit soldiers in the smaller hospitals that the bigger shows missed.

Gypsy Goes to the Dogs. Animal lover Gypsy appears in ads for Voila Pet Foods. The ad was seen in various magazines during 1969.

Gypsy and Johnny II. Gypsy guested on *The Jonathan Winters Show* for the second time. The broadcast date was May 1, 1969. Other guests that evening were Cliff Arquette, George Lindsey and the Young Saints.

Gypsy Greek Goddess. In 1969 Gypsy and actor Larry Storch traveled to Greece for the opening of a new casino in Athens. The unlikely pair were in Athens during the month of June 1969.

USO SHOWS

in association with

THE HOLLYWOOD OVERSEAS COMMITTEE

presents

Gypsy Rose Lee

VIETNAM COMING SOON!

FOR DETAILS CONTACT
YOUR SPECIAL SERVICES OFFICER

Patriotic to the end, Gypsy made two tours of Vietnam with the USO and the Hollywood Overseas Committee. This photograph shows the cover of the promotion material that publicized her second tour. Circa 1968/69.

Gypsy's Touched by an Angel. Gypsy appeared on the short-lived *The Della Reese Show* on August 11, 1969.

Gypsy's Down Under Again. Gypsy made the front page of Melbourne, Australia's *Newsday* on October 13, 1969. She is shown fishing on a boat, flanked by friends Bob and Dolly Dyer. The title for the article, excerpted below, was supplied by Gypsy:

Above, left: Gypsy, curlers in her hair, brings a smile to a member of the U.S. Navy. *Right:* Gypsy Rose Lee, iconoclast and legend, is seen boarding a helicopter as she heads to her next destination, where she will entertain more troops. Within a year cancer would take her life. Circa 1968/69.

"Goddam Comedy of Errors."

The most famous stripper since Salome — Gypsy Rose Lee — has just spent a week in paradise. But paradise turned a little sour.

What was going to be an idyllic week's fishing in the beautiful Barrier Reef waters of Cairns, in north Queensland, turned into one of the greatest debacles of the age.

And Gypsy was not amused ... the food was bad, the weather was rough, the fish wouldn't bite, and when they did...

While the former burlesque queen struggled with a 300 lb. marlin, everything went wrong. Her host, TV's Bob Dyer, was lucky to escape with his life, when a gaff rope entangled his leg and nearly pulled him overboard.

Worse was to come. Gypsy broke Bob's favorite rod.

The lady who spent 30 years of her life losing her clothes almost lost her head as a very angry black marlin did what it could to avoid capture.

Gypsy Cooks with Mike. *The Mike Douglas Show* often featured cooking segments, which were always a hit with television viewers. The results could be hilarious, especially when Douglas was cooking with the likes of Carol Channing, Martha Raye, Carol Burnett, Minnie Pearl, Phyllis Diller and Jimmy Durante. In 1969 Douglas compiled a book of celebrity recipes in *The Mike Douglas Cookbook.* Gypsy's recipes, like her "Linger Longer Omelet," below, joined those of other celebrity chefs including Vincent Price, Ann Miller, Shelley Winters, Zsa Zsa Gabor, Kaye Ballard, Della Reese and Sammy Davis, Jr.

Gypsy Rose Lee's Linger Longer Omelet

¼ lb. Italian link sausage sliced ¼ inch thick
¼ green pepper cut into ¼ inch strips
1 Tb. olive oil
½ sliced onion, ⅛ inch thick
1 small potato, peeled, sliced ¼ inch thick
½ tsp. salt
1 slice prosciutto cut into ½ inch strips

1 tomato, peeled, sliced ¼ inch thick
2 Tbs. chopped pimiento
6 eggs
1 Tb. chopped parsley
1 Tb. olive oil
Garlic

Sauté sausage and pepper in 1 Tb. oil over low heat 4 to 5 minutes or until sausage begins to brown. Add onion, potato and salt. Cover and continue to cook, stirring gently occasionally, 5 to 10 minutes or until onions are transparent. Add ham [prosciutto] tomato and pimento. Cook until tender. Drain excess fat.

Break eggs into mixing bowl. Add parsley. Beat with fork until frothy. Add sausage mixture.

The Over the Hill Gang. In 1969 ABC began their season by introducing a new format: made-for-television movies. One of the most entertaining movies shown that year was *The Over the Hill Gang.* All of the lead actors were well-known character actors with plenty of experience in movies and television including Walter Brennan, Edgar Buchanan, Pat O'Brien and Chill Wills. They played a team of lawmen who were once a part of the legendary Texas Rangers. Other Hollywood veteran's in the cast include William Benedict, Myron Healey, and Elmira Sessions.

In what would be her final screen appearance, a radiant Gypsy played the character of Cassie. Cassie was a longtime admirer of these four one-time Texas Rangers, their one-member-only fan club. The final gunfight took place at Cassie's Corral.

The made-for-television movie was popular enough to have a sequel titled *The Over the Hill Gang Rides Again.* The second installation had Fred Astaire as a special guest star. Had she lived, Gypsy would have probably saddled up for this one too.

• 1970 •

In his book, *Gypsy & Me,* Erik Lee Preminger writes of his mother's courageous battle with cancer. She called Erik to tell him that a spot had been found on her lung. An operation was required immediately. Gypsy had asked that they wait until her son could arrive. She called Erik at his office in New York, and broke the news. Within an hour Otto Preminger had Erik in a limo, bound for the airport.

When he arrived at his mother's bedside, she broke the news that it was cancer. Initially, he thought it might have been tuberculosis. After an exploratory surgery, doctors found that the cancer had spread too much for it to be removed. Gypsy told her son that they thought they might be able to use radiation to "knock it out."

Famous for her tenacity, Gypsy fought until the end. Her belief that she could beat the odds never flagged.

Erik remembered accompanying her to one of her radiation treatments. As they passed by the other patients, she told Erik she could not be upset with God for giving her "… this horrible disease." She quietly told her son "… I've had three wonderful lives, and these poor sons-a-bitches haven't even lived one."

Gypsy was fond of saying, "I have everything I had twenty years ago … it's just lower." Even at age fifty-eight "everything" seems to be in place. Circa 1969.

Gypsy's Final Bow. Gypsy dies on April 26, 1970.

Newsweek. The following excerpts are from a remembrance to Gypsy that ran in *Newsweek* on May 10, 1970:

> "Did you ever hold a piece of candy or a toy in front of a baby, just out of his reach?" Gypsy Rose Lee once said, trying to explain her act. "Notice how he laughs? That's your strip audience."
>
> What the lady didn't mention was that she had probably stolen the candy from the baby to begin with. Of all the great women — from Mistinguett down to the ineluctable Tempest Storm — who have given their most to the quintessentially American art form of public undress, nobody put less actual flesh on the line than Gypsy Rose Lee. Yet she hocked it with such polished comic brass, and wisecracked about it offstage with shrewd PTA bawdry, that she remained the world's idea of a prima strippa for more than three decades, right down to her death in Los Angeles last week of cancer at 56.

Afterword

Noralee Frankel

"Let Me Entertain You," proclaims Gypsy in the musical *Gypsy*. Robert Strom's book, *Lady of Burlesque: The Career of Gypsy Rose Lee*, does that and more. The book is arranged chronologically by year, which in Gypsy's case is no small feat. Figuring out what goes where in Gypsy's life or if an event actually happened makes writing about her a challenge. As Kaye Ballard wrote, "The truth about the facts of her life never mattered to Gypsy as much as the presentation of those facts."

As the fictitious Dr. Gregory House has concluded, "Everybody lies." Gypsy certainly did. Gypsy invented powerfully compelling and seemingly plausible stories about herself. She made up tales about her age, stage name, first strip, relationship with mother, and the worst lie of all, her son's father. Robert Strom manages to keep it all straight or when it is hopelessly confusing, gives the reader Gypsy's various versions of an event.

Best of all, *Lady of Burlesque* offers the reader a chance to read some of Gypsy Rose Lee's own articles. The piece on "They Need It for Bullets!" is hysterical as Gypsy humorously complained about trying to be an exotic dancer during World War II with all the material shortages. Her article for *Flair* magazine describes her experiences on the carnival circuit so vividly readers feel they are touring with her. The *House and Garden* article discusses her fabulous house in New York City; while "How to Catch a Musky" places the reader in the boat with Gypsy as she fishes for the elusive "big one" with the same tenacity with which she approached her career.

Gypsy loved to write and she took great satisfaction in it. With the same drive she brought to stripping, Gypsy wrote an autobiography and two mystery novels. Although the thrillers are credited to "Craig Rice," I am convinced from Gypsy's correspondence that Gypsy authored these books. Her letters and her interviews have the same style as her writings. Her letters to her third husband, painter Julio de Diego, were the basis of the article for *Flair*. Her written work demonstrates her voice. So unless Craig Rice also ghosted Gypsy's personal correspondence, Gypsy wrote her own books. As Gypsy pointed out, others edited them.

The intensity of Gypsy's written word was reflected in the way she lived. As Phyllis Diller in her interview with the Robert Strom noted, "Gypsy really *lived* her life. She made every moment of it … *interesting*." Gypsy acted on stage, radio, and television, raised money for political and social causes. She was elected vice president of her labor union, the American Guild of Variety Artists (AGVA), and edited its newsletter. All her activities were rooted in her identity as a stripper, even while she repeatedly tried to leave her primary occupation. She overcame professional adversity, failure as a Hollywood actress, hideous reviews of the Broadway play she wrote, censorship and blacklisting, and difficulty in finding another career after she ceased to strip.

Parts of her autobiography hint at the truth. Even though her mother never forced her into stripping, Gypsy always displayed ambivalence about her chosen profession. She spent much of her time trying to leave burlesque for other venues, including movies, serious theater, and writing, but these failed to yield the income she craved, so she always returned to strip tease. Finally too weary to continue, she gave up stripping in her forties when she was still much in demand.

Ultimately, sometimes in spite of herself, Gypsy's lasting fame rested on her career as a stripper, her autobiography, and the musical. Strom's book contains plenty of material on the various revivals of the brilliant musical. As each woman takes her turn as the driven, ruthless, stage mother she interprets the role just a little differently, with a distinctive nuance. The part of the vulnerable "no talent daughter" is particularly difficult since it demands innocent softness in the beginning and a sexual toughness by the end.

Publicity helped Gypsy a great deal. From her rise in burlesque in the 1930s until her death in 1970, Gypsy was one of the most interviewed and photographed women of her time. Reporters flocked to her because she perfected the art of being quotable. Gypsy always went for the punch line rather than the straight line in interviews and her writing, even if by doing so she skewed the truth. She hid behind wit and glibness. Clever articles sprinkled with pictures of a woman whose legs seemed to go on forever graced girlie magazines and the respectable mainstream *Life* and *Look*.

Modern readers cannot fully appreciate Gypsy Rose Lee's fame. Strom includes just a sample of the articles about her in magazines and newspapers. Popular authors of the time such as J.P. McEvoy, Gladys Hall, and Richard Lauterbach, wrote about her. *Liberty*, *The Saturday Post*, and *Cosmopolitan* published J. P. McEvoy's articles. Besides a play McEvoy also wrote several novels. Gladys Hall, a flourishing fan magazine writer, tried to capture Gypsy's personal side. The prestigious Richard Edward Lauterbach, who wrote a long article about her in *Life* magazine was the Moscow bureau chief *Time* magazine. Eliot Elisofon, her friend and lover, photographed her at various times for *Life* magazine. Besides being a photographer, Elisofon was an artist, art collector, author, and filmmaker. Other famous photographers such as Alfred Eisenstaedt and Arnold Newman also photographed her. Newman's portrait has been part of a Smithsonian exhibition on prominent women at the National Portrait Gallery. Given all the articles that he had to research, Robert Strom handles all the complexity of this unforgettable woman's career. His masterful touches allow the reader to have an understanding of her life.

Noralee Frankel is the author of Stripping Gypsy: The Life of Gypsy Rose Lee, *Oxford University Press, 2009.*

Appendix A: Gypsy's Letters to *Inner Sanctum Mysteries*

Between January 4, 1941, through August 28, 1941, Gypsy wrote thirteen letters to her friends, editors Lee Wright and Charlotte Seitlin at Inner Sanctum Mysteries, regarding her work on *The G-string Murders*. The original letters were donated, by Gypsy, to Princeton University. The collection is missing one letter. However, the editor of *Inner Sanctum Mysteries* printed a pamphlet containing all thirteen letters, which were heavily edited for the pamphlet. Here are the unedited letters, from Princeton University Library's Gypsy Rose Lee Collection. Gypsy wrote these letters while she was on the road. They are all on the stationery of the various hotels she stayed at.

HOTEL AMBASSADOR
CHICAGO, ILLINOIS

Dear Miss Seitlin: January 4, 1941

Thank you for your letter. I was very happy to know that you and Mr. Weidman approve of the background for my story. (I am quite a fan of his.)

About a skeleton: It hadn't occurred to me but I will try to beat one out this afternoon. There is a possibility that I will stay in Chicago for some time and would like to get this publishing business off my mind. It's like being all made up, ready to go on ... and not knowing what theatre you're playing.

Sincerely,
GYPSY ROSE LEE

HOTEL AMBASSADOR
CHICAGO, ILLINOIS

Dear Lee Wright: January 13, 1941

Thank you for Craig's book. It is my favorite.

I did want to get a clean copy of the manuscript for you. (The corpse steps out takes second billing now. She has been ill and I haven't had a chance to talk to her. She read the first pages of G.S.M. and suggested the business of my knowing the Princess.) I dropped the original in the bathtub and most of my notes were on it. The carbon (in all colors) was fuzzy, forgive me.*

Would ten thirty Monday be too early to see you? I have so damned many things to do, my plane arrives at nine something, I'll go directly home and wait for a call from you. I hoped to squeeze you in between my dentist and my agent. They're both nice guys but if you'd rather there's an hour and a half between Mike Todd and J.P. McEvoy.

GYPSY

*That bath tub line reads badly now that I look it over. You see it takes almost an hour to soak off my body paint so I do my rewriting while I wait.

HOTEL AMBASSADOR
CHICAGO, ILLINOIS

Dear Miss Wright: January 20, 1941

Thank you for the books, I finished one yesterday. My first reaction was to tear my own manuscript in many small pieces. After I spoke to Miss Rice I felt better. She told me that the changes would be a simple job. (For her, perhaps) and she is writing me in detail. We discussed methods of murder for several hours, Thursday we are meeting again.

The murderer in G-String is not a mad man. That annoys *me* too much when I'm reading a mystery … I did think that he (The doorman) would be the guilty party. He wouldn't have to be insane to want those women out of the way. I wanted the reader to sympathize with him. A great many will probably think it's a good idea to clean up the Burlesque theatre, anyway.

Miss Rice was delighted with the advance publicity on her books. She told me that Simon and Schuster were undoubtedly the best publishers! As for my cooperation on promotion of G-String Murders — if and when — I'll do my specialty in Macy's window to sell a book. If you would prefer dignified, make it Wanamaker's window. There has been so much publicity about it already that I'm a little embarrassed. (The book I mean — not the specialty.)

I do want to finish it before I leave Chicago and I'm certain that with Miss Rice helping me I will.

Sincerely,
GYPSY ROSE LEE

HOTEL AMBASSADOR
CHICAGO, ILLINOIS

Dear Lee Wright: February 2, 1941

Instead of trying to rewrite these few pages I'm sending them on as is. The publicity boys here have me booked for a solid week and I'd know if this is the right approach. (This rented Royal is about as unregal as the Princess.)

How's about Moey getting the toilet? He could be built up a little from the first chapter. Then at the end I can throw him in as a suspect…. Do you like Sarah Jane? The guessing game just occurred to me this morning, if I think it over I can "suggest" better places to Stachi.

When Biff comes in — start of next chapter, he says, "This is a hell of a way to get your name in the papers." I'll be talking about the wedding gown and then he says, "Why didn't you tell me you wanted me to make an honest woman outta ya?" Then I say "he was crazy, wasn't he?" and the money gag of stock holder comes out. Russell could have found the G string caught on his coat when he picked La Verne up and put it in Biff's pocket because he was afraid. The glitter on the elevator … Stachi had sent the Hermit a _____ something earlier. He had the G string and was waiting for the moment to kill La Verne … as he placed the papers or whatever it is in the box the fringe came loose. Dolly was going to tell me who the Princess was the night she got drunk in my room … Biff was going to tell me the same thing the night we went to the Dutchman's O.K.?

Would it make Dolly more of a character to have her a belly roller? I don't have one and what is a home without a mother? What is Burlesque without a belly roller? If I take Dimples out of the first chapter … the white henna and etc. I can use her for Jannine. Alice I'll sweeten a little more, the Princess you said was set.

How is Gee Gee? Sandra with the ice on her breasts can be in a frozen condition every time we see her. The sink is full of ice for her breasts and the cocoa butter and etc.

My masseuse just made an entrance so I'll get my ass pounded a little and while she's working I'll try and figure a couple of good places to dump the corpse — mine that is,

Regards,
GYPSY

HOTEL AMBASSADOR
CHICAGO, ILLINOIS

Dear Lee: February 19, 1941

Thanks for the long letter; I got so excited about your suggestions that I bought me a new type-writer. They told me the small type was more dignified — so — naturally Lady Lee had to get it and now I'm damned if I read the print. (I thought the blue ribbon was sexy.)

I'll do everything you suggest, but I do wish I had your copy of the script. Mine is too dirty to show to Craig. I saw her yesterday, incidentally. She is very happy with her radio show (and her husband) but she said she'd read it and if there wasn't too much work to be done I could depend on her.

She also suggested that The Esquire might be interested in the first chapter as a shortie. (Cut, of course) I could take the stuff I want for the book and add to what is left ... leaving the blackout "You've worn your last pair of pants." Whatever they gave me I could figure was the Davis money.... I know they don't buy articles written by women but in my case they may make an exception... yes?

That is unless you think it may not be good publicity for the book. I rather thought it would help, but I don't know from those things. If you like the idea let me know. AND ... if the Wm. Morris agency calls you about me, I have no agreement with them. They would like to think so but I'm up to my ass in agents and I'll be damned if I'll let them walk in here. They have been calling me long distance and sending me wires about the Modern Age publisher wanting the book. With their ten % in mind of course. In the first place I never heard of the Modern Age and second I don't want to know from agents.

Five of them took me into court four years ago — when I was in Burlesque not one wanted a piece of me, when I got the Hollywood contract — and I do mean when *I* got it — they all sued! The Judge was an angel ... he called them pimps and etc. And when I said I was willing to pay ten percent, he split it up between them. That contract cancelled all others (one had a literary clause in it). They are such schmoozies they think I've forgotten. Since then I've bought them all out ... with the exception of the Wm. Morris office ... and they're the worst of the lot. In the four years they've handled me they haven't gotten me so much as an Elks smoker! NOT ONE DATE! The guy's name is Het Manheim, he's the cutie that is trying to make with those publishers.

The real laugh is that when the story broke that I was writing a book one of them called me and said that they wanted me to do a murder mystery with a Burlesque background. It's a wonder he didn't tell me that he had a terrific title — The G-String Murders.

I think that's all, gotta make with the book words.

Regards,
GYPSY

RIVERSIDE THEATRE
MILWAUKEE, WISCONSIN

Dear Lee: February 26, 1941

How do these chapters sound? I've tried so hard to make the characters different but I don't like to draw a picture of each one; there are so many and I'm afraid the descriptions would slow up the works. La Verne being Stachi's grand daughter is wonderful. The new gimmick about La Verne is wonderful. I have her singing a little more often so the readers won't forget that she is the Prim.

Does this sound good for a dust jacket; a picture full length, of a stripper? Semi nude. The G String actually silver flitter. (Very inexpensive, that flitter business.) And a separate piece of paper pasted on the skirt, like birthday cards, you know? The customers can lift the skirt and there's the G-string sparkling gaily. It is strictly gag business but it might cause talk. More than the Fortune painting. I asked Vertes if I could use the drawing he did of me for the back where they say; about the author ... it is like a drawing of me, half dressed pounding on the typewriter between shows. Just in case you liked it. He said he would be delighted. Dammit I love furriners! Aside from the hand kissing they really make like gents.

Is Louie "in" the raid scene enough now? It seems to me like he is definitely La Verne's lover now, which gives him a motive, jealousy, for the murder. As for Russell, he has his little reason, too.

Moey COULD be a hired killer, couldn't he?

Moey would have a motive for the Princess, and the idea being that he took advantage of La Verne's death by having his killer struggle too.

The Chinese waiter ... well I did think that I would have La Verne the one that was fascinated by the weed instead of Gee Gee. She can take the thing out of the box when Gee Gee opens it.

I'm going to take out the business of the waiter seeing a man doing the strangling. In that way the princess could have killed La Verne. Fear of being exposed? and Dolly could also have a motive.

Any way I know you are a busy girl so I'll write it first, and discuss it later. Keep this copy, in case I lose mine and if you have time write me to Riverside Theatre Milwaukee about changes you want made in the second draft.

> Love,
> GYPS

ORIENTAL THEATRE
CHICAGO, ILLINOIS

Dear Lee: March 5, 1941

The week in Milwaukee was a busy one. (Excuse A for not writing sooner, and B, my plans were uncertain.)

I will definitely be in the city the first of April. Holy week and all that funny business closed the show for a while. Two weeks maybe. I was supposed to play San Francisco but Todd won't let me go.... It's nice to be so popular only in Frisco I would have made more money. However the two weeks is a god send. I must get this damn book settled in my mind. Craig should be in to see me soon and we are going to discuss it. There has been too much publicity already, it will be a back number before it hits the presses if I don't get my ass and heels together.

After the fifth show I'm usually too tired to sit at the typewriter. I'm so mixed up I don't know where to start. We do six today but by hook or crook the first chapter will be smoothed a little. I hate that gag about not knowing whether to begin with the Princess or the Party or etc. It reminds me of a vaudeville act that comes out and explains that the scenery didn't arrive, the music was lost and his partner broke his leg but "with the kind indulgence of the audience he will try to entertain them." We call that "Copping a plea." When I tried to write it really sounded like I was apologizing. AND so damned many books start that way.

I know ... tried and true ... but even so the entire theme of the book is different from the usual Murder Mystery and I don't like the ... please forgive my inaptitude ... beginning. If I can whip up something different, may I?

(The manager just came back to tell me that there is a committee of local virgins catching the show to see if I really do take off my pants.) Being cancelled out of the Oriental Theatre would be a fitting climax to my stinking career. Two policemen stood in the wings all week in Milwaukee. They couldn't believe "That was ALL I did" and were scared to death to take their eyes off me. They really thought the second they left I would peel off a few layers of skin. WOE. WOE. And me with no breakfast yet.

After the show they were all here, brass buttons badges 'nall. I showed them a piece of net and told them it was a pair of bloomers so they left covered with smiles. But I have a hunch they'll be back. So if I'm not in jail I'll call you first.

> Best regards,
> GYPSY
> The Girl with the Diamond Studded Navel.

Still no food!

FAIRMONT HOTEL
NOB HILL
SAN FRANCISCO, CALIFORNIA

Dear Lee:										May 15, 1941

This damn San Francisco jaunt came up so suddenly that I had no time to call you. It's only for two weeks though, and just to prove to you that I haven't deserted "G-string" because I'm back to wearing one under separate cover you will find. I didn't retype the whole thing, just added to your copy. I loved your notes; I was reading along and saying, to myself, "I like this chapter fine" and at the end I'd come across, "What happened to Jake?" in your hand-writing. Hurt me ego ... that's wot.

I gave Louie The Grin a mouth like a torn pocket ... Dwight Fiske version. Then when I was complimenting myself on that stroke some guy gives me, "Oh, yes. I read a book about a man that had HIS mouth sewed up."

Remember when I was beefing about Chicago? All on account of it was a saloon? Well, this time it really is a saloon. The stage is six feet long and two feet wide which is a dandy coffin, but no dandy for me, and of course the orchestra needs some room. It means that Mother Lee has to crawl around thru the tables while she does the act that skyrocketed her to fame. After the first performance last night my new boss dropped in, green suit and all. "Why don't you get out and mingle a little?" he asked, leering at me. "All the time you stay cooped up like a butterfly in a cage!" I was sewing on organdie ruffle on my second act G-string, making little stitches like a nun. That sort of got him, too. "It's bad for your eyes," He cautioned. "Better I should rent you a sewing machine."

One good thing about the place is that it gives me a chance to break in my new number. The costume is wonderful and the lyric — well, just because I wrote it is no reason why I should hide behind a bushel.

(My gawd — The boss' accent is rubbing off! But on me!)

The lyric: I was certain the mooches wouldn't get it but God love 'em they laughed anyway. There must be something amusing about a naked woman talking. Most of the fan, muff, and bubble dancers keep their mouths shut then I come along with dialogues and they laugh at anything.

My suite has a terrace that overlooks Telegraph Hill and the big bridge. I love it. If I could only get organized I'm sure I could get some words written. But as soon as I go to work I start worrying about my legs and my waistline. That means an hour a day with a masseuse and half hour exercising, then an hour swimming. By then it's time to get undressed for my show. All that for a measly two thousand a week (with tips).

I'll call you when I get home, in the meantime write me here if anything comes up. And I hope you like the added words.

Best,
GYPSY

FAIRMONT HOTEL

NOB HILL

SAN FRANCISCO, CALIFORNIA

June 16, 1941

Monday morning

Dear Lee:

Did you get the mailing envelope of words? I just sent another batch, the last ones are rolled up in an envelope on account of I couldn't find the right sort of thing to send them in.

I have been working on the last chapter. It is a bitcheroo. I've really gotten to the point that I don't give a damn who killed 'm. Incidentally, the pages I sent you are a first draft. I'll kick them around a little when I get this damn motive off my mind.

I hope I marked the inserts carefully enough. Most of the stuff goes in the second chapter. How I got that business in the tenth, I'll never know. Must have been drunk.

The enclosed clipping was in the Sunday paper. Herb saw your letter when he had cocktails with me on Friday. He thought it was wonderful and I was sorry I didn't have some of the others to show him. He said he could understand why I wanted Simon and Schuster to publish my book if I received mail like that. I told him that the mail had nothing to do with it. It was all because Richard Simon was so beautiful.

The post office just called again. They don't want to take the manuscript because it was rolled up, and it was typewritten. What sillies they are. I told them to send those words damn quick and to stop calling me. If he wanted to see me could he come to the saloon. Trying to tell me like I didn't know from post offices! Then he said he would appreciate it if I would at least put a few stamps on it. "Not the full amount of course … that would be asking too much."

Did I tell you that I had eaten clams every day since I arrived? Well, I had to stop. I was getting with hives. Still feel a little ill from them. They have open air trolleys here in Frisco, and just to make my trip complete I had to go slithering off, sick to my stomach, all bumped up with hives and I still slide off the damn trolley. My bottle of rum went crashing to the street, the manuscript scattering all over and me with no pants on sprawling on the avenue. It must have been a pretty sight. If we don't do any business tonight I'll know the reason. You can't give it away and expect to get paid for it too.

(The post office called again. I owe you twelve cents on the first batch of words. So help me Gawd I'm going to get me a carrier pigeon.)

I'll be here one more week. Held over by popular demand! Then I play the Bowery in Detroit. Then home, I hope.

Best regards,
GYPSY

FAIRMONT HOTEL
NOB HILL
SAN FRANCISCO, CALIFORNIA

Dear Lee: June 20, 1941

I received your letter this morning. Made me feel like a stinker for not sending you the words sooner. The trouble was that after reading them over and over I decided that they were too rough to waste postage on. However I have started rewriting them, and to prove to you that I HAVE been at it, I'm sending them anyway. I have carbons and I hope the general idea is all right because I'm using this as a guide.

The first six pages of the last chapter stink so I kept them but if I can only keep these press guys out of my hair for a day or two I should finish them fast like a mouse.

I'll be here for two more weeks, closing around the twenty-fifth. Then I'm going to Malibu for a week, vacation bent, and bejeesus I'm going to get it. Then I open the seventh in Detroit for a week. The fifteenth I SHOULD play Pittsburgh for two weeks but I'm getting so weary. I may come home right after Detroit. I'll call you the day I get in town in any case.

Bye, and I hope the new things will do.

GYPSY

BOOK CADILLAC HOTEL
DETROIT, MICHIGAN

Dear Charlotte: June 7, 1941

The batch of letters arrived. I'll handle the press agent first thing; Bill has been Mike Todd's man for a couple of years. He understands me and I adore him. As far as you're concerned I think you covered everything with your letter, but with me he can handle double in brass. I have enough dates booked to carry me through the winter and I don't like the kind of publicity these out of town boys dream up. I need someone with vision, bejeesus, and Bill has it. The press agent in this city has an idea that he could "get a break" if I were arrested. Nice thing. All the time and money I spend trying to keep out of the clink and he wants me in. No, Bill is a smarty pants and I like him.

Now we get down to the decent and indecent proposals:

A.W. is much too pretty for me. I like my men on the monster side. A snarling mouth, evil eye, broken nose … if he should happen to have thick ears, good! And I like a little muscle, hair on the chest, none on the head. A nervous tic excites me and if with all these things he wore green suits.... BANK NIGHT!

My saloon career prospers. I've been held over for another week. Broke all records they tell me. (As if I didn't cast the house myself.) As soon as I knew, I moved out of that flea bag of a hotel. Swimming pool or no swimming pool, I couldn't stand the lobby characters. Talk about running a relay; my poor behind was black and blue from the waist down. Even when I walked fast I got it. They must have been practicing the art of the quick pinch. I had to brace myself in the corner of the elevators because the slow guys camped there. The elevators in the Book Cadillac are like Tommy Manville's bedroom; all mirrors. Even on the ceiling. It gives the men ideas but it makes them nervous at the same time so I guess I can get out of these damn tin pants. (They were beginning to chafe ... the warm weather and all).

Please give my love to Janet. I'll be home the twenty-second of July. I'm taking a month off regardless. These late hours are giving me the "Yaddo" pallor.

Love to Lee, too.

GYPSY

BOOK CADILLAC HOTEL
DETROIT, MICHIGAN

Dear Lee: July 21, 1941

When your letter arrived I got ambitious. I always do, for that matter. Being so far away from people that I can discuss plot, motive, blood and bodies with, I get stale. I really have finished the last bit of it but I wanted to wait until I got home and copied it before I showed it to you. I've padded it so that you'd think it was a Wodehouse being sold to Red Book and paid for by word.

These inserts are rough but I'll clean them up later. Couldn't you hold off with the editing until I get home? I have fifty pounds (weighed by the T.W.A.) of new words. None of them are sacred to me but in some cases there is an improvement.

When the coffee is good and we sell out the night before I find out I write better. If I have night lunch with a smarty pants like Saroyan, I want to spit on the whole damned manuscript. (The coffee was good, and we sold out, but it didn't work this morning.)

Some stupid son of a bitch dropped in yesterday and killed a quart of my good liquor while he told me that HE had the idea of doing my murder mystery with my title! He tops it off with "You know," he says, "*I* know your age, and believe me you look swell!" Am I glad that I keep myself prepared for people like that. I tell you, I wouldn't be without those micky finns for anything in the world! Simon and Schuster will rue the day that you brought the Belle of the Bistros into your fold. (His name is Shannon Cormack in case anything happens to me.) The city editor of the Free Press writes murder mysteries. He's dining with me tonight. Just called this minute.

Everything is all right. Cormack works for the Free Press. Get it? An example of what I'll go through for a literary career.

I'll call you Monday.

Love, Gyp.

HOTEL ONONDAGA
SYRACUSE, NEW YORK

Dear Charlotte: August 28, 1941

"This is my last State Fair ... so please be kind...."* Indeed it is, too. They can have their Mud Operas. I do not care for some. First the rains came, then it got cold. You should have seen my bare blue behind waving in the breeze! If there's such a thing as a blue pickle I'm it. Believe me, I could tie a bow on each goose-pimple.

The orchestra is the local American Legion Band. Instead of a piano they have two tubas. They dug up an accordionist for my number (better they should have dug up a couple jew's harps). The dressing room is across the muddy race track, I have to wade over to the grandstand for each appearance, and speaking of dressing rooms! It's a tent with peekholes. No shelves, no chairs, no mirrors or lights. Ten of us manage to get made-up by kerosene lamps. The other nine are high acts. (Hang by the teeth, the neck and etc.) Even in the cold weather they smell strangely. Maybe I should be glad it isn't warm.

When I saw the rain I went to a local store and bought two confirmation dresses; I put them together and made a little creation. It isn't Chanel but the audience is so far away they can't tell if I have a dress on or not. During the afternoons they currycomb the horses in our dressing room and if I smell a little gamey when I get home blame it on the trotters.

We broke all records though. (One hundred and one Fairs.) I put the money in the grouch bag and tonight I'm off to the Hub. The enclosed is an interview. He'd love to have a book, but you can do as you please about it. (He DID mention S. and S.)

I hope they can do something about getting the book out earlier than the fifteenth. And I do want to see the Galley things. I want to be able to tell people ... "Teddibly soddy ... cawn't make it tonight ... I have to check my Galley proofs."

Best to everybody. I don't suppose Lee is back yet but say hello when you see her. (Oh, I had a letter from Wolcott ... he said he'd read the book if it killed him. Also mentioned that my boy friend, Janet, was spending the week end at Bomossen and asked me to join them. I didn't receive the letter in time to answer it. I did send a pillow cover from Atlantic City though. I was going to send you taffy from Atlantic City, but after breaking my sixteen hundred dollar set of china on the damned stuff I decided against it.)

                                              Love, Gypp.

*Remember that little ditty?

Appendix B: Last Will and Testament

A document bearing the title of "Last Will and Testament of Rose Louise Hovick" was received by William G. Sharp, County Clerk on May 8, 1970.

The Will and Testament reads:

I, ROSE LOUISE HOVICK, also known as GYPSY ROSE LEE, of 1240 Cerrocrest Drive, Beverly Hills, California, being of lawful age and of sound and disposing mind and memory, and not acting under duress, menace, fraud, or the undue influence of any person whomsoever, do hereby make, publish and declare this my Last Will and Testament and do hereby expressly revoke all former Wills and Codicils to Wills made by me made, in the manner following, that is to say:

FIRST: I direct my Executors to pay my just debts, expenses of last illness and funeral expenses as soon after my death as is convenient.

SECOND: I declare that I am unmarried at this time; and that I have one child, a son, ERIK KIRKLAND, who is over the age of twenty-one (21) years and who resides at 1240 Cerrocrest Drive, Beverly Hills, California.

THIRD: I hereby give, devise and bequeath all of the rest, residue and remainder of my property and estate, both real and personal, of every kind and nature wheresoever situated, including property over which I may have any power of appointment, to my son, ERIK KIRKLAND.

FOURTH: Except as otherwise provided in the Will, I have intentionally and with full knowledge omitted to provide for my heirs.

FIFTH: I declare that those of my heirs, if any there be, whether now living or who be born hereafter who are not herein specifically mentioned or provided for, have been intentionally omitted by me, and that I have intentionally made no provision for any such heir or heirs, and I hereby generally and specifically disinherit each, any and all persons whomsoever claiming to be or who may be lawfully determined to be my heirs-at-law, except as otherwise provided in the Will. If any such heir, or heirs, or any person who, if I died intestate, would be entitled to any part of my estate, shall either directly or indirectly seek to establish or assert any claim to my estate or any part thereof, excepting under this Will or to defeat or change any part of the testamentary plan of this Will, and succeed in establishing his or their rights by final judgment of a court competent jurisdiction, then and in any or all of the above-mentioned cases and events I hereby give and bequeath to such a person or persons the sum of ONE DOLLAR ($1.00) each, and no more, in lieu of any other share or interest in my estate.

SIXTH: I appoint as Executors of this Will my son, ERIK KIRKLAND and WILLIAM FITELSON of 580 Fifth Avenue, New York, N.Y. If one of the Executors are unable or refuse to act, then the remaining Executor shall act alone. I direct that no bond be required of any of said persons as Executors. I authorize my Executors to sell any property of my estate, and to hold, manage and operate any property and any business belonging to my estate at the risk of my estate, and not at the risk of my Executors, the profits and losses therefrom to insure or be chargeable to my estate as a whole.

Gypsy's Last Will and Testament was signed on November 15, 1969. It bears the full signature

Rose Louise Hovick, below that she has noted A.K. and signed Gypsy Rose Lee. The document was admitted to probate on June 1, 1970.

The probate order and decree were entered at the Superior Court of California, County of Los Angeles on December 9, 1971. This document reads as follows:

Estate of ROSE LOUISE HOVICK, also known as GYPSY ROSE LEE, and as ROSE LOUISE DE DIEGO, deceased.

ORDER APPROVING FIRST REPORT AND FOR
PRELIMINARY DISTRIBUTION UNDER WILL

Attorneys appearing for Petitioner: Shearer, Fields, Rohner and Shearer.

The first report and petition for preliminary distribution, and supplement thereto, of Erik Lee Kirkland, as executor of the estate of said deceased, coming on this day for hearing and approval by the Court, all notices of said hearing having been given as required by law, the Court, after hearing evidence, and finding that the consent of the inheritance tax attorney is filed, and it appearing that it will not cause any harm to said estate and is for the best interests of said estate and those interested therein, approves said report and grants said petition as follows:

It is Ordered, Adjudged and Decreed by the Court that said has in his possession belonging to said estate, an accounting being waived, a balance of $424,658.60, of which $271,257.68 is in cash, and the remainder consists of the property described in said account at the value of the appraisement, and said report is hereby approved and allowed accordingly; that the sum of $7,109.36 is hereby allowed said attorneys on account of statutory fees; that the sale of personal property described as a 1956 Rolls Royce, four door sedan, Type SC 120, for the amount of $8,250.00, of a 1959 Fiat Convertible Sedan, for the amount of $220.00, of certain of furniture, clothing and miscellaneous personal property, for the amount of $20,875.00, of certain of the decedent's works of paintings, for the amount of $64,540.00, as more particularly set forth in said petition and hereby approved.

It is further Ordered, Adjudged and Decreed by the Court that the hereinafter named distribute shall not be required to give any bond before receiving any portion of his distributive share of said estate; and that by virtue of the terms of the last will of said deceased, there be and hereby is distributed at this time, to Erik Kirkland, the following:

Cash in the sum of $158,000.00;

Works of Paintings, appraised at $81,090.00 as follows:

    1 Gomaire, Marcel, water color, Woman, 16 × 12;

    1 Grosy, George, water color, Butcher, 23 × 17;

    1 O'Keefe [sic], Georgia, pastel, Lillies, 20 × 16....

Appendix C:
The Auction of Gypsy's Estate

The Estate of Gypsy Rose Lee was auctioned off by Sotheby, Parke-Bernet of Los Angeles. There were exhibitions on March 6, March 8 and March 19 of 1971. The actual auctions were held on Tuesday March 9 at 8 pm and March 10 also at 8 pm.

The auction catalog was divided into ten parts to represent the various rooms in Gypsy's Beverly Hills home, and has been reprinted courtesy of Sotheby's.

FIRST SESSION

Tuesday — March 9, 1971, at 8 P.M.

DRAWING ROOM

1. Pair of Sheraton Black Painted Side Chairs, with caned seats and resting on turned legs. Circa 1800.
2. Regency Style Ebonized Card Table, the hinged top inlaid with brass and raised on cabriole legs ending in gilt-metal sabots.
3. Gilded Bronze Table Lamp, the stem in the form of a seated cherub.
4. Wrought-Iron Torchere, with a tray top and resting on a tripod base.
5. Unusual Table Lamp, in the form of a frog, the bronze shade inlaid with colored glass.
6. Empire Style Occasional Table, with a black marble top, the base with ormolu mounts.
7. Attractive Pair of Empire Table Lamps, each formed of four lights and resting on loin paw feet, carved with acanthus leaves.
8. A Pair of Empire Style Occasional Tables, with triangular black marble tops, the tripod base of each terminating in lion paw feet.
9. A Pair of Italian Ebonized Occasional Tables, each with a hinged cover and inlaid with burl walnut.
10. Louis XV Style Gilt-Metal Fire Screen, in the form of a fan with pierced panels.
11. A Pair of Louis XV Style Gilt-Metal Chenets, each of rococo form depicting a cherub seated among scrolling foliage.
12. Large Ebonized Side Cabinet, of break-front form, the front with four cupboard doors.
13. A Pair of Metal Table Candelabra, hung with spear-shaped drops.
14. Victorian Wrought-Iron Occasional Table, with a pierced top and resting on a tripod base.
15. Gilt-Metal Table Lamp, in the form of a Corinthian column.
16. Bronzed Metal Figure, entitled Priere du Soir, resting on a black marble base and signed Moreau.
17. Empire Style Occasional Table, with a black top, the column with gilt metal mounts.
18. Dresden Porcelain Figure of a Monkey, depicting the figure climbing a chain with a lemon.
19. A Fine English Regency Harp, the instrument with an elaborate brass nameplate, the freestanding front column supported by weighted monopodiea. Signed J.A. Slumpff, London, 44

Great Portland Street, Portland Place. Circa 1840. (Received as part payment for Gypsy's performance in the road company of *The Threepenny Opera*.)

20. A Fine Set of Four Sheraton Black Painted Armchairs, the oval crestings and rails decorated with panels after Angelica Kaufman, the caned seats with squab cushions and raised on turned saber lets. Circa 1800.

21. Mason and Hamlin Baby Grand Piano, contained in an ebonized case. Serial No. 35975. Together with a piano stool.

22. A Pair of English Cut Glass Table Candlesticks, each hung with spear-shaped pendants.

23. An Attractive Pair of Louis XVI Style Gilt-Metal Table Lamps, the legs hung with swags of flowers and surmounted by flame finials.

24. Victorian Upholstered Armchair, covered with green velvet.

25. Unusual Austrian "Blinking Eye" Clock, the dial painted with a portrait of a maiden, the whole contained in an ebonized shadow box. Circa 1850.

26. ESTEBAN *SURREALISTIC STUDY*. Head of a woman with flowing hair before a turquoise background. Signed and bearing the inscription "Para Julio De Diego y Gypsy Rose Lee" Oil on paper. 15 × 11½ inches.

27. RUBY BERNATSCHKE *ROSE*. White rose before a green background. Signed with initials. 6¾ × 5 inches.

28. RODOLFO MO *THE FLOWER WOMAN*. Roses climbing from the head and shoulders of a woman in a black dress and a hat with fruit decoration. 20 × 16 inches.

29. W. ASHTON *HAYSTACKS IN FRANCE*. Gray sky, birch trees to left. Signed and dated 1904. On canvasboard, unframed. 8 × 12 inches.

30. AV KUIOUTCHIAN *AUTUMN OUTING*. Peasants in gay costume in a cart behind two white horses followed by another cart and horses. Signed. 9¼ × 12¼ inches.

31. AMERICAN SCHOOL, 20th Century *SURREALIST LANDSCAPE*. Two figures before a monolith, a golden city in the background. 12¼ × 8 inches.

32. CAROL BARBER *VIEW FROM A WINDOW*. *A woman seen dressing* behind the window of a townhouse, red buildings to right. Signed and dated '55. On canvasboard. Carol Barber was a member of Gypsy's 1955 tour. 18 × 14 inches.

33. JOHN DECKER *TWO WOMEN*. A seated young woman in a hat, another woman to her left, in tones of red. Signed. On canvas mounted on a board. 16½ × 13½ inches.

34. AMERICAN SCHOOL (?), 20th Century. *MOTHER AND CHILD*. Semi-abstract composition in pastel tones. Indistinctly signed and dated '36. Oil on cardboard. 36 × 30 inches.

35. RUTH SACKS *MARINE*. Two sail boats in the foreground. Oil on canvasboard, unframed. 8 × 10 inches.

36. PHIL PATCHEN *"THE SUNSHINE GIRL."* Woman's face in a sunflower. Signed; also signed, titled and dated 1966 on the reverse. 7 × 5 inches.

37. AMERICAN SCHOOL, 20th Century *MALE NUDE*. Semi-abstract in tones of red, green and brown, suggestion of a figure to left. Poor condition. 40½ × 20 inches.

38. RUVOLO *BIRD*. Abstract composition of a black bird before a pink and red background. Signed and dated '49 (?). On masonite. 11¾ × 8 inches.

39. JULIO DE DIEGO *ELEMENTS OF RECONSTRUCTION*. Surrealist composition of men and cranes, a Greek temple and a city in the background. Signed and dated '43, also titled on the reverse. 28 × 35 inches. Provenance — Associated American Artists, New York. Possedoit Gallery, New York. Exhibition — Brussels, Galerie George Giroux, *Exposition d'Art American Contemporain*, 1948 No. 20. [*Note*: Gypsy and Julio De Diego were married in 1946.]

40. JULIO DE DIEGO *ARRIVAL*. Surrealistic composition of terraced buildings and trees. Signed and dated '45, also titled on the reverse. On masonite. 24 × 30 inches.

41. JULIO DE DIEGO *DANGEROUS CATS*. Three stylized tigers, bones of their prey in the foreground. Signed and dated '44, also titled on the reverse. On masonite. 36 × 48 inches.

42. Gilt-Wood Carved Figure of a Cherub Playing a Cello. Together with a paper mache figure of a cherub playing a harp.

43. A Pair of Wrought-Iron Table Compotes, the circular tops supported by figures of peasants.

44. A Pair of Iranian Pottery Figures of Cats, decorated in polychrome.

45. Silvered Metal Compote, the body molded with a cherub and winged griffin.

46. Lead Cornucopia, the body molded with a grotesque mask and resting on hoof feet.

47. A Pair of Terra-Cotta Jardinières, with incised bodies.

48. Chinese Penwork Box, the interior fitted with a sewing compartment, the whole decorated with chinoiserie designs. Circa 1810.

49. Decorative Compote, the interior inlaid with seven miniatures. Together with a small box.

50. Polyorama Panoptique, the viewer with an accordion action. Together with a small collection of slides depicting prominent landmarks. Circa 1830.

51. Gilt-Metal and Glass Flower Lamp, the stem of bulbous form and resting on tripod shell feet.

52. Victorian Brass Spill Holder. Together with a cast iron covered urn.

53. Bronze Jardinière, the circular bowl supported by three Bacchanalian figures.

54. Chinese Pigskin Trunk, the cover and sides decorated in a famille rose palette and depicting figures and pagodas.

55. A Collection of Shellwork, each piece elaborately inlaid.

56. A Collection of Shellwork, each piece elaborately inlaid.

57. Victorian Tole Coal Scuttle, with porcelain handles and later decoration. Circa 1860.

58. Victorian Tole Kettle on Stand, decorated with exotic birds and flowers. Circa 1830.

59. George III Style Cut Glass Table Candelabra, each of the three branches supporting drip pans and with two spear finials, the center stem supporting a star finial.

60. American Pressed Glass Rummer. Together with three pressed glass fan-shaped dishes.

61. Unusual Early Victorian Circular Centre Table, the centre decorated with a scene of Wellington surrounded by his staff and being crowned by Wing Victory, the border depicting Wellington's rise to dukedom from the Battle of Assaye, 1803 to the Battle of Toulouse. Circa 1820.

62. A Regency Settee, with out-scrolled arms, the seat rail decorated with chains of flowers on a simulated rosewood ground, the whole upholstered in lime-green velvet.

ENTRANCE HALL

63. A Pair of Brass Hanging Wall Lights, with pierced globe bodies.

64. A Pair of Torcheres, one side symbolic of Night, the other of Day, each holding a flaming torch.

65. Victorian Papier Mache Tripod Table, the top inlaid with a mother-of-pearl chessboard. Circa 1850.

66. Gilt-Metal Table Lamp, in the form of three figures playing pipes.

67. A Pair of Victorian Circular Footstools, each covered in green velvet. *Gypsy covered these herself.

68. Victorian Green Upholstered Easy Chair, with one arm and a buttoned back.

69. Victorian Wrought-Iron Kitchen Door Knocker, in the form of a hand holding a ball. Together with another, smaller.

70. EDWARD MILLMAN *STILL LIFE WITH FISH*. Colorful semi-abstract composition. Signed and inscribed "For Gypsy and Julio." 7¾ × 10 inches.

71. RUDY BERNATSCHKE *CORNER DRUG STORE*. Red brick Victorian building in a city. Signed and dated 1944. Gouache on paper. 15 × 12¾ inches.

72. SILK EMBROIDERED PICTURE *MOTHER AND CHILD*. In reds and blues. Overall 12½ × 10½ inches.

73. N. GASBARRO *PEACOCK ON A WALL*. With a brightly colored tail, perched on an ornamental balustrade before a lake. Signed and dated 1941. 47 × 32 inches.

74. JOSE CLEMENTE OROZCO *FIGURE STUDY*. Four men in work clothes, one hiding his face in his hands. Signed. India ink and wash. 12½ × 9½ inches.

75. ARA *HOMAGE*. Peasants lined up before a priest attended by a boy with a candle. Signed. 11½ × 18¾ inches.

76. GOLYARV *APPLES*. One sliced in half, two other green apples on a white cloth. Signed and dated '63. Oil on panel. 3¼ × 3½ inches.

77. JULIO DE DIEGO *UNDERWATER ADVENTURE*. A woman and two others fishing, surrounded by fantastic fish. Signed and dated '41. Crayon on paper. 11¾ × 15¼ inches.

78. JULIO DE DIEGO *"ALLEGORY TO A COLD NIGHT, JANUARY, 1948."* Surrealistic composition of a man with a red umbrella and a flower, a woman to the right. Signed, titled, dated and inscribed "To Gypsy." Gouache on paper. 11½ × 14¾ inches.

79. JULIO DE DIEGO *THE SHEEPHERDER.* Fantastic figures around a sheep. Signed and dated '43. Together with another surrealistic drawing. Pen, ink and canvas on brown paper. 12 × 9 inches and 11½ × 8¼ inches.

80. JULIO DE DIEGO *BIRTHDAY COMPOSITION.* Surrealistic woman and other figures. Signed and inscribed in a banner "Happy Birthday Gypsy Love Julio, New York, January 9, 1948.

81. JULIO DE DIEGO *MAN WITH AN UMBRELLA AND FLOWER,* in a blue poncho before a brown background. Oil on cardboard. 13½ × 6¾ inches.

82. JULIO DE DIEGO *CARNIVAL SIDESHOW.* Numerous figures beneath a tent. Signed and dated '49. Watercolor. 5¼ × 6¾ inches.

83. JULIO DE DIEGO *COMPOSITION.* Surrealistic head and heart. Signed and with the words "Gyp Muchas Felicidades En El Dia de Tus Cumple Amos con Amor Julio New York 9 de enero de 1948" on a banner. Crayon and ink. 12 × 9 inches.

84. MARCEL VERTES *THE ARTIST PAINTING FLORA: A THREE PANEL SCREEN.* Two girls in a spring landscape, the lady artist attend by a doe. Signed. Oil on paper. Each panel: 69½ × 21¾ inches.

85. MARCEL VERTES *GYPSY.* Seen nude from the rear before a red curtain. Signed and inscribed "To Gypsy dear son vieil ami." Crayon. 11¼ × 8¼ inches.

86. NEAR EASTERN BRASS EWER, the body of globular form and with a hinged spout.

87. WROUGHT-IRON CHANDELIER, supporting six lights and with an elaborate pierced body.

88. VICTORIAN CIRCULAR CENTRE TABLE, painted with roses.

89. AN UNUSUAL PAIR OF VICTORIAN WALL MIRRORS, formed of prints, the faces removed to display mirrored surfaces.

DINING ROOM

90. ROYAL WORCESTER "BLIND EARL" DINNER SERVICE, each piece decorated with rosebuds and leaves and with lobed gold rims, comprising —

1 footed compote	1 rosewater bowl	6 coffee cups and saucers
1 coffee pot	1 sucrier and cover	6 dinner plates
1 milk jug	6 teacups and saucers	6 side plates

91. VICTORIAN WROUGHT-IRON FLOOR LAMP, with a milch glass globe.

92. WROUCHT-IRON CONSOLE TABLE, with green painted D-shaped top.

93. A PAIR OF PARIS PORCELAIN SPILL VASES, the polychrome bodies encrusted with flowers and birds.

94. SET OF TWELVE WROUGHT-IRON DINING CHAIRS, with caned backs, the seats with squab cushions.

95. MARCEL VERTES WOMAN WITH A POODLE. Red-haired woman in a lavender dress holding a poodle on her left shoulder, green background. Signed. 23½ × 20 inches.

96. VICTORIAN WROUGHT-IRON JARDINIERE, in the form of a basket, supported by a stag's head, the pedestal in the form of a tree stump.

97. WROUGHT-IRON CAMPANA-SHAPED GARDEN URN.

98. VICTORIAN WICKER-WORK TWO-TIER OCCASIONAL TABLE.

99. GORHAM SILVER-PLATE TELEPHONE RECEIVER HOLDER, inscribed "Gypsy."

100. WROUGHT-IRON BREAKFAST TABLE, of circular form and resting on quadruple supports.

101. A SET OF FOUR WROUGHT-IRON CHAIRS, en suite with the preceding.

102. AMERICAN GLASS PITCHER, decorated with playful children in the manner of Mary Gregory. Together with two tumblers and a shot glass, all with similar decoration.

103. COLOR PRINTS BY CHARLES GEOFFROY AFTER GRANDVILLE THE ET CAFÉ: Man dressed in tea leaves and coffee beans. FLECHE-D'EAU: Woman adorned with reeds and climbing flowers stepping into a pond, watched by three fish. ROSE: Seated woman in a dress embellished by rose leaves and bud beetles paying court to her. Published by Garnier Freres, Editeurs. Each: 8¼ × 6¼ inches.

104. COLORED PRINT MANDRAGORA MAS. Flowering mandrake planet. 16 × 11¾ inches.
105. FRENCH PORCELAIN BUTTER TUB AND COVER. Together with porcelain covered container.
106. AMERICAN PRESSED GLASS BUTTER TUB, in the form of a swan. Together with a cut glass carafe.
107. VICTORIAN SPILL VASE, in the form of two hands.
108. SILVER-PLATED TEA SERVICE, comprising teapot, sucrier and milk jug, each piece with an etched body.
109. A PAIR OF LOUIS XV STYLE GILT-METAL TABLE CANDLESTICKS, in the form of seated cherubs on rococo bases.

KITCHEN

110. A SET OF TEN COPENHAGEN BREAKFAST CUPS AND SAUCERS, A COPELAND DINNER SERVICE, each piece with a gadrooned body.
111. A COPELAND DINNER SERVICE, each piece decorated with fruit and flowers, comprising dinner plates, teacups and saucers, coffee pot, milk jug, sucrier and cover.
112. ENGLISH FISH SERVICE, each piece of similar decoration, comprising plates, teacups and saucers.
113. TWO SIMILAR CONTEMPORARY PITCHERS. Together with a stylized platter, each inscribed A.A.A.
114. TREEN MORTAR AND PESTAL. Together with a circular chopping block.
115. KIRIKI DE DIEGO *KITCHEN SCENE*. A dismayed woman being bitten by a large green fish on a kitchen table. Signed and dated 12/49. Gouache. 9 × 7½ inches.
116. A COLLECTION OF FOUR PERSONALIZED LIQUOR BOTTLES, dating from road shows in the 1940's. *Painted for Gypsy by her husband, Julio De Diego, while they were working on *The Royal American Shows* (a carnival) together.
117. A MISCELLANEOUS GROUP OF METALWORK, including four chocolate molds.
118. A SET OF TWENTY-FOUR PRESSED GLASS KNIFE RESTS.
119. A QUANTITY OF MISCELLANEOUS PORCELAIN.
120. A QUANTITY OF MISCELLANEOUS TOLE.
121. CAST-IRON INKWELL. Together with another, in the form of a baked potato.
    121 A. Framed painting of a Cherub with bow, oil on panel.
    121 B. Lovers observed by Cupid. Oil on panel.
    121 C. Tole Chandelier, decorated with flowers.
    121 D. Pair of Smaller Chandeliers, similar to the preceding.
    121 E. A Group of Biographies and Autobiographies, all inscribed to Gypsy.
    121 F. A Group of Five Novels, all inscribed to Gypsy.
    121 G. Miscellaneous Group of Picture Frames (Lot).

[END OF FIRST SESSION]

SECOND SESSION

Wednesday — March 10, 1971, at 8 P.M.

122. AMERICAN MAHOGANY CARD TABLE, on rope turned legs. Circa 1830.
123. A PAIR OF METAL TABLE LAMPS, with cherub form handles.
124. MAPLE OCCASIONAL TABLE, on cabriole legs.
125. A PAIR OF BIEDERMEIER FRUITWOOD SIDE CHAIRS, with rush seats. Circa 1840.
126. BRASS STUDENT'S LAMP, the double sided frame with ruby glass shades.
127. A COLLECTION OF TEN MINERAL EGGS. Together with a crystal egg, six with metal holders.
128. GEORGE I ARMCHAIR, with a pressed splat back and outscrolled arms, with a leather drop-in seat and raised on cabriole legs ending in pad feet. Circa 1730.
129. SMALL FRENCH TULIPWOOD SIDE TABLES, with a hinged top and raised on square tapering legs. Circa 1780.
130. A PAIR OF MAHOGANY SIDE CABINETS, on a square tapering saber legs, each with a tambour fronted compartment.

131. A PAIR OF DIRECTOIRE STYLE OCCASIONAL TABLES, the bases in the form of fluted columns.
132. A PAIR OF TOLE TABLE LAMPS, the black painted bodies resting on square plinths.
133. A PAIR OF GROTESQUE COMPOSITION TABLE LAMPS, one in the form of a gargoyle, the other in the form of a monk. *Gypsy bought these figures in a souvenir shop near Notre-Dame Cathedral, Paris, and made these into lamps herself.
134. LOUIS XV STYLED COFFEE TABLE, with a square top and raised on cabriole legs.
135. WROUGHT-IRON FIRE GRATE, on lion paw feet.
136. GREEN PAINTED RATTAN CHAISE. Together with a similarly painted work table.
137. LOUIS XV STYLE CANED BERGERE, the cresting rail craved with flowers and with similar carving on the apron.

CELLAR

138. TWO LOUIS VUITTON STEAMER TRUNKS, one lettered "Gypsy Rose Lee."
139. FANNY BRICE *NUDE DRYING HERSELF*. Green background. Signed. Oil on canvasboard, unframed. *A gift from Miss Brice.
140. ARA "*COME ON YOU THIEFS AND MURDERS*." Priest exhorting a frightened crowd of peasant. Titled and inscribed on the reverse. Unframed. 25 × 20 inches.
141. JULIO DE DIEGO *DECOY AND HUMMINGBIRD*. Surrealistic bird with red wattle in a garden, four hummingbirds overheard. Signed and dated '44. On masonite, unframed.
142. JULIO DE DIEGO *RUG*. Executed by Gypsy Rose Lee. Fish and other surrealistic figures. Diamond shape 40 × 58 inches.
143. MARCEL VERTES *GIRL IN A GREEN HAT*. Wearing a purple poncho and green trousers, holding a staff entwined with violets. Unframed. 108 × 72 inches.
144. MARCEL VERTES *BARE-LEGGED GIRL IN A GREEN WRAP*. Seductively playing a lute, resting her head on a Police Gazette. 108 × 72 inches.
145. MARCEL VERTES *GIRL IN ORANGE AND PURPLE*, holding a mandolin entwined with leaves. Signed. Unframed. 102 × 72 inches.

UPSTAIRS HALL AND MINSTREL'S BALCONY

146. BRASS TABLE LAMP, with a beaded shade.
147. GEORGE III CHINOISERIE HANGING CORNER CUPBOARD, of bow-fronted form. Circa 1760.
148. VICTORIAN WROUGHT-IRON OIL LAMP, with a frosted shade.
149. VICTORIAN TRIPOD TABLE, with a velvet patchwork cover.
150. A SET OF THREE GILT-WOOD SIDE CHAIRS, with "bamboo" frames.
151. LARGE UPHOLSTERED EASY CHAIR, covered in buttoned yellow velvet.
152. BRONZE TABLE LAMP, in the form of a putto standing on a fluted column.
153. PAINTED TRIPOD TABLE, the top well-decorated with a still life of flowers.
154. AMERICAN STYLE MAHOGANY BUREAU, of inverted breakfront form, the hinged flap elaborately inlaid with brass and mother-of-pearl.
155. DRESDEN PORCELAIN SLIPPER. Together with a bisque slipper.
156. WEDGWOOD-BLUE JASPER CACHE POT AND COVER. Together with a mahogany Canterbury.
157. VICTORIAN TABLE CLOCK, with an enamel dial and flanked by a cherub.
158. MAHOGANY TORCHERE, with a circular top. Together with a mahogany Canterbury.
159. A PAIR OF VICTORIAN X-FRAME CHAIRS, the arms carved with acanthus leaves and upholstered in beige velvet.
160. A TERRA-COTTA URN STAND. Together with an ebonized occasional table.
161. VICTOR PHONOGRAPH AND STAND, with elaborately decorated trumpet, the stand inlaid with floral marquetry.
162. MARCEL VERTES *GYPSY TYPING*. Gypsy nude, wearing a fantastic hat and long gloves, seated before a typewriter. Signed and inscribed *To Gypsy*. Brush and ink. 29½ × 21½ inches. Note: This drawing was used by Gypsy as her trademark.

163. JULIO DE DIEGO *"THE PILLS MAKERS THE PHARMACIST AND THE ANGELS."* Brightly colored caricature of Gypsy and her husband taking pills made by devils, attendant angels attempting to dissuade them. Titled and inscribed *News Item: Gypsy Rose Lee takes pill between shows. Ah!! Julio De Diego takes pills for gallbladder chronic cholecystitis. Ah!! in mirror print.* Watercolor. 8¼ × 13 inches.

164. MARCEL VERTES *SOUVENIR DU 14e RUE BURLESQUE 1935.* Gypsy on stage in a long dress, her hands on her hips. Signed, titled and dated 1940. Gray wash. 16 × 20 inches.

165. MARCEL VERTES *GYPSY ON STAGE.* Three spectators on a balcony watching Gypsy nude on stage, the orchestra in the foreground. Gray wash. 16 × 20 inches.

166. MARCEL VERTES GYPSY COMME CENTAUR. Gypsy as a centaur, pursued by a male centaur in the distance. Titled. Watercolor. 8¼ × 11 inches.

GYPSY'S BEDROOM AND DRESSING ROOM

167. A PAIR OF WROUGHT-IRON CIRCULAR GARDEN SEATS, on tripod legs.

168. VICTORIAN EBONIZED SIDE CABINET, the door inset with a porcelain clock depicting a river landscape.

169. EBONIZED MANTEL CLOCK, with engine turned brass dial and enameled chapter ring, the lower section depicting an automaton in the form of a dolphin drinking from a rotating fountain.

170. A PAIR OF VICTORIAN FRAMED PRINTS ON GLASS, both of young girls, one holding a rabbit, the other with flowers.

171. A FINE VICTORIAN PAPIER MACHE THREE TIERED STAND, the lower tier inlaid with a view of Windsor Castle, the whole well-decorated with mother-of-pearl, gilt and flowers. Circa 1860.

172. UPHOLSTERED CHAISE, covered in green cut velvet.

173. TWO SIMILAR WROUGHT-IRON TORCHERES, both with circular tops.

174. VICTORIAN PAPIER MACHE OCCASIONAL TABLE, the circular top inlaid with a pagoda and highlighted with mother-of-pearl inlay.

175. VICTORIAN BLACK PAINTED COAL SCUTTLE, the sides with ring handles.

176. VICTORIAN PAPIER MACHE SPOON-BACK CHAIR, inlaid with insects and flowers, and raised on cabriole legs.

177. A PAIR OF CAST-IRON TABLE LAMPS, in the form of a putto in rococo bases.

178. VICTORIAN PAPIER MACHE WORK TABLE, the lobed top inlaid with mother-of-pearl with a spray of flowers, and resting on a tripod base.

179. VICTORIAN PAPIER MACHE TRAY, the center decorated with a woman playing a musical instrument. Together with a Victorian papier mache tea caddy.

180. MALACHITE BOX, of triangular shape with gilt trim. In original Russian protective case. * Purchased during a tour of Russia.

181. AUBUSSON CARPET, with a wine red field and a separate floral medallion border.

182. AN ELABORATELY FRAMED COLLAGE, containing assorted seashells and photographs and newspaper clippings in Gypsy's career. *Created by Gypsy.

183. PAIR OF EMERALD AND DIAMOND EARCLIPS, the gold mounts set with two cabochon emeralds suspending two pear-shaped emeralds with a total approximate weight of 3.80 carats, sixteen small rubies, twenty-four emeralds and numerous rose cut diamonds.

184. SNAKE BRACELET, in Victorian style and constructed of wire mesh and enamel.

185. THREE HAIR ORNAMENTS, of yellow metal, one in the form of a crayfish on a ginger twig with heart-shaped pendants.

186. MUSICAL CIRCUS STABLE of brass, in the form of a male acrobat supporting a woman holding balances and both supported by a three-tiered wooden stand of red, white and blue.

187. TWO WOOD AND LACE FANS. Together with a Spanish-style simulated tortoise-shell hair comb.

188. TWO HANDBAGS, one beaded blue purse, and the other in tapestry.

189. TWO HANDBAGS, one beaded in mauve and silver, the other crocheted depicting a stylized blue heron.

190. THREE BEADED BAGS, one gold and silver with a pearl snap, one of Indian material, the third black.

191. METAL INKSTAND, depicting a young boy in the eighteenth century dress leaning on a tree stump with lizard, signed Knapp. Together with a Victorian match holder, of cast iron.

192. A GROUP OF NINE HOTEL KEYS, including keys from:
     Semiramis Hotel, Cairo
     Albergo Excelsior Italia, Florence
     Marhaba, Mazagan
     Hotel Reina Cristina, Algeciras
     Hotel McKinley, Canton, Ohio
     Crawat, Luxemburg
     The Dorchester, London
     Hotel de la Sirene, Meaux
     1 unidentified with prancing stag enclosed in cartouche decoration.

193. PORCELAIN VASE, depicting a group of deer in elegant clothing.

194. EUROPEAN SCHOOL, 20th Century. *A SHERHERDESS CARRYING A CHILD ON HER BACK.* Watercolor. 8¾ × 6½ inches.

195. AMERICAN SCHOOL, 20th Century. *GYPSY'S DOG*: A Mexican hairless. On masonite. 12 × 10 inches.

196. BERNATSCHKE *FEMALE NUDE*. Seen from behind, holding a green drapery. 11½ × 9¾ inches.

197. VICTORIAN PAPIER MACHE STANDISH, with two cut glass wells. Together with a peacock feather fan.

198. TWO SIMILARLY DECORATED FLOWER HOLDERS, each with a glass bud liner.

199. CAST METAL TABLE LAMP, in the form of a winged cherub holding a torch.

200. A COLLECTION OF FIVE CAST-IRON BOOTS, including a pair of high buttoned shoes.

201. VICTORIAN CENTRE TABLE, with a wrought iron base and metal top.

202. VICTORIAN PAPIER MACHE OCCASIONAL TABLE, the circular top decorated with grapes and vines.

203. VICTORIAN WROUGHT-IRON BED, the headboard with elaborate scrollwork and hung with lace.

204. A COLLECTION OF FIVE VICTORIAN PINCUSHIONS, including one in the form of a shoe.

205. A PAIR OF VICTORIAN RUBY GLASS SCENT BOTTLES, the covers decorated with miniatures.

206. CUT GLASS SMELLING SALTS BOTTLE. Together with a cut glass covered box.

207. VICTORIAN PAPIER MACHE WORK BOX, with hinged cover, the whole inlaid with mother-of-pearl.

208. REGENCY STYLE DESK, the top with projecting corners, the whole painted with chains of flowers and raised on "bamboo legs."

209. VICTORIAN PAPIER MACHE WORK BOX, the hinged front opening to reveal a velvet lined interior, the exterior decorated with sprays of flowers and leaves.

210. PAINTED WALL MIRROR, containing a circular plate.

211. VICTORIAN TOLE CANISTER, the front with a beveled mirror plate.

212. A SMALL COLLECTION OF DRESSING TABLE ARTICLES, including a papier mache glass case, and a collection of miniature metal shoes.

213. VICTORIAN SEWING STAND. Together with a smoker's tray in the form a Near Eastern woman.

214. MILCH GLASS TABLE LAMP. Together with a small marble top occasional table.

215. SEWING MANNEQUIN, covered in moiré silk.

216. UPHOLSTERED VICTORIAN EASY CHAIR. Together with another, covered in green velvet.

VICTORIAN GUEST BEDROOM & BATHROOM

217. A SMALL VICTORIAN POLYPHON, contained in a fitted mahogany case. Together with six discs.

218. TOLE TOP OCCASIONAL TABLE, decorated with a peasant woman feeding bird.

219. VICTORIAN MAHOGANY WORK TABLE, with a pair of flaps and two drawers in the frieze.

220. A PAIR OF VICTORIAN ROSEWOOD SIDE CHAIRS, upholstered in buttoned emerald velvet.
221. VELVET ROSEWOOD SETTEE, with a buttoned back and upholstered similarly to the preceding lot.
222. VICTORIAN TOLE BED, grained to resemble walnut, the head and footboards with cast metal crestings, the whole resting on dolphin feet.
223. COLORED REPRODUCTION *FEEDING THE CHICKS*. Little girl in a landscape feeding bread to chickens. 27 × 20 inches.
224. COLORED PRINT *MISCHIEF*. Two small children pouring ink and water in a waste basket full or their father's papers. Published by H. Schile, 36 Division St. N.Y. 26 × 21¾ inches.
225. VICTORIAN AVIARY, contained in a glass dome and resting on a mahogany pedestal.
226. CIRCULAR MARQUETRY OCCASIONAL TABLE, on a tripod spindle base.
227. VICTORIAN STEAMER TRUNK, covered in embossed copper, and with tin mounts.
228. CIRCULAR VICTORIAN WALL MIRROR, in a mahogany shadow frame.
229. EARLY WROUGHT-IRON SEWING MACHINE, decorated with flowers and resting on lion paw feet.
230. VICTORIAN TOLE TEA CANISTER, the front with a mirrored beveled door.
231. THREE VICTORIAN LACE PARASOLS, each with natural wooden handles.
232. VICTORIAN HALL STAND, the upper section with a coat rack, the lower section for umbrellas. Together with a collection of Victorian parasols.
233. CHINESE BLACK LACQUERED LOW TABLE, inlaid with mother-or-pearl. Together with a Victorian photograph frame.
234. SHERATORN BLACK PAINTED ARMCHAIR, with a splat back and velvet seat.
235. VICTORIAN EBONIZED BOOK TABLE, with a circular revolving top above two tiers.
236. A COLLECTION OF SEVEN PORCELAIN ASHTRAYS, the body of each molded with a pipe.
237. VICTORIAN TABLE LAMP, with a painted globe and base.
238. A QUANTITY OF MISCELLANEOUS PORCELAIN.
239. LOUIS XV STYLE GILT-METAL MANTEL CLOCK, with a white enamel dial.
240. VICTORIAN ROSEWOOD DESK, with a hinged top enclosing small drawers and pigeon holes, the whole raised on turned legs.
241. METAL FLOOR LAMP, the column encrusted with porcelain flowers.
242. A PAIR OF CAST-METAL TABLE LAMPS, in the form of children.
243. MINIATURE VITRINE CABINET, in the form of a sedan chair. Together with a covered box with an etched glass cover.
244. TWO WALL APPLIQUES, each in the form of a mirrored giltwood bat.
245. GILT-WOOD STOOL, the shell-form top supported by a dolphin.
246. GILT-METAL TABLE LAMP, the base in the form of dolphins. Together with a gilt-metal stand.
247. VASELINE GLASS BOOT. Together with another spill vase.
248. EMPIRE STYLE PAINTED COMMODE CHAIR, the whole painted with anthemion and swans. Monogrammed G.R.L.
249. UNUSUAL CEILING FIXTURE, in the form of a dragonfly, the wings and body formed of multicolored beads.
250. ART BRONZE TABLE LAMP, the frame molded with holly leaves and glass berries.
251. GILT-WOOD FLOOR LAMP, on a turned stem.
252. A PAIR OF UPHOLSTERED EASY CHAIRS, with arched ends and each with a single arm and covered in buttoned velvet.
253. BRONZED METAL TABLE LAMP, of a female swimmer.
254. VENETIAN GONDOLIER'S CHAIR, with an X-frame base, the whole decorated with flowers on a green ground and covered in salmon velvet.

GARDEN & GARAGE

255. A PAIR OF LEAD GARDEN TUBS, with monopodiae handles and resting on terra-cotta plinths.
256. A PAIR OF WROUGHT-IRON WALL LIGHTS, the bodies elaborately molded with clusters of grapes.

257. A PAIR OF WROUGHT-IRON CHAIRS, with elaborately scrolling backs and feet.
258. A PAIR OF JAPANESE LEAD FIGURES OF CRANES.
259. A PAIR OF CAST-IRON STOOLS, each with a fan medallion top.
260. WROUGHT-IRON BREAKFAST TABLE. Together with four chairs *en suite*.
261. 1956 ROLLS ROYCE Silver Cloud S/1. By Freestone & Webb. (Body No. 1791) Four-door sedan in beige and black with beige leather interior. This attractive and unusual automobile was used by Gypsy on her European tour of 1959 and subsequent American tours. The custom seats recline into beds, a feature which provided a comfortable place to rest during the tiring road shows. Other at-home conveniences include the two compartments in the front passenger door, one containing a tea service for two with water heater, tea kettle, cups, napkins, etc. The other compartment with another tea kettle, water jar and thermos bottle. The back of each front seat fitted with retractable utility tray for luxury touring. The automobile has an AM-FM radio with speakers fitted in all four doors. The car is fitted with a right hand drive and automatic transmission. Overall condition very good. The car has excellent Gates Airfloat Supreme white-wall, 8.85/9.15 4-ply tubeless tires. The odometer reads 47,230. [*Authors Note:* The crowning touch of the interior is a cut glass bud vase mounted on the dashboard which Gypsy purchased at Portebello Road on the way to pick up her car. The Rolls dealer's only concern was that the vase at least be cut glass and she assured him that it was.]

Appendix D: Broadway

The Original Production of *Gypsy: A Musical Fable*

Gypsy *Starring Ethel Merman Opens on Broadway, 1959*

The original production of *Gypsy* opened at the Broadway Theatre on May 21, 1959. When its run there ended on September 9, 1960, the show was moved to the more intimate Imperial Theatre. Ethel Merman and company gave a total of 702 performances. The show received eight Tony Award nominations: Best Musical, Best Actress in a Musical: Ethel Merman, Best Actor in a Musical: Jack Klugman, Best Featured Actress in a Musical: Sandra Church, Best Scenic Design, Best Costume Design, Best Director of a Musical, and Best Conductor and Musical Director.

Legendary Broadway critic Brooks Atkinson wrote two reviews of the original production of Gypsy. In the first, which ran in the May 22, 1959, *The New York Times* pronounced: "Good Show!" and in the second, which ran in the May 31, 1959, *The New York Times*, focused on Mama Rose: "Merman in 'Gypsy'; Topflight Performance in New Musical Play."

Of course, Brooks Atkinson wasn't the only New York based critic to review *Gypsy*. The following reviews all appeared in the May 22, 1959, issue of New York City newspapers:

- "'Gypsy,' Ethel Smash Hits" by Frank Aston. *New York World-Telegram and Sun.*
- "Miss Merman Has Her Best Role in 'Gypsy,' a Real-Life Musical" by John Chapman. *New York Daily News.*
- "'Gypsy' a Dynamic Musical" by Robert Coleman. *New York Daily Mirror.*
- "'Gypsy'" by Walter Kerr. *New York Herald Tribune.*
- "Huge Night for Merman and Her Fans" by John McClain. *Journal American.*
- "Ethel Merman Has Another Success" by Richard Watts Jr. *New York Post.*

There have been numerous revivals of the musical *Gypsy* since Gypsy Rose Lee's death. Critics from *The New York Times* have reviewed every production.

Gypsy *Starring Angela Lansbury Opens in London, 1973, and New York, 1974*

This was the first revival of *Gypsy*. The cast was led by the incredible Angela Lansbury. In 1974 the production moved to Broadway where it played at the Winter Garden Theatre from September 23, 1974, and closed on January 4, 1975, after 120 performances. Angela Lansbury won the Tony Award for her portrayal of Mama Rose. Zan Charisse (Louise/Gypsy) was nominated as Best Featured Actress in a Musical. Arthur Laurents, who wrote the book for the musical, was nominated for Best Director of a Musical.

At the Drama Desk Awards Angela Lansbury won as Outstanding Actress in a Musical. Director Laurents took home the award for Outstanding Director of a Musical. Zan Charisse and John Sheridan (Tulsa) each received a Theatre World Award the year.

- "Theater: 'Gypsy' Bounces Back with Zest and Lilt" by Clive Barnes. *The New York Times*, September 24, 1974.

Gypsy *Starring Tyne Daly, 1989*

The production starring Tyne Daly as Mama Rose was the second Broadway revival of *Gypsy*. It opened at the St. James Theatre on November 11, 1989, where it ran through January 6, 1991. The production was then moved to the Marquis Theatre for a run beginning on April 8, 1991, and ending on July 26, 1991. Tyne Daly and company turned in 476 performances.

Like Angela Lansbury before her, Tyne Daly won the Tony Award for Best Actress in a Musical and the Drama Desk Award for Outstanding Actress in a Musical. The Drama Desk Award was also given to the producers for Outstanding Revival. Other Drama Desk nominees were John Hadary (Herbie), and Crista Moore (Louise/Gypsy). Crista Moore and Robert Lambert (Tulsa) also won the Theatre World Award. Arthur Laurents returned once more to direct the show he had written.

- "*Gypsy* Is Back on Broadway with a Vengeance" by Frank Rich. *The New York Times*, November 17, 1989.

Gypsy *Starring Bernadette Peters, 2003*

The third revival of Gypsy, with Bernadette Peters as Mama Rose, ran for 451 performances at the St. James Theatre. It opened on May 1, 2003, and closed on May 30, 2004. This production was directed by Sam Mendes. The talented Tammy Blanchard was Louise/Gypsy. Blanchard had recently received rave reviews for her performance as the young Judy Garland in a television movie about Garland's life. Bernadette Peters and John Dossett (Herbie) were both nominated for the Tony and Drama Desk awards. Tammy Blanchard took home the Tony Award for Best Featured Actress in a Musical.

- "New Mama Takes Charge" by Ben Brantley. *The New York Times*, May 2, 2003.

Gypsy *Starring Patti LuPone, 2007*

Patti LuPone, like Bernadette Peters and Angela Lansbury, is a Broadway icon. She amazed audiences in the original production of *Evita*, and numerous revivals of Broadway's classic musicals: *Anything Goes, Company, Oliver!* and *Sweeny Todd*. With this, the forth revival of *Gypsy*, made the show the most recorded Broadway musical. Arthur Laurents returned to direct his show for the third time. Laurents was 90 when the show opened on March 27, 2008, and 91 when it closed on January 11, 2009. He was nominated for the second time as Best Director of a Musical; unfortunately he did not win. As expected, Patti LuPone won both the Drama Desk Award and the Tony Award for her portrayal of Mama Rose. Her costars, Boyd Gaines (Herbie) and Laura Benanti (Louise) also won. The show won the Tony for Best Revival of a Broadway Musical.

- "Patti LuPone in *Gypsy*: Light the Lights boys! Mama Rose Hears a Symphony" by Charles Isherwood. *The New York Times*, August 15, 2006.
- "Whatever Happened to Mama Rose?" by Ben Brantley. *The New York Times*, July 16, 2007.
- "Patti's Turn, If Not Always Rose's" by Charles Isherwood. *The New York Times*, August 5, 2007.

Television Adaptation

Gypsy *Starring Bette Midler, 1993*

In addition to the Broadway revivals of *Gypsy* there was a television adaptation starring the "Divine Miss M," Bette Midler, as Mama Rose, in 1993. Cynthia Gibb portrayed Louise and Jennifer Beck portrayed Dainty June.

Expectations were high among Midler's fans and the fans of *Gypsy*. Some, this author included, felt that Midler was unable to transcend her own larger than life image, but the general consensus was that she turned in a fine performance.

Bette Midler won the Golden Globe Award for Best Actress in a Miniseries or Television Film and the film was also nominated for twelve Primetime Emmy Awards, including Outstanding Made for Television Movie and Outstanding Lead Actress in a Miniseries or a Movie for Midler, and won for Outstanding Individual Achievement in Music Direction (Michael Rafter).

- "TV Weekend; Midler Takes Her Turn In Mama Rose's Spot" By John J. O'Conner. *The New York Times*, December 10, 1993.

Appendix E: Discography

That's Me All Over, 1958. An LP featuring twelve pieces that Gypsy used over the years. Gypsy's never really sings, she performs this material in a recitative fashion (not unlike Rex Harrison in *My Fair Lady*). This record is on the Westminster label. The album includes the classic "I Can't Strip to Brahms" and also has terrific versions of Cole Porter's "I Sleep Easier Now" and Rogers and Hart's "The Heart Is Quicker Than the Eye."

Gypsy Rose Lee Remembers Burlesque, 1962. Another LP featuring songs and routines that Gypsy used in her act for many years. She is joined by several unbilled comedians while recreating scenes she learned from the great comedians of vaudeville and burlesque. This album is on the Stereooddities label. It was released originally released in 1962, and was later re-released as *An Evening with Gypsy Rose*.

Gypsy *Soundtracks*

With the original production of *Gypsy* in 1959, the film in 1962, the first revival in London and New York in 1974, the second revival on Broadway in 1989, the television film in 1993, the third Broadway revival in 2003 and the fourth in 2008, *Gypsy* has become the most recorded Broadway show.

Gypsy Original Broadway Cast, 1959. The first Broadway soundtrack of Gypsy is available on Columbia Broadway Master Work (SK 60848). This CD includes bonus tracks of the following previously unreleased material: "Some People," "Mr. Goldstone / Little Lamb" both of which are sung by Ethel Merman, "Momma's Talkin' Soft" sung by Laura Leslie, and "Nice She Ain't" sung by Bernie Knee.

Gypsy Original Motion Picture Soundtrack, 1962. This soundtrack is available on the Rhino Movie Music label (RZ 73873). Like the 1959 Broadway soundtrack this CD offers bonus tracks. They are all outtakes of Rosalind Russell singing the following songs: "Some People," "Small World," "You'll Never Get Away from Me," "Everything's Coming Up Roses," "Together Wherever We Go," and "Rose's Turn" (film version). It also includes the album version of "Rose's Turn." The "Dainty June and Her Farm Boys" is touted as a "previously unreleased full version."

Gypsy Original London Cast Recording, 1974. This version is available on the BMG/RCA Victor label (60571-2-RG). This production of *Gypsy* opened on May 29, 1973, at the Piccadilly Theatre and starred Angela Lansbury.

Gypsy Original Cast Recording, 1990. This recording is available on the Elektra Nonesuch label (79239-2). This production was the third Broadway revival of *Gypsy*. The show opened at the St. James Theatre on November 16, 1989, and starred Tyne Daly. The booklet from this CD has notes by author/director Arthur Laurents.

Gypsy Original Soundtrack Recording, 1993. This is the soundtrack for the television film of Gypsy and is available on the Atlantic label (82551-2). Bette Midler starred as Mama Rose.

Gypsy The New Broadway Cast Recording, 2003. This version is available on the Angel Records label (7243 5 83858 2 3). This cast featured Bernadette Peters.

Gypsy The 2008 Broadway Cast Recording, 2008. This CD is available on the TIME LIFE label (M19659). This revival of *Gypsy* starred Patti LuPone as Mama Rose.

Kay Medford in Gypsy (with Alyn Ainsworth and His Orchestra), 1969. A studio album on the MFP label. This is a unique listening experience for the true *Gypsy* fans and dedicated collectors. Kay Medford played the mother of Gypsy's friend Fanny Brice in the Broadway production of *Funny Girl*. Kay Medford was a brilliant performer, once described as a "… veteran scene-stealer…." She delivered lines with a poker face, and a very dry delivery. However, Miss Medford was not a singer. Nevertheless, this is an interesting take on Mama Rose. Kay Medford's supporting cast included Sonya Petrie (June), Lorraine (Gypsy), Jimmy Blackburn (Herbie), Richard Fox (Tulsa), and as the strippers who sing "You Gotta Get a Gimmick," Janet Webb, Janette Gale and Betty Winsett.

Appendix F: On Screen

Films

You Can't Have Everything—1937
Ali Baba Goes to Town—1937
Sally, Irene and Mary—1938
Battle of Broadway—1938
My Lucky Star—1938
Stage Door Canteen—1943
Belle of the Yukon—1944
Babes in Baghdad—1952

Screaming Mimi—1958
Wind Across the Everglades—1958
The Stripper—1963
The Trouble with Angels—1966
Around the World with Mike Todd—1968 (A
  documentary of Mike Todd's life)
The Over the Hill Gang—1969

The Gypsy Rose Lee Show—1966 to 1968

The New York Public Library is the home of the Billy Rose Theatre Collection, which houses the Gypsy Rose Lee Collection. The collection includes the following episodes of *The Gypsy Rose Lee Show*, here listed by episode number.

Episode # 350. Filmed on August 29, 1966.
  Guests: Eliot Elisofon and Christine
    Schmidtmer.
Episode #410. Filmed on November 21, 1966.
  Guests: T.C. Jones and Aleene.
Episode #411. Filmed on December 5, 1966.
  Guests: Woody Allen and Richard Deacon.
Episode #437. Filmed on December 19, 1966.
  Guests: Sally Rand, Iris Adrian, and Harry
    Richman.
Episode #439. Filmed on December 19, 1966.
  Guests: Sylvia Vaughn Thompson and Ketty
    Lester.
Episode #441. Filmed on January 9, 1967.
  Guests: Monica Sheridan, Nanette Fabray
    and Pamela Rodgers.
Episode #442. Filmed on January 9, 1967.
  Guests: Jack Albertson and Nanette Fabray.
Episode #447. Filmed on January 10, 1967.
  Guests: Eartha Kitt, Laine Kazan.
Episode #448. Filmed on January 10, 1967.
  Guests: Irwin Corey and Jan Hampton.

Episode #450. Filmed on January 10, 1967.
  Guests: Sallie Blair and Bert & George
    Bernard.
Episode #452. Filmed on January 17, 1967.
  Guests: Pat Carroll and Else Tyroler.
Episode #456. Filmed on January 18, 1967.
  Guest: Ethel Merman.
Episode # 461. Filmed on February 20, 1967.
  Guest: Liberace.
Episode #462. Filmed on February 6, 1967.
  Guests: Van Johnson and Patsy Kelly.
Episode #467. Filmed on February 7, 1967.
  Guests: Rose Marie, Joe Flynn, and Pat Mon-
    tandon.
Episode #468. Filmed on February 7, 1967.
  Guests: Joe Flynn, Ketty Lester and Paul
    Mayer.
Episode #475. Filmed on February 20, 1967.
  Guests: Dom DeLuise and Katharine Ross.
Episode #479. Filmed on February 21, 1967.
  Guests: Phyllis Diller and Judge Noel Can-
    non.

Episode #482. Filmed on March 6, 1967.
 Guests: Bob Crane and Fannie Flagg.
Episode #484. Filmed March 6, 1967.
 Guests: Rosemary Clooney, Rosemary De
 Camp, and Melody Patterson.
Episode #499. Filmed on March 28, 1967.
 Guests: Jack Carter and Paula Stewart.
Episode #503. Filmed on April 24, 1967.
 Guests: Robert Goulet, Gale Storm, and
 Frank D'Amico.
Episode #504. Filmed on April 24, 1967.
 Guests: Marie Wilson and Gale Storm.
Episode #506. Filmed on April 25, 1967.
 Guest: Richard Deacon.
Episode #509. Filmed April 25, 1967.
 Guests: Woody Allen and Selma Diamond.
Episode #510. Filmed on April 25, 1967.
 Guest: Robert Q. Lewis.
Episode #511. Filmed on May 8, 1967.
 Guests: Mary Ann Mobley and Laura Labby.
Episode # 514. Filmed on May 8, 1967.
 Guests: Celeste Holm and Coleen Gray.
Episode #517. Filmed on May 9, 1967.
 Guests: Red Buttons, Norman Wisdom, and
 Anne Rogers.
Episode #519. Filmed on May 9, 1967.
 Guests: Pat Carroll, Larry Casey, and Edith
 Quaglin.
Episode #525. Filmed on May 23, 1967.
 Guests: Shelley Berman and Betsy Palmer.
Episode #526. Filmed on May 22, 1967.
 Guests: Paul Lynde and Gretchen Wyler.
Episode #527. Filmed on May 22, 1967.
 Guests: Yvonne De Carlo and Paul Lynde.
Episode #528. Filmed on May 22, 1967.
 Guests: Theodore Bikel and Maria Cole.
Episode #533. Filmed on June 5, 1967.
 Guests: Nanette Fabray, Ronnie Schell, and
 Suzy Creamcheese.
Episode #534. Filmed on June 5, 1967.
 Guests: Iris Adrian and Kay Stevens.
Episode # 542. Filmed on June 19, 1967.
 Guests: Agnes Moorehead and Donna
 Archibald.
Episode #547. Filmed on May 20, 1967.
 Guests: Ketty Lester, Betsy Palmer, and Fern
 Warner.
Episode #549. Filmed on May 20, 1967.
 Guests: Joan Shawlee and Leslie Fono.
Episode #560. Filmed on July 4, 1967.
 Guests: Nichelle Nichols and Sergio Franchi.
Episode #567. Filmed on July 18, 1967.
 Guests: Beverly Garland and Kay Ish.

Episode #568. Filmed on July 18, 1967.
 Guests: Irwin Corey and Steve Volk.
Episode #604. Filmed on August 28, 1967.
 Guests: Pat Carroll and Nanette Fabray.
Episode #605. Filmed on August 28, 1967.
 Guests: Ella Logan, Pat Carroll, and Nanette
 Fabray.
Episode #613. Filmed on September 11, 1967.
 Guests: Allan Sherman, Imogene Coca, and
 Trudy Dye Ferrand.
Episode # 614. Filmed on September 11, 1967.
 Guests: Imogene Coca, Leningrad Circus.
Episode #636. Filmed on October 23, 1967.
 Guests: Patricia Bain and Bob Crane.
Episode #638. Filmed on November 6, 1967.
 Guests: Theodore Bikel, Buffy Ford, and
 Warren Jacober.
Episode # 651. Filmed on November 11, 1967.
 Guests: Ben Blue and Richard Deacon.
Episode #655. Filmed on November 21, 1967.
 Guests: Julio de Diego and Anaïs Nin.
Episode #656. Filmed on November 21, 1967.
 Guests: Julio de Diego and Eliot Elisofon.
Episode #658. Filmed on November 21, 1967.
 Guests: Rod McKuen, Gisele MacKenzie,
 and Hugh Masekela.
Episode #664. Filmed on December 4, 1967.
 Guests: Eddie Foy, Jr., Pat O'Brien, and Flip
 Wilson.
Episode #667. Filmed on December 5, 1967.
 Guests: Wilfred Hyde-White and Arthur
 Cort.
Episode #673. Filmed on December 5, 1967.
 Guests: Pat O'Brien and Donna Jean Young.
Episode #682. Filmed on January 2, 1968.
 Guests: Nanette Fabray and David Barrett.
Episode #683. Filmed on January 2, 1968.
 Guests: Carl Reiner, Nanette Fabray, and Pat
 Morita.
Episode #685. Filmed on January 2, 1968.
 Guests: Barbara Feldon, Suzy Parker and Bob
 Crane.
Episode #689. Filmed on January 18, 1968.
 Guests: Rip Taylor and the Marquis Chimps.
Episode #690. Filmed on January 10, 1968.
 Guests: Lainie Kazan and Carmen McRae.
Episode #697. Filmed on January 22, 1968.
 Guests: Vidal Sasson, Beverly Adams, and
 Ann Elder.
Episode #701. Filmed on January 23, 1968.
 Guests: Ella Logan and Richard Deacon.
Episode #702. Filmed on February 23, 1968.
 Guests: Colleen Gray and Fred Kimball.

Episode #703. Filmed on January 23, 1968.
  Guests: Richard Deacon, Ella Logan, and
      Shirley Bright Boody.
Episode #704. Filmed on January 23, 1968.
  Guests: Anne Jeffreys, Abby Dalton, and
      Anne Lund.
Episode #707. Filmed on February 5, 1968.
  Guests: Colleen Moore and Gayelord Hauser.
Episode #709. Filmed on 5, 1968.
  Guests: Jack Sheldon and Paula Wayne.
Episode #710. Filmed on 5, 1968.
  Guests: Jack Sheldon and Paula Wayne.
Episode #712. Filmed on February 6, 1968.

Guests: Ed Ames, April Olrich, and Nigel
  Pegram.
Episode #714. Filmed on February 6, 1968.
  Guests: Ronnie Schell, Anne Marie
      Bennstrom, and Willie Restum.
Episode #716. Filmed on February 19, 1968.
  Guests: David Frost, April Olrich, and Nigel
  Pegram.
Episode #718. Filmed on February 19, 1968.
  Guests: Fannie Flagg, T.C. Jones, and Irene
  Junita.
Episode #721. Filmed on February 20, 1968.
  Guests: Chita Rivera and Paul Lynde.

The Jonathan Winters Show—August 1968.

The Mike Douglas Show—Gypsy was Mike's co-host for a week beginning on September 23 and ending on September 27, 1968.

The Name of the Game—Gypsy played Rosetta Stewart. Her co-stars were Tony Franciosa and Juliet Prowse. This episode was "Shine On, Shine On, Jesse Gil." The show was broadcast in 1968.

Appendix G: A Remembrance

The November 1988 issue of *Washington Magazine — Showcasing the Best of the Evergreen State* featured articles about "Washingtonians Who've Changed the World." Gypsy was classified as one of the most influential stars in the 20th century, and was the first Washingtonian under the heading "Entertainers."

"Naked Genius: Gypsy Rose Lee's Greatest Fantasy Was Herself."
by C.R. Roberts

It was 1918 and Rose Louise Hovick was four years old when she made her show business debut singing "I'm a Hard Boiled Rose" for the lodge members assembled at Knights of Pythias hall in Seattle. Her parents divorced shortly thereafter, and later that year she traveled with her mother and sister south to Hollywood.

Or perhaps all that happened in 1917. Perhaps Rose was only three. Different sources tell rather different stories.

The Hovick family lived on Fourth Avenue North, near Queen Anne Hill, or else they lived in West Seattle. Take your pick. Her stepfather was a chiropodist. Her grandfather ran the baggage room at King Street Station. Her father was a reporter for *The Seattle Times*. Her great-great-grandmother was a member of the party stranded by the famous blizzard that struck Donner Pass and invited members to dine on each other. Her great-great grandmother had the luck and pluck to survive the experience.

Or so goes the story that Rose Louise Hovick used to tell.

She was given the name Gypsy Rose Lee by Herbert I. Moss, a burlesque impresario. That's what she says in her novel the *G-String Murders*. Elsewhere it is said that she was given the moniker by Florenz Ziegfeld, he of "Follies" fame, who once employed her.

If you care which story is true, take your pick. Rose lets you make up your own mind.

She will tell you that the Rolls-Royce she drove was specially made, which it was, but she fails to mention that she bought it used. She will tell you that her house in New York has 28 rooms, which it did, but she neglects to say that she only lived in six of those rooms, having rented the balance out as apartments.

The monogrammed Rolls and the mansion were illusions. They were to be seen and appreciated, loved and admired, but they were not real. They were not as real as Rose would have you believe. The truth hid somewhere beneath the paint. These were fantasies, stories, and the merchandise of romance.

And so, too, was Gypsy Rose Lee. She was not only a stripper, she was the dream of The Stripper. She was the name. She was Gypsy, forever on the road, mysterious, dangerous. She was Rose, soft as velvet, stemmed by thorns. She was queen-mother to all the crimson extremes a young man knows.

Her talent was the heat she gave the spark that ignited imagination. Imagine, she said, what secret pleasures rest beneath my feathers. Think hard what waits below this lace. Look for yourself, she said, within this intimate mirror. Hear the story I'm here to tell. Listen with your eyes wide open. See whatever it is you need to see.

She knew what we wanted to see. She knew that we do not always want to know the whole and naked truth.

Reviewing her autobiography, *Gypsy*, John Steinbeck wrote: "I found it irresistible. It's quite a performance. I bet some of it is even true, and if it wasn't, it is now."

It is true that Gypsy Rose Lee was an author. In 1941 she wrote *The G-String Murders*, a mystery concerning homicide among strippers. She followed this in 1942 with *Mother Finds a Body*. She was, for a time, something of a Sitwell, presiding with the literary likes of Christopher Isherwood and Carson McCullers in her New York salon.

She was a playwright, having written *The Naked Genius* in 1943. The play was about a stripper who wrote a successful murder-mystery novel. Gypsy Rose Lee played a starring role in her own fiction.

She was three times a wife and three times divorced. She married a businessman first, then an actor, then a painter. She never married the man she loved most — Mike Todd, "Mr. Elizabeth Taylor"— and it was only after he had grown to be a man that she told her son who his father was.

She was a speed-reader. She read Shakespeare and Freud. She was given to taking up hobbies as she did husbands: for a time she knitted, then she upholstered furniture, then she made quilts, then she bred tropical fish. She collected antiques. She watched television. She very much enjoyed working in her garden.

She was one of those very few celebrities whose fame obtains from the fact of their fame. Rarely did she play the performer, as the years went on — more often she was simply herself.

She was the quizmaster on "Think Fast," an ABC-TV game show during the 1949-50 season. She hosted her own talk shows, in 1958 and 1965, and was for several years the hostess of "The United States Steel Hour." She was a regular guest of Jack Paar. Her stories always concerned herself.

Her talent was her ability to become and then continue to be Gypsy Rose Lee. Who she was was who she was.

She was a name.

She had beautiful legs and bad teeth. She suffered dental problems throughout her career. She smoked heavily and died of lung cancer. There was pain behind the mask.

She was as poor a mother to her son as her own mother had been to her. She was selfish and overbearing, manipulative and melodramatic. She was strong and courageous.

When she was on stage, on camera, in the spotlight, she never gave less than her best. She had and maintained, standards.

She made toe socks for wounded GIs during World War II and toured the front-line hospitals with the USO in Southeast Asia during the 1960s. She could hurt people closest to her and she could charm multitudes. She knew what we needed. She knew the power that illusion owns.

Because she knew what it was like to be poor, hungry and disappointed, she knew how best to use her special and most unusual talents to lift a spirit, bring forth laughter, cause happiness. She made a difference because she knew the possibilities that life could offer, and she knew how to show the way.

The way was never to show it at all. Leave a hint, leave a scent, but never show it all. Show the music, not the notes. Explore the expectations. Expose what you cannot see, and never will. Hide the mundane answers. Paint the truth. Entertain. Imagine this. Imagine that.

Gypsy Rose Lee proved how real illusions can be. She showed us how it is our nature to want the things we cannot have. She taught us the ways of the sweet frontier.

Bibliography

Alexander, H. M. *Strip Tease: The Vanished Art*. New York: Knight Publishers, 1938.

Ballard, Kaye. *How I Lost 10 Pounds in 53 Years: A Memoir*. New York: Back Stage Books, 2006.

Britten, Benjamin, Donald Mitchell, and Philip Reed. *Letters from a Life: The Selected Letters of Benjamin Britten, 1913–1976*. Berkeley: University of California Press, 1991.

Carr, Virginia Spencer. *Lonely Hunter*. New York: Doubleday, 1975.

Castelluccio, Frank, and Walker Alvin. *The Other Side of Ethel Mertz*. Manchester, Connecticut: Knowledge, Ideas & Trends, 1998.

Cerf, Bennett. *Try and Stop Me*. New York: Simon & Schuster, 1944.

Diller, Phyllis. *Like a Lampshade in a Whorehouse*. New York: Jeremy P. Tarcher/Penguin, 2005.

Douglas, Mike. *The Mike Douglas Cookbook*. New York: Funk & Wagnalls, 1969.

Drutman, Irving. *Good Company: A Memoir, Mostly Theatrical*. Boston: Little Brown, 1976.

Flinn, Caryl. *Brass Diva: The Life and Legends of Ethel Merman*. Berkeley: University of California Press, 2007.

Frankel, Noralee. *Stripping Gypsy: The Life of Gypsy Rose Lee*. New York: Oxford University Press. 2009.

Garebian, Keith. *The Making of Gypsy*. New York: Mosaic Books, 1998.

Goldwyn, Liz, and Jennifer Augustyn. *Pretty Things: The Last Generation of American Burlesque Queens*. New York: Regan Books, 2006.

Havoc, June. *More Havoc*. New York: HarperCollins, 1980.

Kellow, Brian. *Ethel Merman: A Life*. New York: Viking Adult, 2007.

Kennedy, Matthew. *Joan Blondell: A Life Between Takes*. Jackson: University Press of Mississippi, 2007.

Knight, Arthur, and Eliot Elisofon. *The Hollywood Style*. New York: Macmillan. 1969.

Laurents, Arthur. *Gypsy: A Musical (Suggested by the Memoirs of Gypsy Rose Lee)*. New York: Random House, 1959.

_____. *An Original Story: A Memoir of Broadway and Hollywood*. New York: Alfred A. Knopf, 2000.

Lee, Gypsy Rose. *The G-String Murders*. New York: Simon and Schuster, 1941.

_____. *Gypsy: A Memoir*. New York: Harper, 1957.

_____. *Mother Finds a Body*. New York: Simon and Schuster, 1942.

Murray, Kathryn. *Family Laugh Lines*. Englewood Cliffs, New Jersey: Prentice-Hall, 1966.

Preminger, Erik Lee. *Gypsy & Me: At Home and on the Road with Gypsy Rose Lee*. Boston: Little, Brown, 1984.

Shteir, Rachel. *Gypsy: The Art of the Tease*. New Haven: Yale University Press, 2009.

Smith, H. Allen. *Low Man on the Totem Pole*. New York: Doubleday, Doran, 1941.

Sobel, Bernard. *Pictorial History of Burlesque*. New York: Putman, 1956.

Tippins, Sherill. *February House*. Boston: Houghton Mifflin, 2005.

Weeks Martin, Jane. *Cooking as You Like It*. New York: Macmillan, 1963.

Index